Illusions
of Power

Illusions of power

The fate of a reform government

MICHAEL SEXTON

SYDNEY
GEORGE ALLEN & UNWIN
LONDON BOSTON

First published in 1979 by
George Allen & Unwin Australia Pty Ltd
8 Napier Street
North Sydney NSW 2060

National Library of Australia
Cataloguing-in-Publication entry:

Sexton, Michael.
  Illusions of power.

  Index
  Bibliography
  ISBN 0 86861 265 0
  ISBN 0 86861 273 1 Paperback

  1. Australia — Politics and government — 1972-1975.
  I. Title.

320.9'94'06

Library of Congress Catalog Card Number 79-53280

Set in 11 on 12 point Plantin and printed in Australia by
Southwood Press Pty Limited, Marrickville NSW

Designed and produced by
Hale & Iremonger Pty Limited

for my mother and father

Contents

Illustrations

The publisher and the author wish to thank the following for granting permission to reproduce illustrations: Herald & Weekly Times Ltd, *Age*, Jean Guyeaux, News Ltd, Advertiser Newspapers Limited, *Canberra Times*, Australian Consolidated Press, John Fairfax Pty Limited.

Abbreviations

ACT — Australian Capital Territory
ACTU — Australian Council of Trade Unions
AEC — Atomic Energy Commission
AGIC — Australian Government Insurance Corporation
AIDC — Australian Industry & Development Corporation
ALAO — Australian Legal Aid Office
ALP — Australian Labor Party
AMA — Australian Medical Association
AMP — Australian Mutual Provident Society
ANOP — Australian National Opinion Polls
ANU — Australian National University
ASIO — Australian Security Intelligence Organisation
CBC — Commercial Banking Company of Sydney
CERC — Cabinet Expenditure Review Committee
CIA — US Central Intelligence Agency
CPA — Communist Party of Australia
CTB — Commonwealth Trading Bank
DLP — Democratic Labor Party

FACTS — Federation of Australian Commercial Television Stations
GMH — General Motors Holden
GNP — Gross National Product
IAC — Industries Assistance Commission
IDC — Interdepartmental Committee
KCMG — Knight Commander of the Order of St Michael and St George
LCP — Liberal-National Country Party coalition
MHR — Member of the House of Representatives
MP — Member of Parliament
MWU — Miscellaneous Workers Union
NSW — New South Wales
OECD — Organisation of Petroleum Exporting Countries
PCU — Policy Co-ordination Unit
PMA — Petroleum and Minerals Authority
PRS — Priorities Review Staff
QC — Queens Counsel
RAAF — Royal Australian Air Force
SMOS — Department of the Special Minister of State
TAA — Trans-Australia Airlines
US — United States of America
VCE — Victorian Central Executive (of the state ALP)

Introduction

Although this book draws most of its material from the Whitlam governments of 1972–75, it is intended to raise general questions about *government* itself — the exercise of political power — in Australia. In the immediate aftermath of 1975 several accounts of the crisis of November and the Whitlam years generally were written, and some provided excellent records of the outstanding events. Even the passage of a relatively short period from the turbulent months of 1975, however, has made it easier to put the only Labor government that an entire generation of Australians has known into some historical context, and to consider some of the questions raised about the Australian political system by the fate of that government.

There have been very few books about how Australian governments function. Only in the 1970s have there been many books about contemporary Australian politics at all, and the majority of those have concentrated on how one party got into office, on how government was gained rather than how it was used. There has been no Australian politician to provide, as Richard Crossman did for the British system, a candid and detailed account of his ministerial activities and his relations with colleagues and public servants.

The fact that this book focuses on certain individuals who were prominent in the Whitlam administration is not intended to suggest that the significance of the events of 1972–75 should be confined to that period. Each of those individuals reflected important aspects of Australian political life in the post-war period. Although the strength and diversity of their personalities affected the interaction of political forces at various times they did not, it will be suggested, affect the ultimate outcome of those forces.

This is, therefore, an examination of how a government elected to office with a moderate program of reform encountered some of the realities of power in Australia. In the face of these realities, that government discovered that many of its own sources of power were illusory.

It is obvious that politicians are not the only exercisers of power in Australia. Often they are singularly unable to influence the course of events. At any time they are subject to the limits imposed by other power-holders — bureaucrats, manufacturers, trade unions, banks, mining companies, media groups and the rest. One of the most important aspects of the Whitlam administration was just how fiercely opposed to change in their own area these groups were, and no doubt still are, and the methods they were prepared to use to resist any alteration to their position.

In many ways the power of these groups is only one facet of a sobering political development which followed the years 1972–75 — the realisation that the difficulties encountered by the Whitlam administration in its efforts to govern are difficulties that will be faced to some extent by any Australian government in the future, no matter what its political complexion. Any government will encounter major problems, as the Fraser government has discovered, in imposing its own designs on an economy as structurally weak as that of Australia and as dependent on stimulation from overseas sources that are themselves under considerable economic pressure. These kinds of problems are obviously magnified, however, by the existence of powerful public and private groups within the community who will resist *any* adjustment to changing circumstances.

It is true that the difficulties are initially — but not necessarily finally — greater for a government which attempts to make substantial changes to the status quo. One reason is that any substantial changes require more administrative capacity and commitment of resources than leaving things as they are. Another is that the greater the change attempted the more violent will be the resistance offered. But resistance is simply a fact of life for a government committed to some change. It lends no credence to the suggestion that the Whitlam government went "too far, too fast". On the contrary, the record demonstrates that it made too many concessions to its opponents.

It was not the government's philosophies or policies that made it so vulnerable to its opponents. Nor was it simply the efforts of those opponents, as constant and as destructive as they ultimately were. The Whitlam government had internal problems that were largely of its own making — among them its failure to impose its priorities on the bureaucracy, to make imaginative appointments, to develop a spirit of unity among ministers. These were challenges that could have been more easily taken up than those of the economic system or the Senate, and when they were not met they reinforced these external forces by weakening the government at its heart.

The Whitlam government is, therefore, no model for a future reform government. But it is a graphic demonstration of the kinds of forces, inside and outside its ranks, that will almost certainly confront such a government. Even in its failures to cope with many of these challenges it has clearly identified some of the solutions to them. In this way it may still have left a valuable legacy.

The National Tally Room, 13 December 1975

1   365 Days

At about 11 pm on 13 December 1975, Gough Whitlam arrived at the Belconnen High School auditorium in an outer suburb of Canberra, Australia's capital. The auditorium, converted into the national tally room for the third federal election in three years, caused by the second dissolution of both Houses of Parliament in eighteen months, was packed with radio and television broadcasters, political party workers armed with calculators, slide rules and tally sheets, lines of telephones, and a wall of onlookers. It was a midsummer evening and shirt sleeves and six-packs of beer predominated among the spectators. As Whitlam walked purposefully to the bank of radio and television microphones that awaited him, a swell of applause rose from the Labor Party workers and the public areas.

Flanked by security guards, his wife Margaret, and members of his personal staff, Whitlam spoke firmly and briefly, losing, even at this time, none of the articulateness and fluency that was his trademark. He was heard in near silence even by the supporters of the new government who had broken out their tulip-shaped champagne glasses to celebrate their victory. Behind him — a dramatic backdrop for the television cameramen — were the huge tally boards that told the story of the most crushing defeat ever suffered by an Australian political party in a national election. Not only had the Labor Party, which Whitlam had led as either Leader or Deputy Leader for fifteen years, failed to regain the government but its representation in the 127-member House of Representatives had been slashed from 65 seats to 36. And in the concurrent Senate election, Labor would match its opponents in only one of the six States. It was clear the Liberal-National Country Party (LCP) coalition had won a decisive majority in both Houses.

Without a glance at the tally board, Whitlam formally conceded defeat. He expressed regret that so many of his colleagues
had lost their seats and called on those voters who had remained
loyal to Labor not to be despondent. Then he was gone — back
to the Lodge, the Prime Minister's official residence where,
through a television console linked to the central computer used
by the Australian Electoral Office, he had been receiving continuous reports of the night's counting which had begun at 8 pm.
It was 33 days since he had been dismissed as Prime Minister by
Sir John Kerr, Governor-General of Australia — the first
Australian Prime Minister to leave office by means other than
death, resignation or electoral defeat.

Exactly a year before, at about 11 pm on 13 December 1974,
Whitlam had presided as Prime Minister over a meeting of the
Executive Council at the Lodge. The Executive Council is the
formal pinnacle of Australia's system of government. It consists
of the Queen's Representative and Head of State, the Governor-
General, and the ministers of the government. Its function is to
formally approve and give legal effect to a myriad of administrative decisions made by the government, from the appointment of ambassadors and judges to the acquisition of land
to extend the runways at one of the nation's airports. Its rules of
operation are enshrined in convention as the Constitution does
no more than establish its existence. One rule relates to attendance at meetings and requires a minimum of three present,
of whom the Governor-General need not necessarily be one; as
he was not on this occasion, being in Sydney to attend a performance of *Romeo and Juliet*. Meetings are usually held at the
Governor-General's official Canberra residence at Yarralumla
but need not be, as the meeting of Friday 13 December 1974 was
not.

In addition to Whitlam, three ministers were present — Jim
Cairns, Deputy Prime Minister and Treasurer, Lionel Murphy,
Senate Leader and Attorney-General, and Rex Connor, senior
member of the Cabinet after Whitlam and Cairns, and Minister
for Minerals and Energy. It was, however, a meeting in little
more than name. The National Executive of the Labor Party —
an eighteen man body representing the eight State and territorial
branches of the ALP — had met in Canberra that day and was to
meet again the next day. In the study of the Lodge, the State
delegates were re-arguing the day's decisions over drinks and
lobbying each other for the morning. Whitlam, Cairns and Mur-

phy were all members of the National Executive because of their parliamentary office. Whitlam and Murphy joined in the National Executive discussions, but got up and left the room from time to time, often for up to half an hour.

They went on these occasions to the dining room where there was an extraordinary gathering of the nation's most senior and powerful bureaucrats, all working with Connor over a set of documents as they had been for some hours before arriving at the Lodge. In the dining room were grouped the Solicitor-General of Australia, Maurice Byers, QC; the Secretary of the Treasury, Sir Frederick Wheeler; the Secretary of the Department of Minerals and Energy, Sir Lenox Hewitt; the Secretary of the Prime Minister's Department, John Menadue; the Secretary of the Attorney-General's Department, Clarrie Harders; and two of Harders' top financial lawyers. Cairns was aware that this meeting was in progress but continued to confer with the National Executive delegates.

By midnight, the group of bureaucrats had settled on the text of a decision that the four ministers would sign and then forward to the Governor-General for his signature, which was necessary even if he did not attend meetings of the Executive Council. The decision was to authorise Connor, as Minister for Minerals and Energy, to borrow for the Commonwealth of Australia a sum 'not exceeding the equivalent of 4000 million dollars in the currency of the United States of America for temporary purposes'. Attached to the authorisation was an explanatory memorandum which stated why the money was necessary at this time. It read:

> The Australian Government needs immediate access to substantial sums of non-equity capital from abroad for temporary purposes, amongst other things to deal with exigencies arising out of the current world situation and the international energy crisis, to strengthen Australia's external financial position, to provide immediate protection for Australia in regard to supplies of minerals and energy and to deal with current and immediately foreseeable unemployment in Australia.

The documents were then signed by all four. When Whitlam was satisfied that they would be given to the Governor-General in Sydney early on Saturday morning, he dismissed the officials and returned to the National Executive meeting. It would last for some hours more but Whitlam, who was to fly out on a six week world trip in the morning, would not have the hangover that many of the delegates would have; rarely, if ever, did he have more than one or two drinks on such occasions.

In many ways the four — Whitlam, Cairns, Murphy and Connor — who had met that night as the Executive Council represented the accumulated strengths and weaknesses of the Labor government. They were, and had been, the most powerful men in that government and the most formative influences upon it. However different they were in so many other respects, they were all aware of this common role they shared and which had brought them together at the Lodge that night. It was perhaps all they had in common. Otherwise their sharply-etched personal and political differences reflected the diversity that is much more characteristic of non-conservative parties — the diversity that brings rare clusters of talents together but also subjects a party to much greater strain and conflict from within its own ranks.

Whitlam — single-minded and meticulous, volatile and impetuous — had been the source of Labor's policy base and administrative framework for over a decade and now dominated its government in a fashion few Labor leaders had attempted. Cairns — earnest and unyielding, eloquent and emotional — had brought politics into the streets and squares in the sixties but now found himself responsible for the management of the national economy in one of its most unstable periods. Murphy — articulate and flamboyant, yet secretive and often politically clumsy — had done much to resuscitate a moribund Senate in the sixties and now saw it emasculating Labor's programs. Connor — ruggedly old-fashioned in clothes and speech, but seeing life as an equation in hydrocarbons — had watched Australians become conscious of foreign control of their natural resources in the early seventies and could now implement his own vision for the nation's minerals and energy wealth. Each deserves detailed analysis for their role in the Labor government and also for their role in the Labor movement in the sixties and the early seventies where lay many of the seeds of their 13 December 1975 defeat.

Not just the participants but the very style and mechanics of the Executive Council meeting of 13 December 1974 reflected many of the central characteristics of the Labor government. At the most basic level nothing could have better exemplified the frenetic pace of those years than the time, 11 pm on a Friday night spilling over into the early hours of Saturday morning, and the locale, the Prime Minister's Lodge, with another meeting being conducted simultaneously in an adjoining room and the ministers alternating between the two.

The basic documents that were intended to constitute the borrowing authorisation, and the explanatory memorandum detailing the reasons for the loan, were only drafted a few hours earlier in the evening and were still the subject of discussion and dispute among those officials who had gathered at the Lodge at 10 pm. And nothing could have been more characteristic than such a dispute. The clash that night between Sir Frederick Wheeler and Sir Lenox Hewitt — both as tough and experienced as any mandarins of the Australian public service in recent years — over whose minister was to be named in the authorisation, was only a dramatic and, for once, documented example of the continual interdepartmental conflict which was to prove so costly to the government during its time in office — but never more costly than in the events leading up to, and arising out of, this Executive Council meeting.

It was, moreover, symptomatic of Labor's larger failure to attain mastery over the bureaucratic machine which alone enabled the wheels of government to turn. The government had initially refused to face up to the structural changes in the public service that were necessary if its major programs were to be rapidly implemented and to the changes in key personnel without which those structural changes could not be feasible. Now, after two years of government, it was much more conscious of the need for new administrative patterns but found the existing organs even stronger and more effective in their resistance than in 1972. Whatever Labor had learned about the bureaucracy in two years, it seemed likely that the bureaucracy had learned more about Labor. Many Labor ministers seemed incapable of grasping the reality that underlay the sort of bureaucratic confrontation that occurred between Sir Frederick Wheeler and Sir Lenox Hewitt — that their departments had long-standing interests which were pursued even to the detriment of the administration as a whole, not necessarily as a conscious process but because many senior bureaucrats would assume the national and their departmental interests to be synonymous. This was not unusual behaviour for any institution and the main problem was not its existence, but the recognition of its existence, so that it could be countered.

Even more obvious ought to have been the fact that the bureaucracy as a whole had certain interests, such as its interest in being the single source of advice to ministers, that it pursued collectively against any government, which is by definition transient in comparison to the public service. Again it is futile to expect the bureaucracy to react in any fashion but defensively to what it sees as an assault on its position. An awareness of the problem is, however, a pre-condition to its solution. Despite its initial fears, the bureaucracy in those first two years had been ineffectively challenged by Labor's long-held resolve to create alternative sources of advice. None of its attempts, including the ministerial staff system which still rankled with senior public servants, had been an overall success and it was significant that present at the Lodge that night as advisers were the departmental heads of all the ministers involved but no member of their private staffs.

If it could be said that departments seldom thought in terms of the government as a whole, this was a comment that could be applied forcibly to many ministers during the first two years of Labor's administration, and could be graphically illustrated by the events of 13 December 1974. As a rule, Executive Council meetings deal with the non-legislative decisions of Cabinet. On this occasion the question of loan authorisation had not been considered by Cabinet or by any other ministers. To a large extent the number of ministers — 27 including the Prime Minister — combined with the fact that all of these constituted the Cabinet, led to this kind of cabalisation and to the situation where people could speak seriously of the economic policy decisions of the first or second 'Kitchen Cabinet' as the small group of ministers in the Prime Minister's confidence changed. But the danger lay in transmitting to individual ministers the impression that somehow their actions could be divorced from those of the Cabinet or the government as a whole.

What was clearly lacking at the end of 1974 was any real notion of *the government* as an entity, with policies and priorities against which individual ministers and departments were required and, moreover, felt required, to test their own programs. In keeping with this seeming lack of appreciation that the government would be judged by the electorate as a unit, Cabinet conspicuously failed to discuss political tactics or the effect of its decisions in electoral terms. This, too, became the prerogative of more Kitchen Cabinets to which ministers might be admitted, or from which they might be excluded, for the most idiosyncratic reasons.

Yet in one sense the unconventional, almost desperate, quality of that night's activity demonstrated Labor's awareness of the forces that had ranged themselves against the government over the last two years. All four ministers who were present had watched while many of the government's most basic programs were consistently defeated in the Senate and resisted by small but effective interest groups in the community. To go outside the parliamentary process to seek loan funds for the government's programs was more likely to appear to them as one of the few means available of avoiding the frustration of some of those programs, than as the undermining of the Westminister system that their opponents would later portray it to be.

In addition, none of them could have any illusions as to the government's chances of seeing out its full term and implementing its programs at a leisurely pace. Despite Labor's re-election only seven months before, the Opposition ranks were already beginning to echo with talk of forcing another election. The realisation that twice each year the government's funds could be cut off by the Senate in an effort to force a premature election and, even more importantly, that neither the Opposition nor some important sections of the community conceded the government's legitimacy even after two election victories, inevitably inspired a sense of urgency that came from living on borrowed time. It had made Whitlam, Murphy and Connor, in particular, determined to let nothing stand in the way of, or postpone, the goals they had set for themselves.

These goals were often grandiose. Whether or not the economic strategy of using $4000 million to fund projects that could not be financed from domestic sources in the foreseeable future was feasible, it could not be denied that it was a spectacular attempt to break out of the budgetary straitjacket that had encased the governments of the industrial world in recent years. Yet paradoxically there was, as with so many of Labor's measures, no attempt to sell the idea to the electorate — an exercise which would not have been dependent on the economic arguments. A case could have been put to the public that the government was seeking loan funds to enable the immediate development of some of the nation's most valuable resources without the necessity for substantial involvement, and so control, by foreign corporations. Such an explanation, even had it done nothing else, would have dissipated some of the aura of secrecy and intrigue that was later to prove so damaging when the loans affair was made public.

For it was another of the ironies of 13 December 1974 that an exercise which to a large extent had its roots in the frustration of Labor's initiatives within the parliament was to supply its opponents with their most consistent ground of attack throughout 1975 and with their immediate rationale for blocking the Budget in October that year. It was supplied to an Opposition hungry for power, which would spare nothing in time or money to capitalise on such a gratuitous endowment.

This, then, was the situation of the Whitlam government on 13 December 1974. It was a government besieged by the most powerful forces from outside — forces that did not recognise it as the country's valid government and who were only awaiting the smallest opportunity to send it tumbling from office. At the same time it was subject from inside to severe pressures of its own making — pressures arising out of its failures to harness the machinery of government and out of the volatile personalities at its head. The obvious danger was that at some point in the future these external and internal pressures would irresistibly reinforce each other and shatter the thin shell of electoral support which alone had prevented the government from disintegrating.

Inside a year the four participants in the Executive Council meeting were to go radically separate ways — most of them unwillingly. Cairns would be dismissed as Treasurer by Whitlam, dismissed from the ministry by the Governor-General after refusing to resign, and finally removed as Deputy Leader of the Party by his colleagues. Connor would resign from the ministry after a series of newspaper articles on his overseas loan negotiations during 1975. Whitlam would be dismissed as Prime Minister and then crushed in a general election. Only Murphy departed, apparently voluntarily, in early 1975 to sit on the High Court of Australia. Perhaps he had his own premonitions about the outcome of events.

There was, however, one other person upon whom the Executive Council meeting was to have a significant impact — Sir John Kerr, who duly signed the loan authorisation in Sydney the next day, as he was required to if it was to take effect. Over the next year he can hardly have relished the charges by the Opposition and the media that the authorisation was of doubtful legality — so doubtful, by implication, that a man who had been a leader of the Sydney Bar, a Federal Judge and a Chief Justice of NSW ought perhaps to have questioned it before giving his approval and to have refused that approval until he was fully satisfied.

It is possible that these charges raised in his mind for the first time the question of how close his involvement should be with Whitlam and his government. As a conservative jurist over many years, he may have asked himself whether their ideas of the law and the Constitution were compatible with his own.

Most importantly, he may have had all these doubts consolidated late in 1975 when, with the Budget blocked in the Senate, Whitlam proposed an intricate scheme of financial arrangements to enable the government to continue its functions after its reserve funds ran out. Whitlam would argue then that the measures were entirely legal but Kerr would recall that this had been argued on a previous occasion, that later grave doubts had arisen and that he had been implicated.

Yet, even with the threatening presence of the Senate brooding over the government day after day, those who left the Lodge in the early hours of Saturday morning should have been able to view the approaching year with a degree of optimism. It was little more than six months since the government had been elected to a second term of office, having been given another chance, albeit narrowly, by the electorate in the apparent belief that it had not yet had a reasonable opportunity to implement its policies and to tackle the economic problems that had dominated the campaign. Ideally the next year would be a time of consolidation, with a run-up to an election sometime towards the end of 1976.

This scenario became more plausible if the Opposition itself were considered. It was in disarray, led by a man in whom most of his colleagues had lost confidence but whom a majority still preferred to his constant and abrasive challenger, Malcolm Fraser. It was only two months since Fraser had tried to depose Bill Snedden in the party room and, although defeated, he had begun at once to organise another attempt. Snedden knew this, as did his party and the government. The result was that Snedden's position was almost untenable and at the end of 1974 the Opposition was effectively without a Leader. It was a situation any government would have relished.

Not everyone in the Labor ranks shared this optimism but not even the most pessimistic would have predicted the year that was to follow — a year of disruption and disaffection that was to reduce the government to a position where it was rendered totally vulnerable in any electoral contest. As it was always in the Opposition's power to bring about such a contest, this was a conjunction of circumstances that the government could not hope to survive.

It was also to be a year of personal disillusionment for many members of the government. After two decades of Opposition, there was likely to be a degree of unreality in the expectations of some. But few of them in 1972 would have accepted that in 1975 unemployment would be a major problem for a Labor government whose commitment to full employment could be nothing less than total. Nor that the government's involvement in the negotiations over the independence of East Timor could evoke the style if not the magnitude of its predecessor's experience in Vietnam. Nor that their support in the electorate would decline most sharply in those groups which had been traditionally Labor's strongest supporters, whose improved welfare had seemed at least one tangible gain of the time in office.

It is worth asking what happened between those two nights a year apart, between that full-bodied if desperate scene of Labor in office and the bleak depression of that converted high school as Whitlam conceded defeat. The bases for many of the events of 1975, both for Labor and its opponents, were laid during the first two years of government and perhaps nothing could have halted their consolidation by the beginning of that year. But this was to be the year when they all culminated to paralyse and finally destroy the Whitlam government.

2   The Titan Gough Whitlam

On 29 October, almost two weeks after the Senate had blocked
the 1975 Budget, thus threatening the survival of his three-year
government, Gough Whitlam, Prime Minister of Australia,
delivered the John Curtin Memorial Lecture for that year at the
campus of the Australian National University (ANU) a mile or so
from Parliament House. After comparing the pressures of war
on Curtin's government with the present crisis in his own
administration, he set out what he saw as some of the basic
differences between Australia's political parties, saying:

> A conservative Government survives essentially by dampening
> expectations and subduing hopes. Conservatism is basically
> pessimistic; reformism is basically optimistic. The great tradition
> which links the American and French revolutionaries of the Age of
> Reason with the modern parties of social reform is the tradition of
> optimism about the possibility of human improvement and human
> progress through the means of human reason. (Whitlam 1975b)

It was not a statement that could possibly have been made by
any other prominent post-war politician on either side, or by few
since Federation. With its attempt to place Australia's parties in
their broad historical context, its drawing on the experiences of
other nations and, above all, its expression of faith in 'human
reason', it represents the antithesis of the mundane, parochial
and paternalistic utterances of most political leaders over those
post-war years. Implicit also in the passage is the respect that
Whitlam had for an audience. In a fashion almost unknown in
the Australian political experience, he treated them as serious
and interested participants in the political process, pressing on
them masses of facts and ideas instead of stale rhetoric. In many
ways those few sentences suggested Whitlam's greatest strength
and weakness — his own idealistic commitment to rational

progress for mankind, and yet his intolerance of, or more commonly, his incomprehension of, those individuals or groups who did not share this commitment.

In 1952, when Gough Whitlam, then 36 years old, entered the Australian Parliament at a by-election for the seat of Werriwa — a safe Labor electorate running through Sydney's southern suburbs including Cronulla, where Whitlam lived, down towards Wollongong — he was an early example of a future development in Australian politics, the educated professional man who had determined on a lifetime career in politics. Although Menzies and Evatt had gone into politics relatively young, they had already established themselves in the front rank of the Bar and could have always picked up where they had left off if political disaster struck. It was still much more common for such men like Sir Garfield Barwick or, even later, Robert Ellicott, to enter Parliament when they had fulfilled all their ambitions in another field. This was not Whitlam's way.

By 1952 he had been at the Sydney Bar for five years and although he made a comfortable living, much of it from landlord and tenant work, his legal career was still very much in its early stages. But during those five years he had indicated clearly that he was prepared to spend all his free time in political activities and was anxious to gain elected office as soon as possible. After joining the ALP in 1945, he gained pre-selection for the Sydney City Council elections as a Labor candidate in 1947. The elections were deferred, however, and in that time he moved to Cronulla where, in 1950, he gained pre-selection for the local State seat of Sutherland, losing at the next election to the sitting Liberal member. The same year he also stood as a Labor candidate for the Sutherland Shire Council but was defeated in this poll also. Throughout this period he was actively involved in a multiplicity of local community groups like the Parents and Citizens Association, the Progress Association and the Returned Servicemen's League. While some of these may have been natural bodies for a young family man to join, the degree of involvement suggests an intention to gain maximum exposure in the area and a clear realisation of the political utility of this kind of activity. It also gives some indication of his enormous reserves of energy and his closely related capacity to throw himself into what would be stultifying tasks. By 1952 his efforts had paid off and he was a member of the national Parliament.

During the rest of the 1950s there was a strange lack of

correlation between the career of Whitlam and the ALP. After narrowly losing the 1954 election, at which it polled over 50 per cent of the votes cast, the Party's latent factionalism erupted into the split which divided it at every level, from local branch members to parliamentary representatives, in every State and in the Federal Parliament. Labor lost elections in 1955 and 1958, with many Party members locked in obsessive sectarian conflicts with former colleagues, conflicts which clouded their reason and destroyed their electoral credibility. While many of his fellow members were fighting the battles of the past, Whitlam was busy laying the plans of the future. He was always busy — researching speeches, reading reports, developing his own indexing system for Hansard because the index supplied was not detailed enough for him. The basic themes of Labor's program, offered to the electorate in 1972, all had their genesis in this period, some of them at an extraordinarily early stage, like the proposal for a national scheme to provide compensation to all persons injured in accidents, whether in automobiles, at work or in the home, which he produced for a Caucus Committee within his first year in the Parliament. Such a scheme was at the heart of Whitlam's developing interests. It would have involved the use of federal funds to deal with a problem that, while common to every part of the country, was being dealt with by time-consuming individual litigation and costly private insurance under different State laws.

It would also have involved a novel use of some of the federal government's powers under the Constitution. It must be recalled that in the 1950s the Constitution appeared as a significant obstacle to the administration of any future Labor government. In the last years of the 1940s, two of the Chifley government's major projects — the nationalisation of banks and of airlines — had been held to violate the Constitution by both the High Court and the Privy Council. In addition it was widely believed that the entire bank nationalisation imbroglio had been one of the factors that cost Labor government in 1949, and it was quite natural that Whitlam's 1957 Chifley Lecture at Melbourne University should have been entitled *The Constitution versus Labor.*

By any standards, Whitlam's interest in this subject was acute. He himself asserts that his decision to join the Labor Party was triggered in 1944 by the opposition of the conservative parties to Curtin's attempt to gain, by referendum, increased federal powers for post-war reconstruction. A full outlet for Whitlam's efforts in this area was provided by the Joint Parliamentary Committee of Constitutional Review that operated from 1956 to 1959. As one of the Labor representatives on the Committee, he steeped himself in questions of federal power and was one of the majority, comprising members of both sides, which recommended referendums to secure increased commonwealth powers in several areas. Menzies was not inclined, however, to follow up the proposals and they were seldom heard of again — except from Whitlam. He had recognised one way to circumvent the nationalisation problem — public enterprises that were established not to monopolise an industry but to compete with existing private corporations — and he was ready in 1972 to propose such bodies as the Petroleum and Minerals Authority, the Pipelines Authority, and the Australian Government Insurance Corporation. He also appreciated the solution to the problem of control over federal funds given to the States — the provision in section 96 of the Constitution that allowed the commonwealth to attach conditions to these grants governing how the money was spent — and would make it a feature of his own government's administration.

Ironically, in view of Whitlam's concern at this time over the national government's lack of powers for economic management, the High Court ensured by decisions it gave during the sixties and early seventies that a federal government could, by 1972, exercise legal powers of regulation over almost every aspect of the national economy, with the possible exception of wages and prices and then only if this was attempted directly instead of by some of the indirect means available. By this stage, management of the economy had become a question not of legal capacity but of political will.

His work on the Constitution had one other important by-product. It developed in him a deep-seated impatience with the role of State governments in Australia. He became conscious of how the division of functions between State and federal governments under the Constitution did not simply affect the distribution of governmental power in Australia but also, by diffusing it among seven bodies, made significant economic and social change more difficult to achieve, making the point with a typical historical and classical allusion that the founding fathers had achieved the same result as if they had followed 'the Hapsburg injunction, *divide et impera,* realising that the entrenched classes find it easier to maintain their hegemony in a divided polity'. (Whitlam 1957) On the grounds of efficiency, therefore, rather than any centralist ideology, he began to argue for a concentration of policy decisions in the hands of the national government, with the actual implementation of programs and disbursement of funds carried out by regional authorities who would be closer to people than State governments and thus less concerned with constitutional pretensions. Again these were early formulations. In September 1953 he told the House:

> The States are neither flesh nor fowl, nor good red herring; neither national bodies nor local government bodies. They have not the means to be national nor the time to be provincial.

To some extent these notions reflected his days as a child in Canberra where he spent the last six years of schooling, the son of a senior public servant there, Frederick Whitlam, who moved his family from Sydney to Canberra in 1927 and became Crown Solicitor for the Commonwealth. For him Canberra never posed the dark threat to State powers that it did for many of his colleagues. But this approach had its real roots in his life in Cronulla and later in Cabramatta, one of Sydney's newer suburbs into which he moved in 1955 when his seat of Werriwa was altered by an electoral redistribution. As these regions on the outskirts of the metropolitan areas of Australia's coastal capitals began to swell with new residents in the immediate post-war years, State and municipal governments — the traditional providers — were unable to keep pace with the demand for schools, hospitals, roads, sewerage, street-lighting and similar amenities. Their absence was particularly obvious to Whitlam because, when he was away from Cabramatta, he was usually in Canberra — a planned city that had an abundance of these services for its small population.

It was also a problem that touched one of his dominant motivations. Just as he had proposed a scheme of national compensation to deal with the sheer waste of resources and inefficiency present in the existing methods of compensating accident victims, he now considered that only the national government could introduce and fund a coherent program of urban improvement that would avoid serious inequalities between different areas in cities like Sydney and Melbourne. Again the national government's role was not premised on ideology but on rationality and efficiency. He never reneged on this view of the States as historical accidents without intrinsic utility. In 1969 he would say:

> More money alone, however, is not a cure-all for the problems of federalism. More money cannot rationalise the 6 State boundaries which were established arbitrarily in London more than a century ago by officials ignorant of Australian affairs. (Whitlam 1969)

Rationality, equality and his outer suburban base were also responsible for one of his earliest and most unswerving causes — electoral reform. It was a source of constant resentment to him that those living in his own populous electorate should find their vote worth less than that of electors in other parts of the State and the nation, most particularly in comparison to rural electorates which were effectively permitted by law to have considerably less numbers than other seats. The cause of one vote/one value was one he would pursue throughout the years of Opposition and later in government. In the last days of government he personally organised a High Court challenge to the still existing inequality between electorates after the Senate had vetoed Labor's legislation for a redistribution.

Central to this crusade for electoral justice was his belief in Parliament, the product of elections and therefore the reason why they must contain no element that might lessen the status of that institution. Towards the end of his campaign opening at Festival Hall in Melbourne on 24 November 1975 he would say:

> My whole public career has been dedicated to the proposition that the reform and change needed in Australia can and must be achieved through democratic Parliamentary means. For fifteen years as Deputy Leader of my Party and Leader of my Party and Prime Minister of Australia, I have maintained that faith. And the Australian Labor Party has held to that faith with me. (Whitlam 1975c)

It was a remarkable statement from someone who had just seen his government destroyed by the use of the parliamentary system. But above all else in the 1950s he had dedicated himself to becoming a parliamentarian. He prepared his speeches assiduously, delivered them with eloquence and earnestness, mastered the intricate rules and procedures of the House of Representatives, served enthusiastically on committees, in short, treated the Parliament — not the electorate — as the centre of his political life. It was his forum for presenting information to the nation and also his means, in the system of questions and committees, of forcing the government to produce information.

Years later, when Leader of the Opposition and sitting beside a swimming pool at Labor Party conference hotels, he would still break off a conversation to have one of his staff make a note for the Notice Paper of a question that had just occurred to him. He saw Parliament as the chief vehicle for educating the electorate about the political system and would never become cynical about that ideal.

To some extent this commitment to Parliament as a means of reform was motivated, however unconsciously, by his own flair for, and ultimately dominance of, the institution. It is a syndrome that Michael Foot identified in his biography of Aneurin Bevan, a British Labour leader from a very different background to Whitlam, but similarly a formidable parliamentarian. Foot said of Bevan that:

> even while the institution was failing so pitifully to mirror the turmoil outside, he acquired a deep respect, almost a love, for the House of Commons. He saw it as a place where, given a proper use of its possibilities, poverty could win the battle against property without bloodshed. Not that he enjoyed, as a substitute for political action, the cosy conventions of the parliamentary game. He never shut his ears to the storms outside ... Yet gradually and imperceptibly — and the fact was of considerable importance for his own future and the Labour Party's — he came to regard Parliament as the most precious potential instrument in the hands of the people. Doubtless his own prowess in the arena influenced his view. It would be harsh to blame a great matador for upholding the virtues of bullfighting. (Foot 1975)

As one of their most formidable opponents, even in these years, Whitlam received considerable attention from the Liberals, but no one in the Parliament was better able to put on the armour of invective. 'Bumptious bastard' for Garfield Barwick; 'Celtic clown' for Hugh Roberton; 'grizzling quisling' for William Bourke who had left Labor for the DLP; these were a few of his jibes. Even when Prime Minister he would still be capable of the quick, clever, brutal comeback. Amid a fracas in the House on 15 November 1973 between Whitlam and Opposition Leader Bill Snedden as to whether a Liberal shadow minister had been drunk at a parliamentary reception the previous evening, the following exchange took place:

> Mr WHITLAM — I invite honourable gentlemen to look at the honourable gentleman's eyes, even this morning.
> Mr Wentworth — On a point of order —
> Mr SPEAKER — Order! The House will come to order.

Mr Snedden — You must be ashamed of yourself.
Mr WHITLAM — You ought to be ashamed of yourself, too.
Look at him: Look at his bleary face.
Mr Snedden — You are being gutless.
Mr WHITLAM — It is what he put in his guts that rooted him.
Mr Snedden — On a point of order. I ask the Prime Minister to
repeat the exact words he just used. I hope that Hansard wrote them
down. Did Hansard get those words?
Mr SPEAKER — Order!

It was in the 1950s also that he developed the themes that he
would pursue for so many years in another area of passionate
interest — foreign affairs and international relations. Influenced
by Australia's separation from other culturally western nations,
but also by a strong disposition against international as well as
national inequalities, he argued for an anti-colonialist and anti-
racist foreign policy, most particularly in relation to Papua New
Guinea which Australia maintained as its own quasi-colony. At
the same time he demanded a recognition of the realities of
international relations, and laid special emphasis on Australia's
refusal to recognise communist China despite the absolute
improbability of its ever being overthrown by the former
government that now occupied the island of Taiwan.
Membership of Parliament also enabled him to inspect issues of
foreign affairs at first hand. Omnivorous in absorbing facts, as
always, he found new mines of information in foreign lands, and
formed a determination often found in Australians who are
conscious of their country's physical isolation, to return to them
at frequent intervals — a determination religiously observed for
the rest of his career.

Thus the 1950s were productive, formative years for Whitlam.
His colleagues were sufficiently impressed to elect him to the
Party Executive in 1959 and to the Deputy Leadership in 1960.
In many ways however, he was still an unknown quantity to
them even in 1960. Evatt had stepped down suddenly from the
leadership to become Chief Justice of NSW and had been
replaced by Arthur Calwell, his deputy. Whitlam was the most
junior of those who stood for the position vacated by Calwell,
and slipped through the middle of the field to win narrowly. The
fact that Calwell and both Senate Leaders were Catholics would
certainly have assisted Whitlam against some of the other
candidates for the deputy leadership who were also Catholics.
The extent to which he was an unknown quantity was to cause
his colleagues a series of severe shocks over the next few years.

In retrospect, it is difficult to recapture the pessimism that had infected the Party of which Whitlam had become Deputy Leader. Disregarding the 1961 election, which was as surprising to Labor in the narrowness of its result as it was to the Liberals, the ALP was then in the middle of one of the most depressing decades of its history. Between 1955 and 1966 it lost five elections for the House of Representatives, the last by the most crushing margin ever. Menzies ran the national government like an indolent ringmaster, doing little between elections but sardonically scheduling the polls to coincide with a period of particularly intense infighting within Labor's ranks. Bitterness that could not be vented upon the Liberals or the DLP was translated into intra-party faction fights — often under the guise of the old dispute concerning government assistance to independent schools — and helped produce the situation in 1969 where the last surviving Labor government in the country was defeated — in Tasmania — to leave the LCP in control of the federal and all State administrations. If the feeling of hopelessness was already strong in 1960 when Whitlam was elected, it would become even more pronounced during his period as Deputy.

For the first three years of their partnership Calwell and Whitlam worked in harmony, but the relationship deteriorated rapidly after the 1963 election to the extent that in January 1965 Whitlam was reported, in what he had apparently intended to be an off-the-record comment, as saying that Calwell was 'too old and weak' to remain as Leader. It was in 1963 that Whitlam began two long term projects designed to significantly improve Labor's national image and ultimately end the exile from power that was eroding its collective will. Both problems had their roots in the Cold War years of the early fifties but were no easier to tackle for the lapse of time. One was the use of foreign affairs in Australian politics; the other the role of the Victorian Central Executive (VCE) in the Labor Party.

For Menzies, issues of foreign affairs had been a consistent electoral bonanza since 1954. In that vintage year of the Cold War, the defection of the Soviet diplomat Petrov, with his tale of large scale espionage and the last minute snatching of his wife from her Soviet guards at Darwin airport, dramatised for Australia the feelings of insecurity that ran through most nations of the West. As the leader of the conservative parties that had traditionally portrayed themselves as more anti-communist and pro-British (now pro-American also) than Labor, Menzies sensed that Labor was vulnerable to the charge of being 'soft' on communism and on the communist threat to the Free World in general and to Australia in particular. And Labor was vulnerable, if only because this issue had also become the catalyst in a long-simmering faction fight that would soon produce the split. By the early 1960s Menzies' orchestration of the foreign affairs and defence issues to raise doubts about Labor's commitment to the protection of Australia, and especially about its enthusiasm for the American alliance, had reached the status of an art form. At the 1963 election, for example, it was the dispute within the Labor Party over the establishment of the US communications station at North West Cape that provided the vehicle for Menzies' standard strategy.

In 1965, however, the test of commitment to halting the communist advance, to supporting the American alliance, and finally the test of loyalty itself, became much stiffer with the introduction of Australian troops into the Vietnam war. Labor would now be in the invidious position of failing to support Australian soldiers fighting in the field. Well aware that Menzies' personal departure in 1965 would not cause any change in these tactics, and that it was not possible for Labor to beat the Liberals at war games, Whitlam initiated his long term campaign to defuse foreign affairs and defence as electoral issues. To some extent this exercise depended on the movement of global political forces but he made a start in 1963 by eschewing Calwell's emotional reaction to the Menzies government's open support for US intervention in Vietnam and by emphasising the practical problems of the war and international reaction against it. Even during the 1966 election campaign he refused to support Calwell's view of immediate withdrawal of the Australian contingent, believing that the electorate would not accept this, although he flatly opposed conscription for Vietnam.

At the same time, he carefully avoided any suggestion of the antipathy to the US alliance and to the US itself that permeated much of the Labor Party as the war dragged on. It was still possible, on his visit to America soon after becoming Party Leader in 1967, for him to be described by Lyndon Johnson as the 'young and brilliant leader of the Australian Labor Party'. He continued to pursue this strategy throughout the rest of the 1960s and at the 1969 election the Liberals found it difficult, for the first time in years, to make capital out of the defence issue.

After 1969, as American and then Australian opinion began to react against the fact that Vietnam was going badly, even this issue became less dangerous for Labor. The march of world events was now in harmony with Whitlam's plan to remove foreign affairs as a permanent electoral liability. The smashing symbol of his success came in July 1971 when he conferred with China's Premier, Chou En-lai, in the Great Hall of the People in Peking. In Canberra Prime Minister William McMahon branded his visit to China, with whom Australia still had no diplomatic relations, as an insult to the US — while in Washington final preparations had been concluded for Henry Kissinger's secret journey to Peking to arrange a visit to China by the US President in ten months' time. When news of Kissinger's negotiations broke a week later, Labor found itself in the dizzy position of seeming more responsible than the Liberals on a matter that not simply involved foreign policy but also related to China — the brooding northern threat of the last 20 years which McMahon himself had described as one of the Liberals' real political assets.

Another asset had been the Victorian Central Executive. If the split was in part a product of the Cold War, then so was the VCE, for it owed its character to the fact that after 1955 Victoria was the stronghold of the DLP. The DLP took almost a third of the Labor Party vote in Victoria and left behind an embattled rump whose sole fixation for many years was to resist encroachment on their control of the party machine, whether from outside by the National Civic Council/DLP, or from inside by members of the Labor Party who wanted to broaden the Party's base of support in the State. Ever alert to a threat to their position, the Victorians sensed Whitlam's plans and became his chief foes within the Party's Federal Executive. In 1966 they led the struggle to have him expelled from the Labor Party for his remark about the twelve-man Executive on national television:

> I can only say we've just got rid of the thirty-six faceless men stigma to be faced with the twelve witless men. (Oakes 1973)

In the very week in which he had begun an intensive by-election campaign for Rex Patterson in the Queensland seat of Dawson, the Federal Executive had made statements about government aid to independent schools that would obviously alienate those Catholics who did not already vote DLP. Despite an upset victory to Labor in Dawson, Whitlam came within an ace of expulsion at an Executive meeting a week later, only being saved by a last-minute change by the Queensland delegates. He had now come to see the state aid question as symbolic in the sense that those who wished to keep the Party's platform firmly opposed to such assistance were essentially uninterested in achieving power and unconcerned that they were crippling the Party at an electoral level. His overwhelming goal was the achievement of government and he saw this spirit of detachment as the greatest single obstacle to the Party's success.

The incident was also characteristic of his rapidly developing 'crash through or crash' style of confrontation. Despite the amount of time he spent at the top of the Party, Whitlam was never really a 'numbers man' in the assiduous sense that many of his colleagues were. Rather than assemble support over a period of time for this attack on the Federal Executive he preferred to simply launch an assault and rely on the merits of his case. It was an approach that presupposed a high degree of altruism and objectivity on the part of his audience, which perhaps explained why so few of his colleagues ever employed it. Just under a year later, however, he had regained enough ground to be easily elected Leader when Calwell stepped down. Thus it was back on to the attack. In June 1967 he told assembled delegates at the Victorian State Conference:

> This conference will exercise its right to elect its own executive; I will exercise my right to repudiate such men as I believe disloyal to the ALP, disruptive of its electoral prospects and destructive of all the ALP stands for.

The next major confrontation came in April 1968 when a meeting of the Federal Executive disapproved of Whitlam's attacks on the Victorian branch and, at the same time, refused to allow one of the two Tasmanian delegates, Brian Harradine, to take his place because of criticisms he had made of other delegates on the Executive. Although Whitlam was now a member of the Executive, along with the Deputy Leader of the Parliamentary Party and the two Senate Leaders, he was on the losing side in all these votes. Next day he resigned as Leader and asked his parliamentary colleagues for a vote of confidence. In a letter to each of them he said:

> It is futile for the VCE to pretend that if I would only abandon my efforts to promote the well-being of the ALP in its State, then the problems of the Party in that State would end. Even if Caucus replaces me, the problems of our appalling and declining electoral

performance in Victoria would still continue: the unrepresentative character of the VCE, the influence of an outside and secret body upon it, its disruptive relations with the Melbourne Trades Hall Council, its strained relations with the State Parliamentary Party, the factionalism of its official publication, the crude partisanship of its articles in the great Melbourne dailies, its inability to sustain branch membership and morale, its alienation of many scores of earnest members. If I were to cease my efforts tomorrow, not one of these problems would be removed and indeed most of them would get worse . . .

My whole approach is based on the obvious premise that we cannot achieve significant economic, social and industrial reforms by political means unless we hold over half the seats in the House of Representatives and win over half the votes of the people of Australia. There will be an undue burden on the Caucus and the other State Executives in winning half the seats in the House of Representatives if Victoria makes no greater contribution than in recent years. We cannot hope to win half the votes unless the Caucus and all organs of the Party represent views which are acceptable to half the people. (Oakes 1973)

This was a full-blooded declaration of war — to which the Victorians responded by setting out to ensure that, once having resigned, Whitlam would never regain the leadership. They were prepared to support Deputy Leader Lance Barnard for the post, and he would certainly have won had he contested it. When Barnard decided to support Whitlam they threw their full support behind Cairns. And they very nearly succeeded. Members of Caucus who would normally have had little sympathy with the VCE, like Fred Daly, voted for Cairns because they resented Whitlam's sudden demand for a vote of confidence. Whitlam won narrowly and probably only because enough members of Caucus feared the electoral consequences of Cairns' leadership, with his general image as the Party's leading left-winger and his regular participation in anti-war demonstrations. It was anything but a vote of confidence in Whitlam. Having survived, he returned immediately, with characteristic single-mindedness, to the struggle for government of which one prerequisite, in his view, was still the replacement of the VCE.

The VCE was finally crushed two and a half years later in September 1970 in Melbourne where the Federal Executive had met to consider complaints against it. Whitlam was by now in an unassailable position after his 1969 campaign which had gained a seven per cent swing and seventeen seats for Labor in the House of Representatives. And the VCE had astonished even some of its supporters by its performance in the Victorian State election in May 1970, not least at the campaign opening when State Labor Leader Clyde Holding, with Whitlam sitting behind him, delivered a policy speech that guaranteed some government aid to independent schools while, at the same time, members of the executive distributed to the press a revised version of the speech that stated that all such aid would be phased out over a period of time. Yet the VCE fought intervention by the Federal Executive to the very last and only the meticulous preparation of the intervention case by the South Australian MHR Clyde Cameron, and his energetic collection of votes, overcame their resistance. Cameron, although long an opponent of Whitlam in the Party, had looked at the results of the 1969 election and observed that Labor had got within seven seats of government, even though it carried only eleven seats out of 34 in Victoria. Cameron's obsessive interest was industrial relations and he wanted to preside over this area in a Labor government. This calculation brought about a conclusion that all Whitlam's years of argument had not been able to achieve.

At the same time as Labor's electoral drive towards government began to accelerate in the last few years of the 1960s, Whitlam continued to co-ordinate an accumulation of material that was translated every two years at federal conferences into pages of detailed policies in the Party platform, ready to be placed before the electorate as a blueprint for change after two decades of conservative government. Still the linchpin of this agenda, and providing the impetus for so many of the policies, was the recognition of the distinctive and difficult character of life in the post-war suburbs of Australian cities. In a 1969 pamphlet of Whitlam's was a passage that even now shows a singular appreciation of this phenomenon:

> Far from establishing communities in any meaningful sense of the word, we are moving in the opposite direction. Sydney and Melbourne, the cities in which most Australians choose to live or are obliged to live, are becoming less and less communities and more and more conurbations-agglomerated, sprawling masses of houses, inhabited by people whom the pattern of urban growth forces to travel further and further to work; taking longer and longer to get there; sharing less and less in common with their fellow citizens; knowing and wishing to know less and less of the common problems and interests of those around them. Hundreds of thousands of Australians in each of our major cities today could not answer even in its most literal sense the biblical question: 'Who is my neighbour?' (Whitlam 1969)

And the conclusion was, as always, undeviating:

It suits the Liberal Party to assert that urban facilities and urban services are matters for the States. Liberals are appalled by the inevitable increase in government expenditure and planning involved in providing better urban facilities and better urban services. They know that the best way to restrict government expenditure on any activity is to claim that it is one for the States, which have fewer financial resources than the Commonwealth. It would be naive and erroneous for Australians to accept the proposition that their national government has no responsibility for the cities and regional centres in which a majority of the nation's population make their homes. (Whitlam 1969)

It was therefore very much the culmination of 20 years of massive personal effort when, on 2 December 1972, Labor was elected to government, although by the relatively narrow margin of nine seats, after 23 years in the wasteland of Opposition.

Of all the survivors of the wasteland — the 20-years-or-more men like Clyde Cameron, Fred Daly, Kim Beazley and Frank Crean — only Whitlam had not been in some measure withered by those endless days of frustration and impotence in the House of Representatives, days of watching Menzies preside languidly over a series of governments while the most active years of their lives drifted away, days of lost divisions and lost causes. It was typical of Whitlam's almost superhuman energy and endurance that he had emerged from this period with the most detailed program in the nation's political history and an undiminished enthusiasm to implement it paragraph by paragraph.

He was, moreover, very much aware that so many of the policies were essentially *his* policies — just as he was aware that he had been largely responsible for neutralising most of Labor's long-standing electoral liabilities and for embodying in his own person the attractions of a reformist party for many who had never voted Labor before. In this mood of assurance and achievement it was not surprising that the government soon became *his* government.

He embarked at once on the implementation of the programs on which he had been working for 20 years. For the central theme of the cities, there was a new department — Urban and Regional Development — to channel increased funds into housing, sewerage, transport and other services in the outer metropolitan areas. In addition it would initiate the long term task of easing the pressure on existing cities by the creation of new centres — the first by an amalgamation of the towns of

Albury and Wodonga located, on opposite banks of the Murray River, at the NSW-Victoria border.

Perhaps the most illustrative element of the urban program was the selection of certain areas — for example, the western suburbs of Sydney and Melbourne — for special assistance in an effort to improve rapidly community facilities that had fallen well behind those of other areas within the same city. In the western region of Melbourne, for example, this involved the upgrading of hospitals, the setting up of community health centres, the provision of migrant welfare officers and additional library and information services. It also extended to the kind of amenities other areas of Melbourne took for granted — public swimming pools, trees and shrubs, the setting aside of some land for parks or simply as open space — but that suburbs like Sunshine and St Albans would have scarcely recognised.

Flowing into these areas at the same time — and into every region — were the greatly increased funds for schools that constituted the most striking of all Labor's commitments to public responsibility. In many ways education expenditure reflected Whitlam's priorities, as its underlying rationale was the creation of equal opportunity — not equality of current condition. It was a program that was premised not on the redistribution of existing resources but on the provision of increased resources that would enable any child to obtain at least the option of an adequate school education. This notion of equality of *access* rather than equality of *means* is captured in a passage from his Chifley Memorial Lecture delivered at the University of Melbourne in August 1975:

> The concept of equality — what I call positive equality — does not have as its goal equality of personal income. Its goal is greater equality of the services which the community provides. This approach not merely accepts the pluralistic nature of our system, with the private sector continuing to play the greater part in providing employment and growth; it positively requires private affluence to prevent public squalor. The approach is based on this concept: increasingly a citizen's real standard of living, the health of himself and his family, his children's opportunity for education and self-improvement, his access to employment opportunities, his ability to enjoy the nation's resources for recreation and cultural activity, his ability to participate in the decisions and actions of the community, are determined not so much by his income but by the availability and accessibility of the services which the community alone can provide and ensure. (Whitlam 1975a)

His government's most visible single measure — Medibank — was based squarely on this model. It provided access to public health insurance for those persons previously unable to afford private insurance but it was to be financed by a levy on taxable income which would have still resulted in lower income earners paying a much greater percentage of their income for health care than higher income earners.

Medibank's other premise was the passion for rationalisation, for efficient use of resources, which Whitlam had maintained during his years in Opposition. He focussed quite naturally on the use of a number of health insurance companies to carry out precisely the same function in specious competition, thus preventing the adoption of the kinds of economies of scale that could reduce the rate of growth of the cost of health care. How strong this passion still remained towards the end of his government can be gauged from a number of passages in an address delivered to an ANU conference in August 1975. Speaking of the role of federal funding, he said:

> At the heart of the program for national involvement lay a view about modern, more contemporary, *more rational* relations between the three levels of government and more modern, more contemporary, *more rational* arrangements for the financing and discharge of functions which modern communities now require their elected representatives to fulfil. (Whitlam 1975b, emphasis added)

And referring to the government's spending on education and urban development, he emphasised that

> these programs had to be defined within a *reasoned framework* of national-state-local relations, financial, functional and administrative.

It was this same approach that attracted him to tariff reform in the economic area as a first step towards the creation of a more efficient manufacturing sector.

Of all the ALP's rationally-based programs, the most representative, for a variety of reasons, was the proposed scheme of national compensation. It embodied Whitlam's genuinely radical view that if social institutions — in this case the system of compensation for personal injuries through litigation in the courts — were not functioning efficiently, they should be scrapped and replaced by a new structure. In addition, as a scheme first put forward in its essentials by Whitlam in 1952, it represented matchless evidence of his persistence and explained his deep commitment to its introduction by a Labor government.

In essence the scheme provided for

— the payment of compensation on a weekly basis to persons injured in motor or other accidents without the necessity of legal action as is generally the case at present.

— the payment of compensation on a weekly basis to all other persons, such as housewives who are injured in accidents at home, who currently have no right to any benefits at all.

While more persons would have been compensated for injury than under existing schemes, considerable funds would have been saved by the abolition of the costly and time-consuming procedures engaged in by insurance companies and their lawyers. In addition to accident compensation, the scheme was to provide sickness benefits to all members of the community. This would have entailed much greater costs, and the funding problems of that side of the scheme concerned even some of his own colleagues.

It was, nevertheless, a classic Whitlam production. *Rational*, in its substitution of earnings-related compensation paid to all persons who suffered injury by accident for random lump-sum awards made to a small percentage of those injured, often after years of delay. *National*, in its reliance on federal funding and its insistence that an injury suffered in one State should be treated no differently from an injury suffered in another State. *Adventurous*, in its pushing to the very edges several of the federal government's powers under the Constitution. *Grandiose*, in its coverage of every person in the country for both accident and sickness compensation. But also, as his critics on the left argued, it was supportive of the existing distribution of wealth by providing greater compensation for the same injury or sickness if suffered by higher income earners. And as his critics on the right alleged, it was hastily drafted, with the result that it was not properly costed with respect to sickness benefits. Moreover it had been prepared without consultation with colleagues, with the result that it overlapped with many current social security benefits and was not designed to fit at all into the existing welfare system.

The national compensation scheme was prepared by a Committee of Inquiry comprising Mr Justice Woodhouse of the New Zealand Court of Appeal, who had reported on a similar scheme for that country and Mr Justice Meares of the NSW Supreme Court. The Committee was established by Whitlam in April 1973 and reported in June 1974. Legislation implementing the scheme passed the House of Representatives in October 1974 but was referred by the Opposition Senate majority to a Standing Committee of the Senate — the Committee on Constitutional and Legal Affairs. Even the Labor Senators on this committee, while supporting the reform of accident compensation, expressed concern about the cost of sickness cover and about the absence of any co-ordination with the existing range of welfare benefits — to the fury of Whitlam who accused them of joining the Opposition to sabotage the government's programs. As a result of the committee's report in July 1975, he was forced to withdraw the legislation and to have it redrafted so that only accidents and not sickness also were covered. This would still not have been acceptable to the Opposition but time ran out before the redrafted Bill could be introduced, as had been planned, in late 1975.

If the Whitlam agenda, painstakingly devised throughout the 1950s and 1960s, emphasised a more rational use of Australia's resources, it assumed a quantity and quality of resources that made efficient use the central problem. By the seventies the distribution of those resources within Australia, and between Australia and the rest of the world, had begun to emerge as an unavoidable issue for governments. It was an issue that became overwhelming soon after Labor took office, and the nations of the west discovered that the effortless economic development of the 1960s had come to an end, at least temporarily. Faced with advice that he would have to choose between parts of his program or sections of the community, Whitlam responded initially with bewildered frustration.

For some months in late 1974 he listened blankly and without response to Treasury advisers who offered the alternative of either inflation or unemployment on a record scale. It was not a situation in which he can ever have envisaged himself when he was contemplating government from the Opposition benches. Nor had he contemplated the prospect of foreign investors cutting back on the flow of capital to Australia or transnational corporations already established in Australia, like General Motors, forcing changes in the government's economic policies by threatening large scale lay-offs of employees. Again a difficult trade-off was involved — on one side the country's need for foreign capital, at least in some areas; on the other side, the desire to retain a measure of Australian control over national resources, and full capacity to apply government policy to all

groups in the community equally.

Uranium mining and export, which became an issue in mid 1973 with the feasibility of the Ranger Project in the Northern Territory then evident, also involved these kinds of considerations including the merits of marketing a product that might be used by purchasing countries to develop nuclear weapons but could be a valuable source of energy for any developing nations that could afford the price. It was an issue that demonstrated sharply the more complex problems which were overtaking Whitlam and his government even as he began to deal with the issues that he had spent 20 years mastering.

Not only the issues but also the machinery of government was to prove much more unmanageable than he could have anticipated. The night of 13 December 1974 demonstrated the extent to which the Cabinet system had broken down. It is a system that was under particular strain in a Labor government where Cabinet had 27 members and some of these, because of the tradition of Caucus election of ministers, would not have been the choice of the Prime Minister. But the manner in which the Connor loan was authorised epitomised Whitlam's reluctance to consult most of his colleagues on any regular basis, and his increasing dependence on small, often transient, groups of ministers, officials or staff for advice. What was most dangerous about this kind of isolation was the enormous weight it placed on his personal ability to judge and evaluate the capacities of his colleagues and others. Yet it was precisely in this area of personal judgment that he was weakest: he allowed Connor to embroil the government in what was probably the most damaging political affair of the post-war years; he entrusted the crucial portfolio of the Treasury to Crean and then to Cairns, although each was in his own way totally inadequate for the position; and he appointed and relied on a Governor-General whose history and contemporary conduct indicated that he could not be taken for granted.

These were all failures of individual assessment. What the bureaucratic feuds that underlay the Lodge meeting suggested was a failure of *collective* assessment in relation to the motivating interests of the bureaucracy under any government. To some extent the strains that developed initially between the Labor government and the bureaucracy were simply caused by the demands of Labor's new and detailed program suddenly placed on a public service grown lazy from years of Liberal government

Opposite: Governor-General Sir John Kerr entertaining
his Prime Minister

when almost no new initiatives were taken. But it was obviously a continuing problem that senior public servants, including those occupying the all-powerful positions of permanent heads of departments, tended to think firstly of the interests of their own departments or of the public service in general rather than of the more abstract notion of the interest of the government as a whole and as a political entity responsible to the electorate.

Yet Whitlam consistently resisted this notion of a conflict of interests. When Labor first took office he rejected the demands of some of his colleagues that the most powerful and established permanent heads would have to be replaced if the government were to make innovations in administration — demands made not because the heads were unsympathetic politically to Labor, although many clearly were, but because they would oppose any changes, such as the introduction of outside advisers to ministers, which detracted from their existing functions. His resistance was successful then, although two years later he would be reduced to complaining to the press that the head of Treasury could not be induced to leave and that he did not know what to do about it.

There was one area, however, where the problems of Cabinet and Caucus and the difficulties of getting programs through the parliamentary and bureaucratic channels and into operation did not impede his natural flamboyance — foreign affairs. He relished it accordingly. It enabled him to combine, free from interference and administrative drudgery, his genuine and long-held anti-colonial and anti-racist ideals for the emerging nations of Africa and Asia with an undoubted desire to stride the world stage in a way that no Australian Prime Minister had yet done. When he described the white South African and Rhodesian leaders as being 'as bad as Hitler' he was not affecting emotion but simply revealing the real anger that he had always felt towards colonial and racist regimes.

In many ways he was now perfectly placed to use to advantage the foreign policy stances he had taken in Opposition when they were slightly ahead of their time. On China, for example, he maintained the initiative seized in 1972. In the case of Papua New Guinea he continued to encourage local leaders like Michael Somare, whom he had first supported in 1970. In Australia's relations with the US, his overall emphasis on the importance of the American alliance (which many in his own party did not support), together with a healthy scepticism for any attempts to involve Australia in disasters like Vietnam, was quite apposite to the mood of an America that now had for the first time some realisation of the limits of its own power and was moving gingerly towards a measure of detente with the Soviet Union after decades of confrontation in all corners of the globe. This was particularly true after Richard Nixon, described by Whitlam with characteristic candour as a 'barbarian' for his Vietnam policies, resigned from the US Presidency in August 1974.

As a genuine internationalist he took Australia's role in the United Nations seriously and used it as another opportunity to demonstrate basic sympathy for the political and economic problems of the Third World. While taking this position of support for the rights of developing countries, he took at the same time a very pragmatic view of the rights of the small nations when they conflicted with international reality or regional stability. It had been the overwhelming demands of reality that had led him to argue in the early 1950s for the recognition of China at the expense of Taiwan. For the same reasons he ignored the storm produced by his decision in 1974 to recognise the Baltic States of Estonia, Latvia and Lithuania as part of the Soviet Union which had annexed them in 1940.

In 1975 it was his concern for the effect of an independent East Timor on the existing powers in the region to the north of Australia, most particularly Indonesia, that resulted in his reluctance to contemplate Australian resistance to reasonably obvious Indonesian plans to annex the former Portuguese colony. This last decision produced a storm, not only from his political opponents but from many members of his own party when, much later in 1976, the extent of Australian acquiescence to Indonesia's aims became clear. It was one of the few occasions on which his opponents inside and outside the ALP were able to assume the more idealistic position.

Ironically he always expected, perhaps naively, idealism in his opponents just as he had expected it in his colleagues, in the public service, and in the electorate. But of all these expectations none had separated him more from most politicians on either side than his belief that if only an issue could be put clearly before the Australian people they would respond to it rationally and with a sense of community purpose. As he said in 1972:

> True it is, the Australian people are predominantly middle class in outlook even perhaps more than income. But there is no inherent

reason why such a people should be immovably conservative. The truth is that we do not really know what the Australian people are capable of. No Prime Minister since Curtin has made any effort either to detect or develop any latent idealism amongst the Australian people as a whole. For the past 23 years fear and division have been the chosen weapons of our rulers. The bluff was called once on the Communist Party Dissolution Act. On the most unpromising ground in most discouraging times, the people did respond to an appeal to reason and freedom, against fear and hate. (Whitlam 1972a)

It follows from a politician's faith in the people that the people should naturally have a similar faith in their politicians. Despite the overwhelming and depressing evidence to the contrary in Australia, he went on to say at the same time:

> We are indeed living in a time of rising expectations. It might be more prudent politically to down-grade the prospects of change as a kind of political re-insurance, but I believe the people should have the highest expectations from their government. I believe deeply that the possibilities of the parliamentary system, far from being exhausted, have barely been tapped.
> The expectations of the people, not the reservations of the politicians, will provide the thrust and direction for the next Labor Government.

Yet even by the end of 1974 it was becoming increasingly clear that he did not meet the expectations of many of the people. It was not so much that he failed to live up to their expectations but that he exceeded them too dramatically.

In the candour with which he acknowledged the nation's problems; in the energy with which he tried to change these situations; in the vehemence with which he confronted opponents to his proposed changes; he projected for many Australians — unused to sharpness of speech or action in any aspect of their lives — a disturbing aura of violence. In a society which tended to obscure its conflicts at both the personal and the public level, he brought those conflicts out into the open, and large sections of the community recoiled from this abrasive intrusion as they would from any display of passion or commitment. Following 13 December 1974, this alienation was to become more and more pronounced until it reached its culmination exactly a year from that date. It would be a year that would finally shake even Gough Whitlam's faith in the Australian people.

3   Prophet without honour Jim Cairns

When Jim Cairns became Treasurer in the Whitlam government on 11 December 1974 it was in many ways a formal recognition of his role, even without the Treasury portfolio, as the dominant force in the government's economic policy and thinking at that time. And although he would be removed from the Treasury by Whitlam in less than six months, thus losing the opportunity to bring down even one Budget, he would remain the reference point in any consideration of economic policy over the government's three years of office. In retrospect it was not an enviable role. Second only to the loans affair, the issue on which the Opposition would focus most effectively and most consistently throughout 1975 and on which they would base their blocking of the Budget in October was the government's handling of the nation's economy and Cairns was singled out as one of their particular targets for criticism.

This was certainly nothing new for Cairns. On 8 May 1970, 70,000 people occupied Bourke Street, Melbourne's main thoroughfare, to protest Australia's continued involvement in the Vietnam war. At their head stood Cairns, Member of the House of Representatives and acknowledged leader in Australia of the anti-war movement in particular, and of the non-communist political left in general. A fluent, lucid, and compelling speaker who could, unlike the majority of Australian politicians, appeal unselfconsciously to the broad ideals of morality and justice, Cairns had become during the past five years the clear leader — both inside and outside the Parliament — of those opposed to the war. He had therefore become the target for government supporters who, despite the LCP's crushing majority in the 1966 election, continued to use the anti-war movement to discredit the ALP and its left wing particularly.

Eighteen months before coming to office, Jim Cairns
addressing a Vietnam Moratorium crowd in Melbourne

In a debate where the terms 'murderer' and 'traitor' were in common parliamentary use, Cairns was consistently branded the
colleague, confidant and champion of communists and their
causes, with the clear implication that he was a communist in all
but party membership.

The government's general approach to the issue is conveyed
by a statement of Deputy Prime Minister McEwen in the House
of Representatives on 7 May 1970:

> Overseas there is a battle in the field against the Communists who
> are trying to drive our troops out, and at home the ALP and the
> civilian Communists are working to defeat our forces on the political
> front.

On 29 May 1968, Paul Hasluck, then Foreign Affairs Minister,
had remarked in response to an interjection from Cairns:

> I am aware that the honourable member for Yarra [Cairns] is a frank
> and open partisan of North Vietnam, but I am speaking on behalf of

the cause that the Australian Government is supporting, on behalf of
the Australian people.

Over the years government backbenchers had often been even
less inhibited than ministers. Commenting in the House on 22
September 1963 on a pamphlet of Cairns' calling for the withdrawal of US forces in South Vietnam, Billy Wentworth said:

> The pamphlet is all directed on a line which is the same as the Com-
> munist line. Idea for idea, paragraph for paragraph, this is the Com-
> munist line. I do not say that the honourable member for Yarra is a
> Communist. I have no evidence that he is a member of the Com-
> munist Party. All that I say — I do not infer this or make any in-
> nuendo but I say it directly — is that his line is the Communist line,
> and this is a matter of very great significance to the country.

The most extraordinary parliamentary performance of the
period in relation to Cairns, one worth reproducing to indicate
the tenor of the time, came from John Gorton, then Minister for
Works, when on 18 November 1965 in the Senate he produced a
series of newspaper reports, mainly from the late forties, which
dealt with meetings of various left-wing organisations attended
by Cairns and also by alleged communists:

> From the time when the Communists openly walked into Korea
> with armed formations and were defeated; from the time when the
> guerrilla forces attempted to overthrow Malaya and were defeated;
> since they began their murder, sabotage and kidnapping in Vietnam,
> supported from Hanoi, they have posed an aggressive threat and the
> only aggressive threat in the world today. These, I think, are the
> enemies of Australia and the enemies of peace.
>
> I suggest it is perfectly correct for Senator McKellar to say that
> these are the people with whom Dr Cairns has associated over many
> years. I have here some facts to back that statement. These are
> newspaper reports, I admit, but none of them has ever been denied
> . . .
>
> On 11 March 1948 the Communist *Guardian* reported the
> following speakers as being at a meeting of the Victorian Prices
> Vigilance Committee, which was a Communist organisation: J. F.
> Cairns — that is, Dr Cairns; Dorothy Cameron, an open and ad-
> mitted member of the Communist Party; J. J. Brown, an open and
> admitted member of the Communist Party and Secretary of the
> Australian Railways Union; P. Malone, an open and admitted Com-
> munist in the Building Workers and Industrial Union; and Thelma
> Lee, an open and admitted member of the Communist Party.
>
> On 13th May 1948 the University Labour Club which is the
> Melbourne University Labour Club and should not be confused
> with the Melbourne University Australian Labour Party Club which

is a completely different organisation — held a weekend conference at Healesville, at which the speakers were: J. F. Cairns that is, Dr Cairns; Ralph Gibson, President of the Communist Party; and E. Lawrie, who was a Communist candidate at elections in Victoria. On 7th September 1949 the Communist *Guardian* reported Dr J. F. Cairns as being chairman of the inaugural meeting of the Peace Council, which was at that time or very soon afterwards branded by the Victorian Executive of the Australian Labour Party, and later by the Federal Executive of the Australian Labour Party as being a subsidiary of the Communist Party. On 15th November 1949 the Communist *Guardian* reported the main speakers at a meeting of Democratic Rights Council, branded by the Labour Party under Mr Chifley as an auxiliary of the Communist Party, as being Dr J.F. Cairns, Rex Mortimer — an open Communist, and A.J. Cregan — an open Communist.

Such performances were of course intended more for the electorate than the Parliament, and over these years Cairns faced twin pressures. He became the chief target of a government campaign that became increasingly virulent as the US position in Vietnam deteriorated. At the same time he was labelled by a number of his Labor colleagues as an electoral liability for the Party because of his involvement in protests and demonstrations.

By the time Labor came to government these experiences, while scarring, had been also strengthening, for Cairns had seen his tormentors proven wrong within a decade — a rare historical satisfaction. It is worth recalling the remarks Menzies made on 13 August 1964, in the course of a debate in the House on the Gulf of Tonkin incident. The American authorities had alleged that North Vietnamese vessels had attacked US ships off the coast of North Vietnam and, as a result of the allegations, the US Congress voted to grant wide-ranging powers for the conduct of the war to President Johnson. Menzies began by referring to a recent speech by Cairns on the subject:

> The honourable member for Yarra is reported, I hope accurately, as having said that Australia should not follow the United States line — of course, we have heard him say that many times — which he defined as pursuing a policy of war which had no basis in morals or justice. He was not talking about some war of the 19th century; he was talking about these incidents that have been engaging our attention; he was talking about these activities of war in the Gulf of Tonkin and, by the way of counter attack, on the shores of North Vietnam . . .
>
> The honourable member for Yarra went on to say, according to the report, that the United States could not claim that it was being attacked in the present Vietnam crisis — I think the crews of the

American destroyers would be fascinated to know that — or that it was acting in self-defence. He says that the United States cannot say that. The US has said it. The honourable member for Yarra is challenging the veracity of the head of the American administration. He is challenging the intelligence and information of the entire Congress of the United States which has every avenue of information available to it.

Against Menzies' remarks need only be placed the opening paragraphs of the chapter on the Gulf of Tonkin incident in the summary of the Pentagon Papers compiled by the *New York Times* in 1971:

> The Pentagon papers disclose that for six months before the Tonkin Gulf incident in August, 1964, the United States had been mounting clandestine military attacks against North Vietnam while planning to obtain a Congressional resolution that the Administration regarded as the equivalent of a declaration of war.
>
> When the incident occurred, the Johnson Administration did not reveal these clandestine attacks and pushed the previously prepared resolution through both houses of Congress on August 7. (Sheehan 1971)

It was the kind of vindication that could only reinforce the implacably self-righteous, almost stoical, approach that Cairns took to life and the imperviousness to criticism from his opponents — or from his colleagues — that had its basis in a prophet-like certainty that he would ultimately be proven correct.

In 1975 Cairns had been a member of the House of Representatives for 20 years. Born 61 years before in Carlton, an inner city Melbourne suburb, his childhood coincided with the 1920s, gay and tinselled post-war years for some but not for Cairns, fatherless after the last year of the war, whose mother found these years an economic nightmare. He finished school in 1931 just in time to encounter the depression years. After being unemployed for almost a year, he found work with a finance house as a clerk on a wage of nineteen shillings a week. He kept the job until 1935 when he joined the Victorian police force — where the pay was better — and became a member of its undercover unit. He also enrolled in the Commerce Faculty at Melbourne University and found enough time over the next five years to graduate with honours and to win a number of Victorian track and field championships.

As a police officer he was not required under manpower regulations to join the armed services when war broke out in 1939 and was in fact discouraged from doing so. He did, however, arrange to have himself drafted into the army in 1944 and he served in it until 1946. After being discharged, he was appointed senior tutor in economic history in the Commerce Faculty at Melbourne University which, like most academic institutions, tended to hire its own best graduates where possible. During the next ten years he continued to teach at the University, rising to the rank of Senior Lecturer, and at the same time, he engaged in research that led to a Masters Degree and later a Doctorate, some of this work being done at Oxford University in 1951 on a fellowship from Nuffield College.

He had joined the ALP in 1947 but had taken no active role in its affairs until his return from England in 1952 when he found the Victorian branch already the battleground for what would be two years later the most violent and destructive split the ALP has ever experienced. Unions and branches were bitterly divided by the struggle for power between supporters of the Industrial Groups, initiated in the late forties by B. A. Santamaria, and their opponents. Cairns himself became a well-known opponent of the Groupers, who controlled the Victorian Executive.

When Evatt decided to meet the Groupers' challenge to his power head-on in 1954 and the Federal Executive dismissed the incumbent Victorian Executive, the divisions that had existed for some years just below the surface in the Victorian ALP erupted into violent conflict. A number of Labor MPs left the ALP to form the nucleus of what would later become the Democratic Labor Party (DLP) and this new party decided to stand candidates against ALP members in all electorates at the next federal election. That election was in 1955 and it was necessary to find a new candidate for the ALP in Yarra as the sitting Labor member, Standish Keon, who had held the seat since 1949, had opted for membership of the DLP. Even without ALP endorsement Keon was a formidable opponent, a fiery and eloquent speaker who had previously been a member of the Victorian Legislative Assembly. Although he had now moved out of Yarra, Cairns was asked to stand against Keon and after the distribution of preferences won the seat by 791 votes. At subsequent elections he held the seat comfortably until 1969 when it was abolished in a redistribution and he moved to the seat of Lalor in Melbourne's western suburbs.

Although the 1950s and 1960s were depressing years for Labor, Cairns rapidly rose to prominence as a parliamentary and public performer. Concentrating on questions of economics and foreign affairs, he was elected to the shadow cabinet in 1958 and remained a member until 1972, excepting the period 1961-3. Whereas many of his colleagues were reduced to sullen submission by continual Liberal supremacy at the polls and in the Parliament, Cairns found a forum, and a challenging outlet for his talents, as an orator and organiser for *non-parliamentary* opposition to the government's war policies. It illustrated the differences between himself and Whitlam, who had become Opposition Leader in 1967 and viewed Parliament first and foremost as the place to undermine the government. Yet Cairns, rather than Whitlam's deputy, Lance Barnard, became the clear countervailing force to Whitlam in the parliamentary party as well as in the public mind and when, in April 1968, Whitlam resigned as Leader to demand a vote of confidence from his colleagues in his clashes with the Federal Executive and the Victorian branch, it was Cairns whom Whitlam's opponents supported. Cairns, needing little encouragement to stand against Whitlam, wrote to his colleagues in the Caucus that the issue was basically:

> Whose Party is this — ours or his? . . . I do not believe that this crisis can be solved by one man getting more of his own way. (Oakes 1973)

The contest aroused fierce passions. Whitlam's supporters predicted that if Cairns were elected Leader the government and the media would use his leftist image to destroy the Party electorally. When the ballot was held Whitlam was re-elected by the close majority of 38 votes to 32 — and it seems unlikely that either man ever entirely forgot the encounter.

In the last few years leading up to Labor's 1972 victory, Cairns was shadow minister for Overseas Trade and Secondary Industry, despite his clear preference for Treasury or Foreign Affairs. In the Caucus ballot that followed the 1972 election, however, he topped the poll after Whitlam and Barnard to become number three in the government — and Minister for Overseas Trade and for Secondary Industry. Neither was a particularly glamorous or satisfying portfolio but Treasury had been given to long-time economics spokesman Frank Crean and Foreign Affairs had been retained by Whitlam. The problem about both Overseas Trade and Secondary Industry was that unless the government as a whole embarked on a program of the most rigorous structural economic change, a minister could do

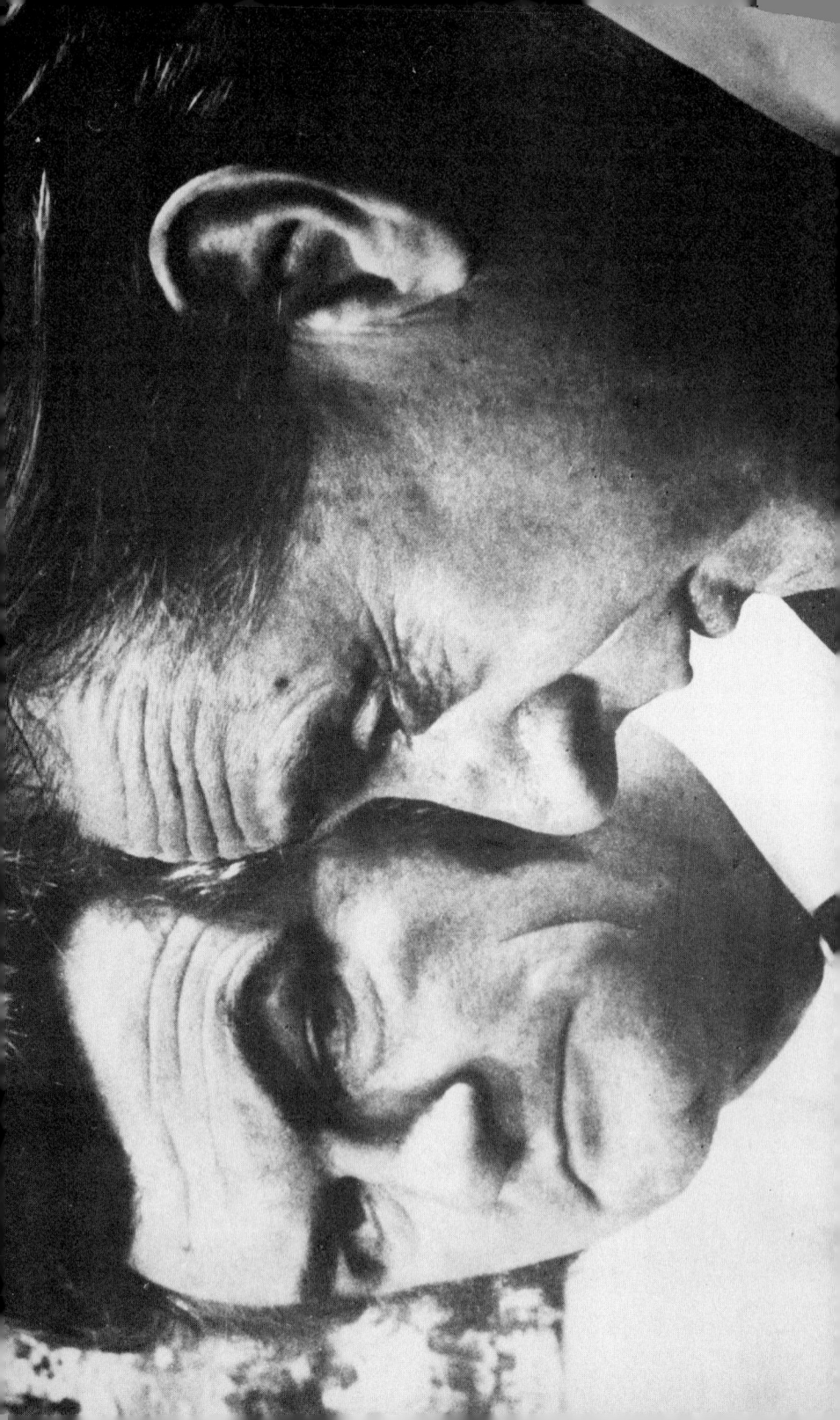

no more than apply band-aid solutions to a manufacturing sector that was in need of major surgery.

As a consequence of this, Cairns found it difficult in the first eighteen months of government to make a significant impact on its direction although Crean's low-key approach to the post of Treasurer created a partial vacuum in the area of economic policy that encouraged him, and others, to contribute on these questions. Yet there was the additional problem of the kind of impact he wished to make. Long considered one of the most radical members of the parliamentary party, perhaps the most radical, he had nevertheless written in 1972:

> How do revolutions take place?
> I think it can be said that they take place in three ways.
> (1) By a serious national economic crisis and breakdown.
> (2) By a sufficiently strong national movement against foreign imperialism and racial domination.
> (3) By invasion of sufficient power or influence from outside to push the indigenous revolutionary forces in the direction history and circumstances were taking them. This is likely to happen only in the security sphere of the Soviet Union or China.
> None of these roads to revolution seems possible, and none desirable, for Australia. If Australia is to develop a society in which power is spread, rather than concentrated in the way that it is now; which is humane and co-operative rather than competitive and acquisitive; or analytical and sceptical rather than credulous — then something different is needed. Something for which hardly any example so far exists. (Cairns 1972)

After the government had left office he wrote that he had accepted that the economic system in general, and the areas of responsibility he was given in 1972 in particular, were not susceptible to radical change:

> For many years before the 1972 election, I was convinced there were severe limits upon what a Labor government could do. I knew that social change cannot be accomplished without the support of 'an appropriate consciousness in the people'. I knew that unless there is support and understanding for social change, there cannot be much social change; and I knew there was little support and understanding for social change in Australia in 1972. It was not going to be possible for the new Labor government even to be reformist. The people wanted jobs, but not necessarily work. They wanted money in wages, salaries, profits or government-provided benefits. This

Opposite: Labor's Treasurer, Jim Cairns, with a
sceptical ACTU President, Bob Hawke

system of jobs and money depended on private enterprise, and unless private enterprise was satisfied, the level of jobs and money would not satisfy the people — and the government would be blamed. If Labor was to remain the government, we would have to keep the system going so that the level of jobs and money would satisfy the people; if that was to be done, we would have to satisfy private enterprise upon which the system depended.

No-one made this clearer to me than the trade-union officials. Whether it was jobs in the boot-trade, in textiles, in motor cars, in Wangaratta, in Launceston, in Western Australia, in factories or on farms, the government was expected to safeguard those jobs. How? By helping private enterprise which provided those jobs. I was well aware when I became a Minister in the Labor government that I would be compelled to follow a policy that would help keep jobs and money at a satisfactory level. There was little support for social change if jobs or money were put at risk and no chance of getting any of it through the Senate. So whatever was done, it would have to be in a way that satisfied the private enterprise system on which jobs and money depended. Given that this was so, if I had not recognised it, and, within reason, been prepared to be guided by it, then I would never have agreed to become a Minister.

In 1972 I became Minister for Overseas Trade and Minister for Secondary Industry. Ironically for one who was by conduct and philosophy among the most radical in the government, I had the Ministries which most required one to be concerned with jobs and money and private enterprise. (Cairns 1976)

One of the difficulties was that Cairns' ideas, while sweeping in appearance, had never been translated into a coherent program of action. In contrast, Whitlam's more conceptually conservative notions were always reduced to concrete form and were often quite innovative in their proposals for implementation. The consistent but non-specific quality of Cairns' theories is illustrated by two statements made over a decade apart. In 1963, writing for a Victorian Fabian Society pamphlet, he said:

Whatever we may choose to call this goal of man's evolution, this unity of all men, there can be no doubt that it is present in all religions and philosophies. There can be, of course, no unity in conditions of conflict, acquisitiveness and violence. There can be unity only in conditions of co-operation, friendship and love. This is the philosophical background of the Australian Labor Party . . . (Cairns 1963)

In October 1974, two months before taking over as Treasurer, he delivered the annual Chifley Memorial Lecture at Melbourne University and told the audience:

I became convinced of the idea that as long as man lives in a society in which he is forced to be acquisitive to survive then he would always bear the marks of self-interest and conflict. But already I had seen that revolutions like that in the Soviet Union did not, and could not soon, make the society in which they occurred much less acquisitive.

To me, the values of co-operation, and even love, and of non-violence, combined with personal and social responsibility became paramount. However, it was clear that society's values depended upon social conditions. So to change the values of a whole society required first a change in social conditions. To achieve this the appropriate kind of economic growth, based on democratic participation, was essential. (Cairns 1974)

Even in relation to specific questions on which he appeared to have long held firm views, he often declined to champion them in the face of contrary departmental or ministerial recommendations although he would later return to his original stand when the issue had lost its immediacy. Yet he seemed unaware of the impression of inconsistency that this conveyed within the government. For many years he had been a critic of the existence of US bases in Australia, the precise purposes and activities of which were concealed from the public and from most parliamentarians. When, as Deputy Prime Minister, he was finally able to demand briefings from the Defence Department on the bases, he made no effort to obtain the information. He had a long record of opposition to nuclear proliferation but on a trade mission to Tehran in March 1975 he promised the Shah that Iran would have access to Australian uranium. Then, in June 1975, when briefly Minister for the Environment, he assured a delegation from the anti-uranium lobby that he believed that Australia's uranium deposits should stay in the ground.

Much later he suggested that one reason why he and Clyde Cameron were both removed from their posts in mid 1975 was that they, more than any other of the ministers, were identified in the eyes of the media with support for wage and salary increases. Yet in a television interview in February 1975 he had made the comment:

Now, I wouldn't want to see a Labor Government in office unless wage and salary earners and other people like that had kept up with the cost of living and perhaps even got a bit ahead of it, but the point I make here is that if that rate of wage increase gets significantly ahead of the rate of increase in the goods and services productivity, then the consequence is not only increased costs, but increased unemployment too, and what I think we have to bring home to workers and to trade union leaders is if they want full employment and they want jobs — and I think they're right in wanting that —

then they have to choose, at a time like this, between jobs and wage increases. (Cairns 1975)

Most of this, however, was in the future. And when Cairns took over as Treasurer in December 1974, he was adding that powerful portfolio to his position as Deputy Prime Minister which he had wrested from Lance Barnard in a Caucus ballot after the May 1974 general election. He had already been acting Prime Minister for two weeks while Whitlam was overseas, and from mid December he would be acting head of the administration for over a month while Whitlam was out of the country. It was a long way from the massed crowds of the Vietnam Moratorium in Bourke Street just over five years before.

Although he had lost Secondary Industry in a general ministerial reshuffle in October 1973, Cairns appeared basically content with the undemanding portfolio of Overseas Trade and the prestige of Deputy Prime Minister. Despite his intermittent interventions in the economic policy area, he had not sought Treasury and at first had considerable doubts about accepting it. Whitlam had first raised the matter with Cairns during the May 1974 campaign, having formed the view that Crean, as Treasurer, must take most of the responsibility for the Liberals' ability to campaign almost exclusively on the issue of the economy.

Cairns was unenthusiastic about Whitlam's suggestion at that stage but he *was* concerned about his role in the government and, soon afterwards, he asked Brian Brogan, an economist from Monash University who advised both Cairns and Whitlam — a unique phenomenon — and had considerable influence on them both, to prepare an options paper on ways that he might gain maximum influence on economic policy since as Deputy Prime Minister he could have his choice of portfolio. Brogan set out three options.

The first was obviously to take Treasury which would itself be strengthened by having the Deputy Prime Minister as its minister. He could then try to bring within the ambit of Treasury the Industries Assistance Commission (IAC), the Prices Justification Tribunal, and the Trade Practices Commission; while at the same time exercising a strong influence on every interdepartmental committee considering aspects of economic policy by means of the Treasury representative on these committees. The whole exercise would be the first step towards a super-ministry that embraced all aspects of economic planning and hived off Treasury's accounting functions to a separate department or to the already existing office of Auditor-General.

The second option was to seek the Labour and Immigration portfolio. This department had the capacity to strengthen its economic information areas and if the Structural Adjustment Board were placed under the control of the Minister for Labour, he could then take control of all adjustment and manpower programs developed by the government to assist both employees and employers to adapt to changes induced by long term economic decisions. The Industries Assistance Commission could also be added to this collection to give him direct responsibility for industry planning policy as well. On a more general level, Cairns had always had a close rapport with the trade union movement and would presumably have Whitlam's support on most issues.

The third option was to take the Department of Special Minister of State, which was basically a collection of leftovers that did not fit easily into any other departments, and to try to convert it into a de facto department of the Deputy Prime Minister, making it the co-ordinating body for all policy matters with long term implications. The Australian Industry Development Corporation and the Priorities Review Staff (PRS) could be brought within the ambit of such a revitalised department, forming a useful base for an effective Cabinet advocate. One of the most attractive aspects of this option was the relatively light administrative load the job would have entailed, thereby freeing its minister for almost full-time application to economic policy questions. A clear disadvantage was that it would take some time to build up such a department, probably more time than either Cairns or the government had at their disposal.

These then were the options Cairns was considering when Whitlam approached him again to take over Treasury. Shortly before Cairns was to leave Australia for a New York visit in October 1974, Whitlam told Cairns that he had decided to offer Crean the post of ambassador in Washington. Cairns expressed grave doubts about the proposal, explaining that there would be strong objections from both Victorian Caucus members and from the Victorian Party machine to the removal of Crean and also to the need for a by-election. Whitlam then suggested a direct swap of Cairns for Crean, Crean for Cairns, in the portfolios of Treasury and Overseas Trade even though his original intention had been to use the occasion of Crean's departure from the ministry as the basis for a major reshuffle of the Cabinet and possibly for fresh elections for all Cabinet posts.

Whitlam added that, should Cairns again refuse the job, he would offer the post to Special Minister of State, Lionel Bowen and in the event of Bowen's refusing, to Social Security Minister, Bill Hayden. What Whitlam was in fact suggesting was that, if Cairns continued to refuse Treasury, Bowen, not Cairns, would be given the inside running for the leadership when Whitlam eventually stood down. Cairn's closest supporters (particularly Urban and Regional Development Minister Tom Uren and Senator Arthur Gietzelt from NSW) would not relish such an arrangement, as Bowen came from a different faction of the NSW ALP, and would place considerable pressure on Cairns. Had the order been reversed, and Hayden been given first refusal, it is possible they would have persuaded Cairns to stand aside for Hayden, and take for himself one of the other options open — the revamped Special Minister of State, Labour and Immigration, or Hayden's own portfolio of Social Security. Whitlam put the proposal to Cairns, now in New York, by telephone, and under these circumstances Cairns accepted Treasury. It was agreed that the swap would be made in mid December — still some weeks away — after Parliament had risen for the Christmas recess.

Over the first two weeks of November, news of the impending dismissal of Crean as Treasurer leaked from a variety of sources and was taken up by the media. In addition the Opposition in the Parliament ensured that Crean was humiliated through a series of questions they put to Whitlam on Crean's future — or lack of it. Crean himself was among the very last to be told, and only then on the morning of 11 November 1974, shortly before Whitlam released a statement of the decision to switch Crean and Cairns in their respective portfolios in mid December.

In addition to the means of obtaining it, there were two other reservations that Cairns would have had at the end of 1974 about accepting the office of Treasurer. One was the state of the Australian economy, the other was the Department of the Treasury itself.

Although it was not yet apparent to most members of the government, the Australian economy was moving into its most severe recession of the post-war years. It was a movement paralleled, to a greater or lesser extent, by all the western industrialised nations over the period 1973-6 in the wake of the

1973 OPEC oil price increase. Once in recession, the Australian economy would demonstrate much less resilience than some of its counterparts, such as Germany or the US, which did not have the same pronounced structural weaknesses.

It had been a tenet of post-Keynesian economic theory that a nation might find itself with the problem of increasing unemployment or an increasing rate of inflation but not both as one would, to some extent, balance the other. The countries of the West were finding by 1974, however, that they could have both and have them at what were then unprecedented levels for the last two decades. At the end of 1974 when Cairns became Treasurer, the figure for the rise in the Consumer Price Index over the year would be 16.3 per cent and for the proportion of the workforce unemployed 5.2 per cent — both post-war records and both indicating no evidence of decline in the immediate future. It was correct but of little use to point out that these problems did not begin with Labor's accession to office. As an OECD Survey in 1972 just before Labor came to office warned:

> In the past two years, after almost a decade of brisk and relatively smooth sailing, the Australian economy is running into troubled waters: domestically, as in most other OECD countries, wage-price inflation has sharply accelerated, while economic activity has slipped down markedly and unemployment has risen. (OECD 1972)

So far as Australia was concerned, the inflation problem had been exacerbated by two particular periods of government action — by the McMahon government's refusal in 1972 to revalue the Australian dollar and its attempt to gain an electoral revival by an over-expansionary Budget in that year; and by the Whitlam government's refusal to raise taxes in 1973 to fund part of its increased expenditure in the areas of education and urban and regional development.

At the root of Australia's economic weakness, however, lay major sectors of manufacturing industry, such as automobiles and textiles, that were (and are) labour intensive and technologically deficient. The result is a cost structure that enables these industries to compete with imports only with the assistance of some of the highest tariff barriers in the world. The perpetuation and entrenchment of this process in the 1950s and 1960s under the meticulous eye of John McEwen and his Department of Trade and Industry had retarded the more efficient rural and mining sectors of the economy, and produced a misallocation of resources that could not be corrected by any government without a long period of consistent reallocation. Measured against other OECD nations — the only comparable economic entities — Australia matched the average annual rate of growth in Gross National Product per head of only three of the 23 OECD countries over the period 1960-73, and its absolute ranking in GNP per head declined from eighth to eleventh position.

Ironically it was a Labor government that was to make the first attempts — however episodic and tentative — to rationalise the least efficient sectors of this ailing economic sector by decreasing government intervention in the form of tariffs and subsidies and allowing market forces to play a greater role, a rare example of a free enterprise approach. Such an exercise might have been economically feasible at a time when the economy was moving ahead strongly, and politically feasible for a government that was electorally secure. Neither condition existed at the end of 1974.

Within a week of becoming Treasurer, Cairns was at the centre of a dramatic demonstration of this fact. In July 1974 the IAC had issued a report on the automobile industry which it categorised as a disaster area; occupied by four manufacturers although only able economically to support two at most; protected by 35 per cent tariffs which amounted to a subsidy of $4000 for each employee each year in the industry; and yet still unable to compete against Japanese imports. The report modestly recommended a reduction of tariffs to 25 per cent over seven years and the removal of one of the four manufacturers. Despite the violent reaction of the auto industry the report was essentially accepted by the government in the context of Whitlam's publicly expressed admiration for the rationalising ideas of IAC Chairman Alf Rattigan.

In mid December 1974 the largest of the auto manufacturers, General Motors Holden (GMH), announced that it intended to retrench 6000 employees because of a fall in sales caused by competition from imports. The announcement was made only a few weeks after the government had agreed to limit the number of imported vehicles to 20 per cent of total sales. Although he publicly attacked GMH's move as a reneging on the recent arrangement regarding import quotas and as blackmail of the government, Cairns presided over a series of meetings between executives of GMH, ministers and the unions involved. Faced by a united front from GMH and the Vehicle Builders Union, with the clear implication that the other manufacturers were also intent on retrenchments, the government caved in. In addition to guaranteeing existing tariffs and import restrictions, it announced a reduction in sales tax on passenger vehicles from 27½ per cent to 15 per cent for three months in an effort to boost sales. In return it received no guarantee from GMH that the retrenchments would not occur but only that nothing would be done for three months. It was the sharpest single lesson to Cairns and his colleagues during the government's terms that it is virtually impossible for a government not electorally secure to implement measures directed to long term rationalisation which nevertheless involved short term dislocation of forceful interest groups.

Nothing had better heralded and typified this rationalisation approach than the 25 per cent across-the-board tariff cut of July 1973. It was even then not so much an approach shared by a majority of Cabinet as an approach adopted by Whitlam and then by Cairns, largely due to arguments by Brian Brogan and another economic adviser, Fred Gruen. It was also designed to have specific short term consequences — an increase in imports that would take up domestic demand pressure and so restrain price increases. Nevertheless it represented a first step towards shifting resources out of inefficient areas like automobiles, clothing, textiles and electrical goods in the long term and into more productive sectors, and provision was made for assistance to manufacturers or employees affected by these policies.

It was argued later that this decision was largely responsible for much of the unemployment increases of 1974. The IAC dismissed this claim in its 1974-5 Annual Report in these terms:

It has been suggested, for example, that reductions in assistance have been a major factor explaining the recent general decline in investment, employment and profitability in manufacturing industry. This appears to largely ignore other changes in the general economic environment, such as demands for higher wages and their effects on profitability, international economic developments and exchange rate movements. For example, a recent study indicates that the various changes made in Australia's exchange rate during the last three years had a much greater effect in the short term on the relationship between the prices of domestically produced goods and the prices of competing imports than the general tariff reduction of 25 per cent in July 1973. Another recent study has suggested that wage rises during the last eighteen months or so have had a much larger impact on current profitability, and hence employment, than recent tariff reductions on the currency revaluations. (Industries Assistance Commission 1975)

Yet once unemployment figures began to rise in the second half of 1974 the rationalist approach collapsed overnight and, for the rest of the government's term, tariffs in numerous areas were lifted to their old levels or, as in the case of the auto industry, above those levels. Both manufacturers and unions increased their pressure on the government and, by early 1975, economic journalists were identifying Cairns — often on the basis of briefings from Treasury — with the government's agreement to increased protection for manufacturers. On 4 April 1975 Kenneth Davidson of the *Age* wrote:

> Never has Australia's political and economic environment been more favourable to industrial pressure for more protection.
>
> Despite conclusive evidence that import competition has played only a minor part in the serious rise in unemployment in recent months, industrialists seeking protection have only to raise the spectre of more unemployment virtually to guarantee any extra protection from imports that they may seek.
>
> Within the bureaucracy the Deputy Prime Minister and Treasurer (Dr Cairns) has become known as 'Dr Yes'. His emotional commitment to planning boils down to a variant of corporate statism not very different from what might be proposed by the National Civic Council.
>
> His attitude is that issues can be decided by men of goodwill in the Government and business getting around the table and reaching a consensus called planning. Unfortunately, other people who may be affected by these decisions, such as user industries or consumers or taxpayers, appear to be under-represented.

By April 1975 rapport between Treasurer and Treasury was non-existent. Even in December 1974 Cairns might have considered the question of his compatibility with what was then the bureaucracy's most powerful arm.

Treasury's power came from its dual role: that of accountant, supervising all government expenditure; and that of policy formulator, advising on fiscal and monetary measures to influence the economy. Its policy role was firmly based on the possession of Canberra's most valuable commodity — information. In addition to its own statistics on public expenditure and its access to all Reserve Bank information, Treasury kept a close watch on the private sector and relied on its representatives in London, Tokyo, Washington, and at the International Monetary Fund and the OECD, to provide a level of economic intelligence no other department could approach. This information was used in collaboration with the Reserve Bank and the Bureau of Statistics to produce the economic forecasts on which Treasury's advice was based. The bulk of this information, however, was not available to other ministers and departments, let alone to the public.

No other department was therefore in a position to offer alternative advice to the government. In the early days of the Labor government it was thought that the Department of Urban and Regional Development might provide this alternative as it had made a point of building up economic expertise, but overall its lack of Treasury's experience and resources restricted its capacity severely. It never emerged as a real source of alternative advice and no other department attempted such an exercise until John Menadue began to build up the economic capacity of the Department of Prime Minister and Cabinet in the last six months of the government's term.

A major problem for the government was that while the economic advice provided was largely monolithic, the institutions that could assist or hinder the implementation of government policy in this area were not. By the beginning of 1975 there was an array of bodies, both inside and outside the bureaucracy, in a position to influence the government's economic strategy either directly or indirectly. The insiders were, apart from Treasury, the departments of Overseas Trade, Manufacturing Industry, Minerals and Energy, Labour and Immigration, Agriculture, Urban and Regional Development, and Special Minister of State (which had a tariff policy branch).

Outside were the Reserve Bank which was responsible for monetary policy; the Conciliation and Arbitration Commission which set minimum and award wage levels; the Prices Justification Tribunal which recommended maximum price levels; the IAC and the Temporary Assistance Authority which recommended the rate of tariff protection and/or subsidies for the rural and manufacturing sectors; the Trade Practices Commission which administered competition policy; and the Grants Commission which channelled federal funds to the States.

Except for the IAC, whose reports were considered by a standing interdepartmental committee, these outside bodies basically operated in isolation from one another and from the bureaucracy also. And within the bureaucracy, advice was tendered individually by departments on a competitive rather than a co-

operative basis. At no point were these diverse and often contradictory strands of economic influence brought together for
Cabinet or its Economic Committee. In the case of the Cabinet's
discussion on the 1975/76 Budget for example, almost 200 submissions proposing large-scale public expenditure were circulated to each minister. The sole body to offer advice from the
viewpoint of co-ordination was the Expenditure Review Committee of Cabinet itself whose officials had considered the aspect
of cost but not that of objectives. Treasury had long dominated
this economic policy jungle. In addition to its basic resources of
a carefully recruited staff and an information monopoly, it
possessed a definable spirit of elitism and enthusiasm unique
within the public service.

Nowhere was this spirit better embodied than in Treasury's
head, Sir Frederick Wheeler, with whom Cairns would have to
work. Wheeler was very much the bureaucrat's bureaucrat. Dry,
diminutive, always dressed in dark suit and dark tie, he worked
long hours and had a relentless dedication to the minutiae of
public service procedures. Fresh recruits to Treasury were in-
variably told the story of how a senior officer who looked
feelingly at his watch while in Wheeler's office near midnight
received a cold enquiry as to whether he was running late for
another appointment that night. Wheeler's passion for exactness
led him to have his telephone calls amplified and recorded by a
stenographer so that there could be no possible doubt about their
contents at some later time.

He had come to Treasury in Canberra in 1939 with a Bachelor
of Commerce degree from Melbourne University and ten years
in the Victorian State Savings Bank. During the 1940s he rose to
First Assistant Secretary and played a part in the formulation of
the major post-war economic policy decisions; attending, as a
member of the Australian delegation, the Bretton Woods Conference which restructured the international monetary scene. He
also became one of the chief advisers to Chifley and, although
the Chifley government lost power in 1949, Wheeler was expected to be the next head of Treasury. But when the job became
vacant in 1952, Menzies passed over Wheeler and gave the job to
Roland Wilson. Wheeler spent the next eight years in Geneva as
Treasurer of the International Labour Organisation, returning to
Canberra in 1960 as head of the Public Service Board.

In 1971 he gained the prize that had eluded him eighteen years
before — Secretary of Treasury — and when Labor came to of-

fice in 1972 he remained in the post despite rumours of purges. Survival was Wheeler's special skill. Later, in 1975, he would demonstrate this again when Whitlam would admit publicly that he had tried without success to remove him from Treasury and a senior minister would attempt to destroy him on the floor of the Senate using material provided by a bureaucratic rival. It is an index of Wheeler's assurance (and of the unique position of permanent heads in the Australian public service) that he could, unperturbed, observe Whitlam, the head of the national government, announce at a press conference that he had tried to get rid of him by offering him the job of Governor of the Reserve Bank but that Wheeler would not be shifted from Treasury. And at the end of 1975, when the Labor ministers departed, Wheeler was still in position as head of Treasury, ready to serve his new masters with a wry smile and very much the last laugh.

Treasury's *esprit de corps* was largely fuelled by the deference it received from other departments. Its domination of the glamorous area of macro-economic policy commanded respect and its more mundane accounting function produced an amalgam of dislike and fear in other departments whose estimates it queried and whose expenditures it scrutinised. Every interdepartmental committee contained the inevitable Treasury representative whose task was to demand justification for all items of expenditure on the project in question and to demolish sloppy submissions.

Yet when Cairns became Treasurer the standing of Treasury was probably lower than it had ever been under any government. The sources of this decline were both distant and recent. Many members of the Whitlam government came to office with the view that Treasury was the section of the bureaucracy most sceptical of Labor policies and most able to thwart their implementation. They also considered that Treasury had deceived and electorally damaged the Menzies government in 1961 and the McMahon government in 1971 (a view stated publicly by McMahon himself) by understating the severity of the deflationary measures it was recommending and by concealing the fact that there had initially been disagreement within Treasury itself as to the likely effect of the measures.

It was partly in response to these feelings and partly in response to the obvious lack of co-ordination among the various bodies influencing economic policy that Labor's Federal Conference at Terrigal in February 1975 seriously debated the

proposition that the ALP adopt as policy the idea of a new department 'to determine medium and long term priorities and to co-
ordinate all Australian government economic and social
programs'. It was strongly supported by Cairns, who still enjoyed the halcyon afterglow of his period as Acting Prime
Minister when he had eclipsed all his colleagues as a public
figure. For his colleagues, however, his present standing was
part of the problem with the proposal for the new department. In
addition to the obvious dangers such a body with overall direction of government priorities posed for their own autonomy in
their particular portfolios, they were all conscious that it would
undoubtedly be headed by Cairns whose power and status would
be even further increased. There was widespread objection to the
idea, some of the most damaging criticism coming from
Whitlam, and from Cairns' long-time supporter Tom Uren. The
conference finally adopted a watered-down proposal to establish
a Department of Economic Planning which would give advice to
and seek advice from various bodies on priorities.

Although no attempt was ever made to establish this body,
soon after the conference a Council of Advisers was set up to
consider the management of the economy. It consisted of the
Prime Minister, the Treasurer, and the Ministers for Minerals
and Energy, Social Security, and Overseas Trade together with
the permanent heads of the Prime Minister's Department,
Treasury, and Minerals and Energy, and the Governor of the
Reserve Bank. It had no support staff of its own and made little
contribution to the development of economic policy, eventually
lapsing later the same year without ever being formally
dissolved. Whatever the suspicions of many members of the
government, therefore, Treasury remained entrenched.

The suspicion was quite mutual. Treasury operated on the
premise that any kind of government intervention in the
economy was inferior to the free play of market forces, even
though it realised that a Labor government would begin from
precisely the opposite premise in many areas. When Labor did
attempt to rely more on market forces, sometimes to a much
greater extent, as in the case of tariffs, than their Liberal
predecessors, Treasury supported these moves but then opposed
any follow-up measures — such as adjustment assistance or manpower policies for firms or employees affected — as being government intervention in the market.

In the six months before Cairns took over, these general

suspicions had hardened into distaste and distrust on both sides. Immediately after the May 1974 election Treasury, led by Wheeler and Deputy Secretary John Stone, had proposed stringent deflationary measures. Whitlam, alarmed in the middle of the campaign by the realisation that inflation was seen by the electorate as the nation's major problem, enthusiastically supported these recommendations for restrictions on expenditure and credit — the famous 'short, sharp shock' policy. At this stage Cairns, now Deputy Prime Minister, was attending the current Kitchen Cabinet which was making most of the running on these questions, the rest of the group being Whitlam, Crean, Hayden and Cameron.

On 22 July Treasury's package of direct and indirect tax increases went to the full Cabinet where it was substantially rejected. Whitlam was bitterly disappointed and blamed Hayden and Cameron for leading the opposition to the measures and Crean for incompetent advocacy of them. With Treasury's policies at least temporarily rejected, the Treasurer discredited in the eyes of the Prime Minister, and the two proponents of alternative views out of favour, there was a yawning vacuum in economic management a month before the Budget was due to be brought down. Although he had put forward no economic alternative until then, Cairns moved in to fill this gap with a Budget strategy paper prepared by Brogan and presented to the Economic Committee of Caucus on 12 August. Essentially it rejected the severity of the Treasury proposals (which Cabinet had already done) and opted at its conclusion, somewhat vaguely, for mild stimulation of the economy:

What choices do we now have?
We could choose the conventional squeeze on credit, demand and wages. This is unacceptable because:
- It imposes unacceptable costs upon the people in unemployment and loss of GNP.
- It imposes most of the costs upon people around average weekly earnings who have not been responsible for inflation. It is fundamentally unjust.
- It is politically unacceptable. A conventional draconian budget would be rejected in the Senate and supply with it. The Government would be seen as imposing vast costs, penalties and losses upon the people, and the Opposition would be seen as protecting them . . .
Put simply, the basic character of the alternative is that maximum production or productivity and the fullest use of capacity consistent with normal demand pressures are much more likely to be effective

than the squeezed output and capacity that comes from monetary, fiscal and wage controls, with their consequent industrial unrest, lower output and productivity. Therefore, now that demand pressures have been cut back to acceptable levels, the budget strategy should aim at a neutral or mildly reflationary budget.

This, coupled with a selective easing of credit restrictions on activities such as housing, should ensure a satisfactory development of demand and output without undue pressures in an upwards or downwards direction in the year ahead. (Oakes and Solomon 1974)

One element that Cairn's proposals had emphasised was that of wages. During 1974 average weekly earnings had risen by almost 27 per cent, chiefly by means of agreements reached between certain key unions and employers outside the context of national wage cases put before the Conciliation and Arbitration Commission. With its proposals for wage and price control powers defeated at the December 1973 referendums, the government was as much a spectator to this process as the Commission. To underline its impotence, the Commission, when wage indexation was introduced early in 1975 in a final attempt to confine increases to national wage decisions, ignored Cameron's argument that higher salary earners should receive only the same increase as those on average weekly earnings and awarded a full percentage increase to everyone. In his August 1974 paper, Cairns suggested tax penalties on individuals for excessive wage increases and greater use of the Prices Justification Tribunal to refuse price rises to companies who had granted the increases. None of these proposals was ever put into practice.

The basic Cairns strategy was nevertheless adopted and he was designated by Whitlam to lead the traditional pre-Budget discussions with business and union interests.

The Budget Cabinet began its week of sitting on 19 August. On the first day several ministers, led by Tom Uren and relying on economists from the Departments of Urban and Regional Development and Manufacturing Industry, alleged that the Treasury submission significantly understated the severity of the measures it proposed to reduce government spending. Most of the Cabinet accepted the charge and Treasury's submission was discredited *in toto.* Expenditure increased 32.4 per cent over the 1973/74 figures. Treasury's reply, in the form of a document circulated to his colleagues by Crean a few days later, indicates its reaction:

I, of course, accept these decisions. But I must say, if only so that Ministers may have a last opportunity to weigh the outcome, that I believe that the impact of the 1974-75 Budget, as framed, will be grossly inflationary and that the end will be that we have dealt effectively neither with rising costs and prices nor with growing unemployment. At the same time, it will worsen our already prospectively difficult balance of payments problems.

There is an interrelationship in all these matters that seems to have been overlooked. Continuous inflation, escalating from the rates presently being experienced, will make it even harder to achieve our full-employment objective. Inflation strikes at the basis of business investment decisions, creates a climate of uncertainty and weakens confidence in the future of the economy and the ability of the Government to meet national economic objectives. It eats into the capacity of the economy to sustain the growth necessary to maintain the work force in viable employment, and to maintain a competitive position in international trade.

In short, I must state my sad conviction that what we have opted for is likely to give us the worst of all worlds. So far from ensuring that unemployment does not rise unnecessarily, our decisions are likely — especially in the longer term — to make it increasingly hard to sustain the level of employment opportunity that has for long been accepted as normal by the Australian work force. At the same time, we have turned away from what may prove to have been our last opportunity to deal effectively with escalating inflation. The result is all too likely to be a vicious circle of spiralling inflation and depressed employment and activity — the classic 'stagflation' situation — coupled with a situation in the balance of payments that only severe action will redress.

But by this stage nobody was listening to Treasury any more.

The 1974 Budget, formally read out in the House by Crean, was known as the Cairns Budget although it really reflected no guiding hand but rather a miscellaneous collection of unrelated spending and taxing decisions by the 27 man Cabinet. And it was to be revised several times in the next six months. To a large extent these revisions were caused by the realisation in September that the tightening of the money supply that Treasury and the Reserve Bank had been overseeing had been biting much harder on the business sector than anyone in the Cabinet had appreciated — or had been informed by Treasury or the Reserve Bank.

The first revision on 25 September was a 12 per cent devaluation of the Australian dollar designed to assist export industries and also industries competing with importers — being roughly equivalent to a 40 per cent increase in tariffs. Treasury opposed the move as inflationary but its advice was rejected out of hand. The decision was taken by the newly diminished Kitchen Cabinet of Whitlam, Crean and Cairns, of whom clearly only Whitlam and Cairns were significant although, when Kep Enderby became Minister for Secondary Industry, he also began to attend these meetings.

The second revision was the mini-budget of 12 November which cut personal and company tax and further eased credit restrictions on domestic and foreign sources of funds. Whitlam stressed the need for stimulation to encourage the private sector. At the same time tariffs on motor vehicle imports were increased as if to symbolise the abandonment of past policies and the substitution of *ad hoc* measures for strategies.

Two further revisions then took place inside three months. On 9 December further taxation concessions were granted to companies and import quotas were imposed on a range of goods. On 29 January additional funding for the States was announced and the capital gains tax established in the August Budget was abolished. Between these came the final capitulation to the auto industry in the face of GMH's threats.

The real position at the beginning of 1975 when Cairns took over Treasury was that the government had abandoned its Budget strategy (itself not a clear policy) and, while no longer relying on Treasury, nevertheless had not been able to find a consistent alternative source of economic advice. Its relations with Treasury can be gauged from Whitlam's public reply in November to the question of whether he considered that Treasury should have at least drawn the figures on the contraction of the money supply to the government's attention:

My God, I do. It damn well will.

Almost as soon as he had become Treasurer, Cairns also became Acting Prime Minister when Whitlam left Australia in mid December 1974 for six weeks. During this period Cairns rode on the crest of a media-induced wave — a study in reasonableness in comparison to the bombastic Whitlam — conveying an impression of genuine involvement in the aftermath of cyclone-ravaged Darwin and the negotiations to halt GMH's retrenchment of its employees. It was the zenith of a public career that inside six months would slide in a precipitate decline to its nadir — a decline that was a phenomenon of both policy and procedure.

In the area of policy the problem was that, even if it had been possible to impose a coherent and detailed program of economic management on Treasury, Cairns had no such program to propose. In his television interview in February 1975 already referred to, he took part in an exchange that suggested how difficult he had found it to adapt his essentially vague ideas to day-to-day administration:

> Dr Cairns: Well I have been saying it, I've done my best and I don't regret it. I think in all these things I feel that I can't regret the influence I've had. I don't lament the result, I've done my best, and what we have is a result of history.
> Robert Moore: But there is a tone of defeatism, I think, coming through your words tonight.
> Dr Cairns: Maybe I would say this, that after two years I can see the position much more difficult than I might have seen it four or five or ten or fifteen years ago. I think the job of changing this society of ours is much more difficult than I might have thought it was ten or fifteen years ago.
> Robert Moore: How much — and we are getting towards the end of our time now — how much, in fact, has the Labor Government changed our society? I mean if there is another . . . if there is an election soon and another party or parties gets in, how much *will* they have to unscramble and how much will they not have to?
> Dr Cairns: Well I think that the changes have not been in economics or in economic management much, but changes that have taken place in the last two years are very important; in our relations with other countries Australia *is* recognised as much more as a genuine independent Australian voice. I think Gough Whitlam as an individual has done more to bring that state of affairs about than anyone else in our history — at least in *this* century.
> I think that there's a great deal more freedom in the community without any undue amount of licence as was predicted. I think people are freer today; they're less concerned with censorship, less worried that things like that might cause trouble, difficulty.
> Robert Moore: But in your own area of economics, I meant. I mean how different is the mixture of the mixed economy now than it was in December 1972?
> Dr Cairns: Not much different, and it can't be much different. This to me is a starting point. The Government is peripheral, its powers are not central. It's got limited scope to do things. We've had 2¼ years — not much in the history of Australia can be done in that time. (Cairns 1975)

Not much different. Even at this stage the twin cankers of helplessness and disillusionment were beginning to take hold. None of this meant that Cairns favoured Treasury's approach to these problems and in the same interview he left no doubt that he considered his department inadequate for the task of economic management when he said:

> The Treasury has a philosophy of neo-classical economics — almost everyone of importance has been trained in one of the university

faculties, Keynesian, they think in macro terms, they think in aggregate terms, they don't think in allocative or priority terms at all, really, and hardly anything that comes from Treasury is other than in macro terms. Mainly today Treasury talks about inflation and the necessity to restrain it still more than it has been. Not unduly concerned about the increase in unemployment; still, I think, believing between the lines that higher unemployment is necessary to give the system the checks and restraints that it needs. The Treasury does think in aggregate terms. (Cairns 1975)

Treasury officers observing the interview no doubt reciprocated the view that their philosophy was incompatible with that of their minister — but they remained stubbornly determined to pursue a policy that they realised was unacceptable to the government of the day.

In the way that so many of the Whitlam government's difficulties were rooted in administration, this mutual suspicion between Cairns and Treasury was extended to a complete breakdown of relations between minister and department caused by procedural problems. Crean as Treasurer had relied almost exclusively on the department to staff his personal office in Parliament House. Cairns was given two Treasury officers to handle correspondence but otherwise had his own staff, including his stepson Phillip who had been with him since he became a minister and Junie Morosi who was appointed his senior Private Secretary in January 1975, despite opposition from a section of the government that was increasingly concerned at the publicity being given to ministerial staff generally. Cairns could no doubt have survived — although with a seriously diminished reputation — the orgy of media trivia that for months surrounded, and was courted by, Morosi and some of the attractive female stenographers whom she appointed to the Treasurer's office. But the structure of the office had other effects. In particular it compounded for Treasury their difficulties in dealing with Cairns.

Treasury's reaction to Morosi can be guessed at from a statement made by Cairns two years later when testifying for Morosi in a defamation action brought by her against a Sydney newspaper. Asked by Counsel for the newspaper if she was involved in Treasury matters, Cairns replied simply of the person who was senior Private Secretary to the Treasurer:

One of the things she isn't interested in is economics.

On a more mundane level the office filing system was later

described by one of the two Treasury officials in the office in the following fashion:

> The files contained inwards and outwards copies of correspondence on electoral matters, representations (including referrals to other Ministerial Offices) and letters to and from organisations and Members of Parliament. Correspondence awaiting filing, and in fact all the outer office files themselves, were in a room that could not be locked and during my time in the office the filing cabinets were almost never locked.
> The filing system was in fact not well kept and has been reorganised over the last month. At the beginning of May there was a large number of loose documents awaiting placement on particular files. If one needed to find the duplicate copy of a letter that had recently been sent from the office one therefore usually needed to look through all the loose documents in order to find it. Regular searches were made when documents needed to be located.

Yet the Treasurer had one of the heaviest administrative loads in the government, with masses of paper, both routine and substantive, coming to his desk each day.

The overall result of this system was that Cairns and his department tended to communicate rather impersonally through the two resident Treasury officers. It became possible for Cairns to settle some economic issues without his department being aware of his decision until afterwards, as in June 1975 when he conducted the negotiations with the failing Tasmanian company, Associated Pulp and Paper Mills, that led to payment of $650,000 to the firm to prevent employees being retrenched.

This situation was further exacerbated by the fact that Cairns spent considerable periods overseas once Whitlam returned at the end of January. During these periods his chief rival in the economic area, Bill Hayden, became Acting Treasurer and was allowed to establish an obvious rapport with Treasury.

Cairns' last performance as Treasurer was in Canberra on 21 May. While Parliament was sitting, Cairns and Whitlam, with Wheeler, Stone, Menadue, Brogan and other officials, met in Whitlam's office to consider the cuts in income tax promised in late 1974. It was decided to compress the reductions into the first six months of 1975 to boost consumer demand, and to offset half this revenue loss with a levy on salaries from 1 July to meet the cost of Medibank which came into operation on that date.

The next day Cairns left for an OECD meeting in Paris. Although the meeting was to last only two days he was not scheduled to return to Australia until 14 June after two weeks in

Switzerland, Egypt and Israel. The OECD meeting was to be attended by Western economic managers at what they saw as a time of crisis. On one heady day, 28 May, Cairns had talks with Henry Kissinger, US Secretary of State, and William Simon, US Treasury Secretary, and breakfasted with Denis Healey, British Chancellor of the Exchequer. On the same day Whitlam telephoned him and insisted that he cut short his trip and return to Australia at once. The glittering world of international economic diplomacy vanished for him even as he looked on it in Paris. Whitlam's call meant the end of his time as Treasurer and, before long, as a minister.

It is quite possible that Whitlam had decided some time before to replace Cairns as Treasurer. In Whitlam's view, Cairns had not produced a coherent program to turn the economy around although this prospect must have been evident to Whitlam before he appointed him. Whatever the ultimate reason, it is clear that Whitlam's immediate grounds for Cairns' removal were provided by a product of Cairns' administrative chaos and made irrefutable by Cairns' absence overseas when the issue broke.

In March and April Cairns had given George Harris, a Melbourne businessman whom he knew slightly, four letters relating to the Australian government's desire to raise loan funds overseas. Harris stated that he would use these letters in Europe during this period to find suitable lenders and he wanted a commission on the deal if it came off. It was the kind of request that a Treasurer receives constantly in the mail but usually ignores. Cairns did not. Two of the letters were non-committal, expressing only a general interest in loan funds, but the remaining two promised a commission to Harris if a loan eventuated although they made it clear that the Australian government, not Harris, would negotiate any loan. One of these letters spoke of an 'commission', the other of a 'once only brokerage fee of 2½ per cent deducted at the source'. During March and April, Harris approached financiers in Europe and the US and on at least one occasion in New York an agreement was made with various firms to divide any commission obtained. Cairns himself had no contact with any of these institutions and, as Harris produced no lenders, the project went nowhere.

Cairns had not mentioned the Harris letters to his department but Treasury's information network was wide-ranging. In late March, Treasury's man in the Australian High Commission in

London notified Canberra of the existence of two of the letters, one of which referred to a commission of 2½ per cent. Wheeler raised the matter with Cairns and gave him a copy of the communication from the London representative. When Cairns conceded that he had given Harris some 'credentials', Wheeler advised that they should be withdrawn at once. Almost a month later Harris called on Australia's High Commissioner in London, Sir John Bunting, to have his letter authenticated. Treasury's London office telephoned Wheeler at once and Wheeler telephoned Bunting to request that the letter be dictated over the phone, which was done. Wheeler again urged Cairns to withdraw any documents that he had given to Harris. Cairns brushed the request aside although he conceded that he did not expect Harris to produce any funds.

It was at this stage that Wheeler decided that he could not accept Cairns' approach on this matter. Convinced that Australia's status as an international lender and Treasury's status as its exclusive negotiator of loans was being damaged by such unorthodox and, in his view, futile efforts as this one encouraged by Cairns (and others encouraged already by Connor) he approached his close colleague Clarrie Harders, Secretary of the Attorney-General's Department, with copies of the two letters, one provided by Bunting and the other by one of the Treasury officials in Cairns' Parliament House office.

Although the verbatim text of the letters was not given to the Attorney-General's Department in an effort to disguise their source, Harders was under no illusions and expressed concern to Wheeler that Cairns had not been informed of what was happening. Wheeler insisted on receiving advice and Harders furnished it from the Advisings Division of his department three weeks later on 28 May, by which time Cairns had left for Paris. Only then did Harders mention the matter to Attorney-General Kep Enderby. Harders would later defend Wheeler as the permanent head who most commonly requested legal advice and argue that he was anxious to be 'even handed' between Treasury and Minerals and Energy, as he had also been asked by Menadue to advise on one of Connor's letters concerning loan raising.

It is difficult to see the similarity between the cases. One involved the head of the Prime Minister's Department, presumably on the direction of the Prime Minister, seeking advice on a letter by another minister. The other involved the head of Treasury seeking advice on a letter by his own minister without the knowledge of his minister or the Prime Minister. The opinion of the Advisings Division was that the letters made Harris an agent of the Australian government for the purposes of introducing it to a lender only, not for negotiating a loan, and guaranteed a commission if a loan was consummated. It was therefore essentially the same as some issued by Connor in December 1974. Despite later suggestions, the parts omitted by Treasury when the letters were sent to Attorney-General's did not alter this position and Harders did not change his opinion when eventually shown them. The same day that he received the opinion, Wheeler gave it to Whitlam and Hayden at an evening meeting in Whitlam's office where Menadue was also present. Ironically he produced at the same time a document that Treasury had received from the Australian Trade Commissioner in Milan which indicated that information on Connor's loan raising activities was leaking out in European financial circles and had found its way to a small German bank. Connor's loan-raising efforts had also surfaced in Parliament and in the Australian press.

That night Wheeler sent the following cable to Cairns in Paris:

> Personal and Confidential and Immediate
> For Treasurer
> From Wheeler
> 1. As your private office will have informed you, the 'K' exercise has been greatly featured in the parliament and the press in recent days.
> 2. I now let you have as an attachment to this message the full extent of a letter which I received from Harders this afternoon.
> 3. Whilst with the acting treasurer and the prime minister tonight on taxation matters inevitably I informed them both of the Harders letter.
> 4. I strongly advise that you take immediate steps to effect an immediate and complete cancellation of accreditations or authorisations (if any) given to George Harris.
> 5. I suggest that you telephone me.
> 6. Given all the circumstances I also strongly suggest that you telephone the prime minister without delay.

It was the communication of someone in a strong position.

After the reference to Cairns' 'private office', presumably in contrast to his publicly appointed Treasury advisers, Wheeler made his third request for a withdrawal of any documents issued to Harris with the clear implication that he had been proven correct on this question. Although he suggested that Cairns contact Whitlam, he was almost certainly already aware that Cairns could not survive and that Hayden would retain him as head of Treasury at least for the immediate future. In the report which he produced for Whitlam on the incident, Solicitor-General Maurice Byers made this assessment of Wheeler's conduct:

> I understand you desire my opinion on the legal questions raised by the documents you gave. I do not think that the Treasury's action in seeking and obtaining the opinion is consistent with responsible government and the implications to which it gives rise . . .
> Suppose the Secretary's immediate subordinate to have sought, without his superior's knowledge, an opinion as to documents given or signed in performance of his duties by the Secretary. And suppose, further, those documents, because of a need to preserve confidentiality, to differ from the ones given. And that, an opinion obtained, it was then (with whatever justification) disclosed, without prior notification to the permanent head. And then down the line.
> I should have thought such behaviour inconsistent with the Public Service Act. It is so because departures from that loyalty the Act postulates are by its provisions attended with penalty.

In the world of the Canberra bureaucracy Cairns was clearly out of his depth. To underline this fact, one of Cairns' earliest responses to Treasury on returning to Canberra on 2 June was to dismiss from Parliament House the Treasury officer who had supplied a copy of one of the letters to Wheeler. Yet the letters had been automatically supplied to Wheeler, because of their subject matter, in accordance with an arrangement agreed to in writing by Cairns in January 1975.

On the morning of 2 June, in a tense meeting, Whitlam told Cairns that there was to be a Cabinet reshuffle later in the week as a result of Lance Barnard's departure as ambassador to Sweden, and that he was to lose Treasury. That afternoon Cairns issued a press statement challenging the idea of the reshuffle. The next day at the Caucus meeting he totally withdrew the challenge, which had attracted almost no support from his former backers, and accepted the post of Environment Minister rather than Social Security which Whitlam had suggested. Cairns was convinced by some of his colleagues that the Environment portfolio could provide a springboard back into power because of its potential appeal to large sections of the community. If he did see himself at the head of a new mass movement based on what had already become in America one of the most emotive issues of the 1970s, it was a dream that would not last more than a month and the remainder of 1975 would be, for him, more like a nightmare.

4   Law and disorder
Lionel Murphy

Of the four ministers present at the Lodge late on the night of 13 December 1974, Lionel Murphy, although not personally involved in the quest for overseas loans, in many ways epitomised the efforts and frustrations of the Whitlam government which were so strongly reflected in the Executive Council meeting itself. As Attorney-General and Leader of the Government in an Opposition-controlled Senate, Murphy was in the frontline of Labor's harassed attempts to implement its programs in the face of legal challenges in the courts, and parliamentary dismemberment in the Upper House.

Always olympian in his energies, often impetuous in his actions, he reacted violently against obstruction whether from his political opponents or from members of his own Party. There could have been no Executive Council meeting if Murphy had not forced his department to prepare the loan documents, disregarding their Treasury-inspired reluctance and then given a legal opinion, again in conflict with his department, to the effect that the loan would not violate the Australian government's borrowing agreements with the States. It was not Murphy's project but he shared Connor's distaste for persons *inside* the government who wanted to limit its actions when it was constantly facing this threat from *outside* as well.

One thing is certain — it was not an unusual hour for him to be engaged in the business of government. Like a lot of barristers his capacity for work — and for flamboyant play — was considerable, and frequently spanned 24 hours at a stretch. Even in the earliest days of the government — in January 1973 — a few weeks after taking over as Attorney-General, he had astonished British and Australian officials in London by calling Foreign Secretary Sir Alec Douglas-Home at 11 pm to say that he would be across immediately to discuss the joint press statement they would be putting out next day on the remaining legal links between Australia and Britain. Soon afterwards he appeared at Home's townhouse, settled the statement with the bemused Foreign Secretary and set off back to his hotel to begin work on some papers for the Commonwealth Law Officers Conference he was attending next day.

Murphy was a product of the same Sydney legal world which had nurtured Kerr and, to a lesser extent, Whitlam who had, however, left it much earlier than the others for politics and never returned. In the 1950s Murphy had been on the opposite side to Kerr in a number of the courtroom struggles for control of important unions. It was a world that engendered not only bitter conflicts but also strong ties between many of those who were thrown together for long periods of time to the exclusion, because of their working habits, of almost all other society. Some of Murphy's closest colleagues in his days at the Bar had been Neville Wran; James McClelland, Labor Senator from NSW and Minister for Labour in 1975 after he replaced Murphy in the ministry; and Michael Kirby, Chairman of the Australian Law Reform Commission to which he was appointed by Murphy, with a judgeship, in 1974. They all owed their positions in some degree to Murphy who had carried the loyalties of the Bar into political life.

He had encountered them all as a barrister in the industrial area in Sydney in the 1950s and 1960s after graduating from Sydney University just after the war with honours degrees in the unlikely combination of law and organic chemistry. In the same way that John Kerr became known for his role in the legal battle for control of the Federated Ironworkers, Murphy's career was accelerated by his involvement in the conflict over the Miscellaneous Workers Union (MWU) which grew during this period to become one of the biggest unions in the country. His work for the MWU ultimately had its political as well as its legal legacies — two of the persons most influential in securing Murphy's ALP pre-selection for the Senate in 1961 were Ray Gietzelt, Federal Secretary of the MWU, and his brother Arthur Gietzelt who himself was elected a Labor Senator for NSW in 1970.

By 1961 Murphy, a QC although still only 39, was a major figure at the industrial Bar. But he was not the choice of the dominant group in the NSW Labor Party for any of the three positions on the Senate ticket for that year. In a surprise result he dislodged John Armstrong, who had been a minister in the Chifley government and a Senator since 1938, to capture the number two position and a certain Senate seat. At this time the Senate was largely a resting place for venerable party stalwarts on both sides and in this sleepy atmosphere Murphy's enthusiasm and aggressive debating skill stood out sharply. So sharply that after the 1966 election he was the left's candidate for the position of Leader of the Opposition in the Senate and replaced the incumbent, Don Willesee of Western Australia.

This office did not make his position in the NSW Labor Party any more secure. Preselections continued to be a struggle right up until Labor achieved government, and in 1970 there was a serious attempt to have him expelled from the Party on the ground that he had 'breached solidarity' by appearing for the MWU in proceedings against another union as part of the extensive legal practice which he still maintained. At a time when all factional divisions in the ALP were described in terms of a left/right dichotomy, Murphy was considered one of the leaders of the left. Actually the factionalism, particularly in NSW, was much more complex and personality-oriented than these labels suggest. What is clear, however, is that a decade of bitter political infighting to hold his position had made Murphy a dangerous opponent — but perhaps also a dangerous colleague.

During that time he had also become a serious rival to Whitlam in the parliamentary Party. Only the fact that they sat in different Houses prevented a direct confrontation, and in 1969 there had been some speculation that Murphy would stand down from the Senate to contest the seat of Hughes in the House of Representatives. Relations between the two were strained throughout this period, as Murphy was a member of the Federal Executive of the Party and voted consistently against Whitlam's attempts to undermine and replace the Victorian Executive. When he resigned the Party leadership in April 1968 in protest at lack of support from the Federal Executive, Whitlam criticised Murphy and the Deputy Senate Leader Sam Cohen, for voting on the Executive against the interests of the parliamentary Party. These were no doubt things that Whitlam recalled when he made his decision in December 1972 to form a government for over two weeks with Barnard alone, rather than with Murphy and Willesee, the other two parliamentary leaders, as might have been expected.

When he did become Attorney-General on 19 December 1972, Murphy unleashed upon his new department an avalanche of ideas. It was a violent shock for the Attorney-General's Department which had been, under Liberal governments, an essentially low-profile supplier of conservative legal opinions on the validity of the actions of other departments. One of Murphy's first directions was to tell them to purchase some books for the department's pitiful library, including the major American law reviews which, unbelievably, were not on its shelves.

The violence of this encounter was nevertheless cushioned and ultimately defused by the presence of Clarrie Harders, the Department's permanent head. Harders had had 23 years in the ranks before becoming permanent head in 1970, and was skilled at adapting to the individual styles of the various Attorneys-General he had worked with over that time. Not only did Harders survive the stormy transition but he rapidly gained Murphy's confidence with his attentive and diplomatic approach. It was a vivid contrast — Murphy, tall, robust, argumentative; Harders, diminutive, softly-spoken, never far from flattery — but one that enabled Harders to go through the Labor years and still be Secretary at their end to greet yet another minister. No wonder he preferred to use the nondescript form 'Attorney' in conversation, even when invited to adopt a first name basis.

Over the next two years Attorney-General's found itself in the forefront of the government's legislative program and also involved in the kind of glamorous exercises that had previously been reserved for departments like Foreign Affairs. One of its first experiences with this higher profile was Australia's challenge in the International Court of Justice to the French atmospheric nuclear tests in the South Pacific. Murphy had the matter brought before the court in May 1973 and later argued parts of the Australian case personally at the hearings in the Dutch capital of The Hague — easily distinguishable in the courtroom by his refusal to wear a wig like other Counsel. With characteristic Gallic disdain, the French government refused to even appear at the court, asserting that it did not recognise the court's jurisdiction over such questions. And with characteristic judicial reticence the court decided, at the end of 1974, that there was no point in deciding whether it had jurisdiction or not because the French had by this time finished their testing in the

Labor's Attorney-General, Lionel Murphy QC, distaining the wig worn by all other counsel, and Maurice Byers QC, later the Commonwealth Solicitor-General, between sessions at the French nuclear test case at the international Court of Justice, the Hague, 1973

Pacific region.

In terms of new programs Murphy pressed Attorney-General's from the outset into developing wide-ranging legislative proposals — based principally on US models — for the regulation of corporate activities and the protection of personal rights. Work began immediately on the re-drafting of the Trade Practices Act to embody the principles of the long-standing US anti-trust statutes: the prevention of, or at least the retarding of, the dominance of industries by one or two giant corporations by restrictions on monopolisation, mergers and price discrimination, although in the 73 years of their operation the US statutes have not dramatically affected the growth or concentration of corporate power, and the techniques adopted from them for Australian purposes may well be even less suitable for a much smaller and naturally less competitive economy. One aspect of the Murphy legislation which advanced well beyond the US model, however, was the emphasis given to consumer protection. The provisions relating to defective products, unfair sales methods, and misleading advertising were stringent and comprehensive and, ironically, they would be the only part of the Act to survive extensive amendment by the Fraser government in 1977.

The Trade Practices Act became law in August 1974 but work had already begun on two further proposals for economic regulation — a Corporations and Securities Act to deal with the financial activities of corporations, particularly share transactions; and a National Companies Act to cover the formation and administration of corporations. Neither was destined to become law. A Corporations and Securities Bill was introduced into Parliament in December 1974 but when it reached the Senate it was referred by the Opposition to a committee from which it never emerged. A National Companies Bill was scheduled to be introduced into Parliament on 11 November 1975 but Parliament was dissolved that day.

In the area of individual rights Murphy's chief project was a Human Rights Act that would adopt the United Nations Declaration of Human Rights as its basis and establish in Australia guarantees of the kind that have always been present in the US Constitution — freedom of speech, freedom of assembly, freedom from arbitrary arrest, freedom from invasions of privacy — together with a commission to which complaints could be made by individuals who considered that they had been deprived of these rights. Murphy took the view that while there was not the consistent denial of personal rights in Australia that existed in many nations, the Vietnam years, when freedom of speech and of assembly were seriously questioned, had demonstrated how fragile was this unwritten consensus. In November 1973 he introduced a Human Rights Bill into Parliament. When it became obvious over subsequent months that the Bill would be defeated in the Senate, it was allowed to lapse and was not re-introduced after the 1974 election.

One piece of legislation which survived the Senate substantially, if not totally, intact was Murphy's Racial Discrimination Act which implemented the 1963 International Convention on the Elimination of All Forms of Racial Discrimination and prohibited conduct that discriminated against such persons as migrants or Aboriginals on the basis of their race, colour or national origin — most particularly in the fields of employment and housing where discrimination reinforced the economic difficulties of minority groups. It became law in 1974. Al Grassby, who had been Minister for Immigration in the first Whitlam government but who had lost his seat at the 1974 elections, was appointed as the Commissioner to whom complaints of discrimination were to be made.

Closely associated with this philosophy of human rights was the Family Law Bill which Murphy initially put before Parliament in December 1973. The legislation proposed two radical changes for obtaining dissolution of a marriage — firstly, that it be made available on evidence of separation without any of the enquiries relating to adultery, cruelty or desertion that had produced so much sordid and irrelevant material in the past and, secondly, that it be granted on the basis of one year's separation, in contrast to the five years then necessary to establish the ground of separation by agreement and the two years necessary to establish the ground of desertion. After a long series of votes not taken on party lines — a rare occurrence in the Australian Parliament — the Family Law Act came into operation early in 1976.

At the same time the Family Court of Australia was set up to administer the Act. Despite the more rational concepts embodied in the new legislation it has not, however, altered the acrimonious and time-consuming quality of most defended divorces because it still — perhaps inevitably — leaves questions of property division and custody of children to be fought out in court unless the parties can agree privately.

Despite his relative isolation over the years in an almost exclusively legal and political environment, Murphy had an appreciation of the significance of access to the law, of how meaningless changes made in for example the Family Law Act were to persons who, because of their economic situation, were in no position to obtain the services of a lawyer. Out of this appreciation came the Australian Legal Aid Office (ALAO). The first ALAOs were opened at Ipswich in Queensland and at Sunshine in Melbourne's western suburbs in April 1974. In little over a year, 30 more offices opened, despite fierce criticism from the Opposition in Parliament and from the legal profession who ultimately sought to have the ALAO dismantled in the courts.

The very placement of offices in areas like Ipswich and

Sunshine was a recognition of the fact that in addition to problems of cost, many persons in the community were reluctant to approach a professional group who appeared so geographically and socially removed from their own lives. ALAO offices were staffed full-time by Australian government lawyers who provided legal advice and assistance on matters of federal law, especially family law, to all persons in need, and on all matters federal and State to persons having a constitutional connection with the federal government — pensioners, migrants, Aboriginals, ex-servicemen. The demand for the ALAO's services was further evidence of the extent of the previously unmet need for legal assistance in the community. Over 150,000 persons sought aid from the ALAO while the first 30 offices were being established and most of these were not substituting the ALAO for a private lawyer but approaching a lawyer for the first time — over two thirds of them with family law problems.

If the idea of the ALAO was an example of Murphy's innovative spirit in relation to the role of law in society, its implementation was an example of his failure to ensure that bodies set up under his authority were run by persons capable of the task. In the case of bodies like the ALAO, the Trade Practices Commission, and the Institute of Criminology, he either chose, or was prepared to accept — at the suggestion of his department — as heads of each of these organisations persons who, with few exceptions, had no talent or affinity for the underlying aims of the organisations. The department certainly lobbied for most of these appointments — most of them in fact were persons from the department — but the final decision was Murphy's. No amount of capable officers down the line in these bodies could ever fully remedy this malaise at the top.

In one further respect, and one reminiscent of the Executive Council meeting at the Lodge, the establishment of the ALAO was characteristic of Murphy's approach to government. It was a swift and, in conventional terms, unorthodox means of achieving something that might otherwise have been frustrated by the Opposition. The way in which the ALAO was established did not involve legislation, which would have taken time to draft and could then have been rejected or amended in the Senate, but simply an administrative decision followed by an allocation of funds from the Budget. The Australian Assistance Plan and the Regional Employment Development Scheme were set up in the same fashion. It was a procedure that, in addition, made legal challenge difficult as a one-line entry in the Budget provided much less scope for constitutional argument than a full-blown statute. The Australian Assistance Plan was challenged in the High Court in 1975 on this very basis but survived by a narrow majority. The ALAO was also challenged but the case had not been heard by the High Court before the government fell. Murphy's point was that the programs were at least *in operation* and had to be struck down rather than rejected in the Senate before they had even got off the ground.

There was, nevertheless, an element of irony in Murphy's reaction to the Senate in 1973 and 1974 since he himself, in the 1960s and early 1970s, had been substantially responsible for building up the Senate's role in examining legislation passed through the House of Representatives. With the enthusiastic assistance of the Clerk of the Senate, James Odgers, he lobbied through the Senate in this period a system of Standing and Select Committees that enabled the Upper House to play a much more active role in the processes of Parliament, including a series of five Estimates Committees that looked at all allocations of funds in the Budget. Given Labor's long term commitment to abolition of the Senate, there was a faintly schizophrenic quality to this exercise and the jibe was made in 1973 and 1974 by some of his colleagues that Murphy was only encountering a monster of his own creation. In practice it was not detailed scrutiny of legislation that was Labor's problem but rather flat rejection — and that power would have been available to the Senate even without its lift in prestige in recent years.

Murphy's efforts in getting these proposals for a committee system through the Senate while still in Opposition indicated that he could be a skilful trader and negotiator even with his opponents. He had always relished the lobbying and scheming among his own colleagues necessary to get his proposals accepted within the Party and he gave some demonstrations of this skill in government also, none being more impressive than the passage of the Trade Practices Act in August 1974 when it was necessary to secure the support of the two Independent Liberals in the Senate, Michael Townley and Steele Hall. But this kind of diplomacy was very much the exception. The pressures on the government from its early days, and Murphy's reaction to those pressures, combined to place him almost from his first days as Senate Leader and Attorney-General at the centre of a series of violent political storms.

Even for a less volatile personality than Murphy the numbers in the Senate after the 1972 elections would have meant trouble for Labor's Senate Leader. With a total of 26 Labor Senators, Murphy faced 34 non-Labor members of the Upper House — 27 LCP, 5 DLP and two Independents, Reginald Turnbull from Tasmania and Sydney Negus from Western Australia. Of the 60 Senators, 30 had been elected in 1967 and 30 in 1970, with the result that the complexion of the Senate in 1973 bore little relation to the mood of the electorate that had just given Labor 49.6 per cent of the vote.

Obviously the government faced defeat whenever the LCP and DLP Senators combined — and both groups had been badly affected by the change of government. For the LCP it was the shock of being dispossessed of power after 23 years during which its exercise had become a comfortable habit. For the DLP it was the even more stunning realisation that they had lost the chief reason for their existence; that after fighting for eighteen years to keep their former colleagues out of government, the ALP had got there despite them and would therefore never have any reason to come to terms with them. In this rancorous setting Murphy could not even be sure that the government would be able to fix routine matters like the hours and days when the Senate would sit, let alone get through legislation that had passed through the House of Representatives. As it turned out he could guarantee neither on a regular basis as the Opposition began a war of attrition from the first day of the 1973 sittings.

That first day, 28 February 1973, also produced the first of the Opposition's concentrated attacks on Murphy himself. The subject of their attack was a series of amendments, made before parliament had resumed, to the rules governing the conduct of divorce cases in the courts. The amendments were designed to effect the sort of changes that were later brought about by the Family Law Act and tried to reduce reliance on the fault of the other party which was then the basis of most divorce applications. Realising that it would take a considerable time to draft the new Bill and get it through Parliament, Murphy had decided upon the amendments as an interim measure while this work went ahead.

Led by Ivor Greenwood, Liberal Deputy Leader in the Senate and shadow Attorney-General, the Opposition alleged that the amendments to the rules were an attempt to change the existing Act by the backdoor, that they were so badly drafted as to be incomprehensible in parts, and that Murphy had bypassed his department to use one of his associates at the Sydney Bar. Murphy defended the amendments strenuously as an attempt to humanise the existing law but over the next two weeks they received a battering from legal commentators in the press and on 15 March the Opposition carried a special motion of disallowance that brought the new rules to an end. The incident served to underline the conflict inherent in Murphy's attraction to cutting corners in government and the Opposition's determination to use its numbers even though no longer in government. On the same day that the rules were disallowed a far more serious confrontation was initiated between these same antithetical forces.

Although he had been one of the delegates at Labor's 1971 Federal Conference in Launceston who had voted against the disbanding by a future Labor government of the Australian Security Intelligence Organisation (ASIO), Murphy soon became dissatisfied with the performance of ASIO, for which he assumed responsibility on becoming Attorney-General. Acting on the advice of Melbourne lawyer and ex-superintendent in the Commonwealth Police, Kerry Milte, he had become convinced that ASIO's decades of concern with what they considered dangers to national security from the left had led them to ignore threats from the right, most particularly from the Croatians who had been responsible for bombings in the Yugoslav communities in Melbourne and Sydney. During the afternoon and evening of 13 March, sitting in his Parliament House suite going through files with Milte, these suspicions flared into the certainty that ASIO was withholding information from him — and doing so only a week before the Yugoslav Prime Minister was due to visit Canberra and would have to be protected.

Shortly after 11.30 pm, half an hour after the Senate had adjourned for the day, he had his staff call the chief ASIO official in Canberra to say that the Attorney-General would meet him on the steps of Parliament House in ten minutes and then proceed to ASIO's Canberra offices immediately. After arriving with the official shortly before midnight at ASIO's offices across Lake Burley Griffin from Parliament House, Murphy spent two hours examining files and among them discovered a file note that discussed the use of training camps in Australia by Croatian terrorists — a report never conveyed to him. Taking copies of some of the files with him he returned, still with Milte, to his Canberra home. There he discovered a further passage that suggested that ASIO (and his own department) were not anxious to highlight any problem of Croatian terrorism in Australia.

Murphy and Milte, having worked through the night, took a 7.30 am flight to Melbourne to examine the files at ASIO's head office in St Kilda Road. ASIO's Director-General, Peter Barbour, had been warned by his Canberra office of this possibility and had told most of the staff not to come to work that day. What Murphy did find, however, was an ASIO headquarters surrounded and occupied by Commonwealth Police and besieged by pressmen. He had agreed in Canberra that the Melbourne files should be sealed until he arrived and the Commonwealth Police, delighted to score off their old rivals ASIO, had responded with a small army and also informed the press. Even the papers on Barbour's desk had been bundled up and sealed in large brown envelopes to await Murphy who spent most of the morning examining documents with Barbour, including the original of the Canberra file that had sparked off the visit.

Over the next two months in the Senate, Murphy faced an almost daily barrage of questions on what became known as the ASIO raid. Although he tried to counter the Opposition with allegations that Greenwood had neglected the Croatian problem as Attorney-General, he had little success in diverting media attention from his own actions. On some days during this period he was so driven into a corner that he simply refused to answer further questions — a humiliating failure for any minister. He was like a fox surrounded by a pack of hounds and the Independent Senator Turnbull caught the mood of the Senate when he said in a debate on the issue on 5 April:

> I am going to speak very little on the question of Croatian terrorism because everyone in this chamber has spoken ad nauseam for 2 days about that subject, and whether an honourable senator says one thing or the other simply depends on which side of the House he is sitting. What disturbs me is the smell of death in this chamber, of people waiting to kill. One can sort of smell this atmosphere of hate which is pervading this chamber and emanating from certain members on the Opposition benches . . . This hatred which is evident in this chamber has been apparent for 2 days. You can notice it; you can see the venom drooling out of their mouths as they wait for the kill. They are waiting and thinking: 'We have got him, we have got the numbers'. It is a numbers game, is it not? We all know that that is so in politics. Now Opposition senators have got something they can triumph on, so they are going to kill someone.

That someone was Murphy. In a move designed to make his

position untenable, the DLP proposed that a Senate committee be established to enquire into the civil rights of Croatian migrants. Such a committee would also consider the ASIO raid and be able to call as witnesses all those present on that occasion. Enraged by constant harassment, Murphy had the DLP motion defeated when it was voted on early in May by suddenly calling off the 'pairs' arrangement under which absent Senators are matched with a Senator on the other side so that the results of votes are the same as if every member were present. If possible, this unprecedented exercise made relations in the Senate worse. It was patently futile, since the Opposition simply recommitted the motion with all its Senators assembled and had it passed a week later. It also became most inconvenient for the government — to whose advantage the pairs system essentially works — when the Opposition refused for some time to re-instate the arrangement. It is the government that especially cannot afford to have members absent and yet has ministers who must travel abroad and meet other commitments. But the scenario was an index of Murphy's dislocation at this time.

A few weeks earlier, at the end of April, Murphy had been the subject of concentrated Opposition and media attack on a separate issue — the execution in Yugoslavia of three Croatians who had been part of a guerilla attack in that country in 1972 but who were also naturalised Australian citizens. When the executions were announced Australia formally protested to the Yugoslav government at not being informed previously. It was revealed in press reports, however, that Murphy had been informed by the Yugoslav ambassador in Canberra three days before the announcement was made (although still after the executions had taken place). Murphy maintained that he had assumed that the information would have been conveyed to the Foreign Minister, Whitlam, by formal channels at the same time. The incident reflected the essential absence of communication between the Prime Minister and the Attorney-General. Whitlam would scarcely have assisted the relationship when before the 1974 election he described the ASIO raid on national television as the greatest mistake of the government.

In one sense Murphy never recovered politically from these early months, and the ASIO raid would still feature in the Liberal Party's 1975 campaign advertising. Yet he always retained strong support in Caucus, partly because of the virulence of Opposition and media attacks on him and partly because he was recognised by those who were not pro-Whitlam as the most significant countervailing force to the emphatic power of the Prime Minister. To this extent criticism by Whitlam only strengthened his position as did the media attacks his supporters suspected were on occasions inspired by members of Whitlam's staff, suspicions that were fuelled by Whitlam's close association with the Murdoch press through its general manager, John Menadue (who had been Whitlam's Private Secretary in the 1960s) at a time when these publications were demanding Murphy's resignation.

Even when the two men were seeking the same objective, communication seemed to be a problem. They collaborated on the plan in March 1974 to gain an extra Senate seat for Labor in Queensland at the next half-Senate election in May by persuading Vincent Gair, former Queensland Premier and, until October 1973, DLP Leader in the Senate, to resign and accept the post of Australian ambassador to Ireland. If this had occurred there would have been six vacancies to be filled for the Senate from Queensland at the half-Senate election, of which Labor would certainly have won three, instead of five of which it would probably have won only two.

It was essentially Whitlam's plan and it succeeded — except that the story broke and Gair did not resign quickly enough to prevent Queensland Premier Joh Bjelke-Petersen issuing the election writs at once for five Senate vacancies only, thus frustrating the scheme at the outset. It was never really resolved in the recriminations that followed whether it was Murphy's or Whitlam's staff who had the responsibility for securing the resignation document.

In any case the error was effectively cancelled when the Opposition used the appointment of Gair as a justification for blocking supply in the Senate in an effort to force an election for both Houses. Whitlam, sensing that neither the economic climate nor sympathy for the government on the issue of blocking supply might be as favourable for some time, accepted the challenge and won narrowly. Apart from the election which it precipitated, the Gair appointment produced a mixed result for Labor — on one hand it gave the government an aura of intrigue and opportunism that would not be easily dispelled, on the other hand it contributed significantly to the political extinction of its long time nemesis, the DLP, since for many of its supporters Gair's actions were the final straw after the wasted

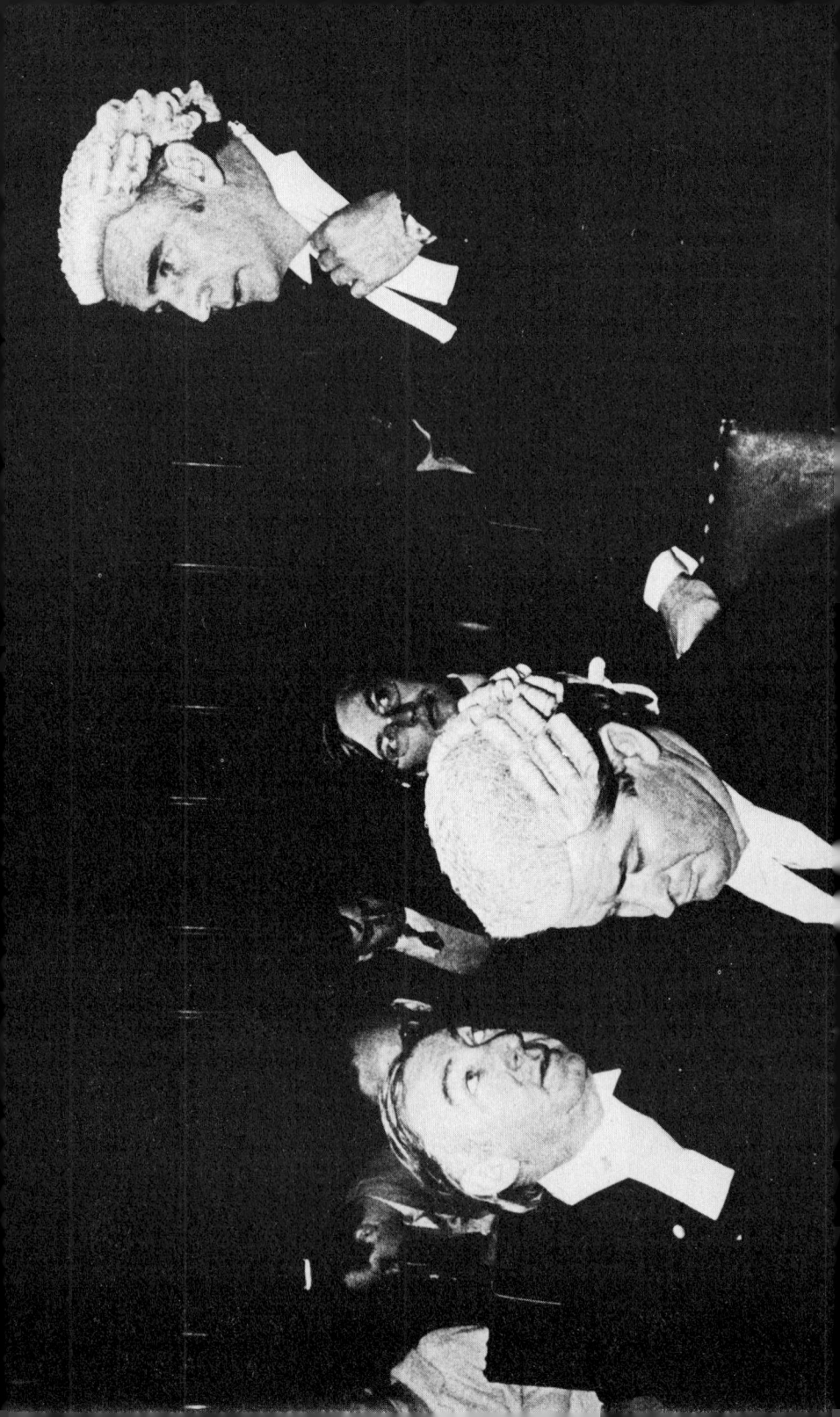

years of voting to keep a Labor government from office.

In the context of the Labor government it is significant that one of the factors affecting the relationship between Whitlam and Murphy in 1973 was a series of press reports explaining how the Director-General of ASIO had approached Whitlam after the raid and received a sympathetic hearing. The reports emanated from ASIO which was merely engaging in the common bureaucratic exercise of having the position of its own unco-operative minister weakened by bringing him into conflict with the most powerful minister, the Prime Minister, and by discrediting him publicly in the press. In addition ASIO was able to hint at the alarm in London and Washington on the part of British and American intelligence agencies who feared that material that they had supplied to ASIO might be disclosed by this or other raids. The head of the CIA's Counter-intelligence Division at that time, James Angleton, later claimed that a complete cut-off of information to its Australian counterpart was seriously considered.

Ironically, neither these incidents nor the raid itself established that Murphy had exercised the kind of control over ASIO that might have been expected to produce such a serious reaction. On the contrary, Labor's dealings with the security services in general, and ASIO in particular, represented a dramatic example of its overall failure to gain meaningful control over the administration of government. It needs to be recalled that security services are a part of the administration and that they reflect the talents and limitations of the bureaucracy as a whole, although they suffer from the additional problem of being very much more isolated in terms of contact with other parts of government and recruitment of staff than other departments.

When Murphy became Attorney-General and found himself in charge of ASIO, it constituted the domestic, or non-military-oriented, wing of the intelligence network. ASIO's formal functions are set out in the Australian Security Intelligence Organisation Act as follows:

(a) to obtain, correlate and evaluate intelligence relevant to security;

JEAN GUYEAUX PHOTO

Opposite: Attorney-General Lionel Murphy QC conversing with Solicitor-General Robert Ellicott QC at the bar table of the International Court of Justice, while Patrick Brazil of the Attorney-General's Department takes notes

(b) for purposes relevant to security and not otherwise, to communicate any such intelligence to such persons, and in such manner, as are appropriate to those purposes; and

(c) to advise Ministers and authorities of the Commonwealth in respect of matters relating to security, in so far as those matters are relevant to their functions and responsibilities.

In its selection of concrete tasks within this broad charter, much of ASIO's work was unchanging routine. The Public Service Board requested ASIO to security-check all public servants and members of the armed forces when they were recruited, promoted to certain levels, or transferred to certain departments. This involved comparing the names of thousands of public servants during the course of a single year with extensive lists, built up over a period of years, of members of all organisations considered to constitute a security risk. In collecting information for its files on these security-risk organisations, ASIO used a variety of techniques but chiefly favoured personal observation and photographing of meetings (many of which were public, as in the case of political groups); newspaper reports of their activities; having one of its officers or a paid agent join them as a member; and using planted microphones or telephone monitors to record their proceedings. It had also on some occasions broken into premises to copy documents of individuals or organisations. The kind of personal information assembled on people included names, addresses, occupations, employers, family and sexual relationships, together with photographic records. It was this information that also formed the basis of ASIO's surveillance of 'subversive' groups and individuals, not because of any connection with public servants, but on the grounds that they represented in themselves a threat to national security.

Espionage by foreign agents in Australia was obviously a further subject of ASIO attention, chiefly by means of surveillance of foreign embassies and their personnel who were engaged, usually with little concealment, in intelligence work. Like the Australian defence intelligence agencies, ASIO exchanged information with the various British and American agencies and kept close links with them through their officers in Australia and ASIO's officers in London and Washington. It also had officers in the Immigration Section of sixteen Australian embassies to screen prospective migrants to Australia.

As the senior members of ASIO contemplated the approach of Lionel Murphy in December 1972 they must have felt uneasy.

Throughout the 1960s, sections of the ALP had alleged that ASIO was acting as the political police of the LCP government by concentrating exclusively on left wing political groups — including all those opposed to Australia's Vietnam commitment — and ignoring right wing organisations. In addition they argued that ASIO was exceeding its powers by exercising surveillance over individuals and bodies which were not dangerous to the nation's security but simply in non-violent political opposition to the status quo. And in the main these allegations were correct.

Although telephone monitoring was only one method of collecting information during this period, it is a reasonable assumption that organisations and persons who were subject to monitoring were also subject to other methods of surveillance and that they indicate the target area of ASIO's activities in those years. On that basis, ASIO's own records of monitoring from 1960-75, prepared for the Hope Commission, demonstrated single-minded attention between 1960 and December 1972 to one political sector only, with the exception of the standard surveillance made in all countries of foreign intelligence agents who normally work out of their national embassies. It was a sector that comprised the Communist Party of Australia (CPA) in its various factions; socialist organisations like the Socialist Party of Australia, the Socialist Youth Alliance and the Young Socialist League; peace movements like the Congress for International Co-operation and Disarmament; anti-Vietnam bodies like the Draft Resistance Movement; militant trade union officials; and a miscellany of radical student groups. All of these were in opposition to the LCP government of the day, and all of them except the CPA and the Socialist parties would have included members of the Labor Party, some of them members of the parliamentary Party and later ministers in the Whitlam government.

ASIO had defined procedures for the authorisation of telephone monitoring:

- The Director-General requested the Attorney-General to issue a warrant under the Act authorising the monitoring, for a period not longer than 6 months, in respect of a specified telephone number.
- The request listed the name and address of the person or organisation subscribing to the number. The Director-General certified the grounds on which he considered the issue of the warrant to be necessary and added in conclusion: 'On the grounds stated above I am satisfied that the telephone service is likely to be used by persons suspected by me or being likely to engage in activities

prejudicial to the security of the Commonwealth'.
- The request specified the date up to which the warrant was intended to remain in force.
- The request, together with an original of the warrant and a copy, were hand delivered to the Attorney-General.
- If the Attorney-General was satisfied, as the Act required, that the information contained in the request substantiated the Director-General's conclusions, he authorised the monitoring by signing the original warrant and the copy which was to go to senior officials of Telecom.

When the monitoring was concluded the Director-General was obliged by the legislation to supply to the Attorney-General a written report on the way in which it had assisted ASIO to obtain intelligence relevant to the security of the Commonwealth, presumably to enable the Attorney-General to better assess future requests for warrants. The ASIO employees who carried out the monitoring had to be individually authorised to do so by the Director-General although the actual interception of telephone calls — that is, the connection of the telephone service to ASIO's monitoring equipment — was in fact carried out by selected Telecom officers who liaised with ASIO. The monitoring itself however — that is, the recording and analysis of conversations — occurred at ASIO's various regional offices and the information obtained was later incorporated in reports and transmitted to headquarters in Melbourne. At headquarters it was examined by the Research and Analysis Branch — the elite of the organisation — who drew conclusions from the material collected by the Operations Branch and prepared briefings for bureaucrats and, on occasion, ministers.

On the evidence available it seems that very seldom over this period was the monitoring likely to assist ASIO to obtain information relevant to the security of Australia. Yet both the Director-General and the Attorney-General of the day were required by the legislation to be satisfied of this likelihood. What commonly characterised the requests for warrants appears to have been a series of flat statements such as the claim that an individual belonged to a socialist organisation like the Socialist Youth Alliance (neither illegal nor professing violent aims) or had taken part in anti-Vietnam demonstrations (of a non-violent nature, for example, during the Australian visit of President Lyndon Johnson in 1967) without any attempt to link these activities to the security of Australia or to suggest how it could be adversely affected by them. These statements would nevertheless constitute the grounds on which the Director-General was satisfied that the monitoring was likely to assist ASIO to obtain information relevant to Australia's security.

To complete the circle, the Director-General's report on the material obtained on the organisation or person monitored would, on most occasions, simply state that additional information concerning their activities (still of a non-violent political nature) had been obtained. Apart from the fact that these reports on their face indicated that such warrants should almost certainly not have even been requested, there is no doubt that this information was used in turn to provide the grounds for future specious requests. In effect, almost all political activity on the left and outside the mainstream of the existing two party system was equated with subversion and made subject to possible surveillance. ASIO's approach to its role was not disturbing so much because of its inherent political selectivity — it could do little damage to anyone by its surveillance except those persons employed in the public service, or those wishing to obtain visas for the US — but because of its obsession with the politics of the Cold War and its inability to adjust to a world that had changed completely over the two decades since the early 1950s. It was most unlikely that genuine national security assessments made in connection with contemporary problems by persons with such a rigid and dated caste of mind could have been adequate for a government of any political complexion.

It is scarcely surprising, therefore, that ASIO viewed the advent of a Labor government with some trepidation. It was also conscious of Murphy's reputation for supporting civil liberties campaigns over the years. So it did not wait for him to arrive. On 15 December 1972, less than two weeks after election day and four days before Murphy took over as Attorney-General, all official telephone monitoring, whether of individuals, organisations or foreign embassies, ceased abruptly. In the case of some offices of the CPA, it was the first break in constant official monitoring since the early 1950s. Having cleared its books on the arrival of the new government, ASIO, like the rest of the bureaucracy, then proceeded to try strenuously to adapt, at least on the surface, to the changed circumstances. In a complete about-face from the last two decades, it made scarcely any requests over the next three years for authority to monitor organisations or individuals engaged in traditional left wing political activities.

Although it had had no occasion to monitor persons in connection with Croatian terrorist groups until December 1972, it suddenly discovered this activity — which was coincidentally a major interest of the new Attorney-General — as a serious threat to national security in the first few months of 1973. The answer to a question on notice in the House of Representatives in April 1973 revealed that at 7 March 1973 only nineteen telephones were the subject of authorised monitoring. What it did not reveal was that all were, except for foreign embassies, Croatian individuals or organisations. Later in 1973 it also discovered Arab terrorism as another threat to national security that seemed compatible with its new 'non-partisan' approach to this question.

In retrospect it seems that the new approach may have been confined to such overt and recorded actions as authorised telephone monitoring. It was disclosed in May 1976 by the *National Times* that surveillance of the Socialist Youth Alliance had occurred in late 1975, while Labor was still in office, by means of a non-ASIO person who had been paid by ASIO to join the Alliance and report on its membership and activities. To have expected ASIO officers — who had spent decades of their working lives operating on the premise that all left wing political organisations were subversive — to put aside those premises or the files built up over many years, was doubtless naive. In the rest of its operations, which unlike telephone monitoring (and that only if the Act's procedures were followed) were not subject to any consistent ministerial scrutiny, there was no real reason to change old habits.

Even apart from the issues of political bias and general incompetence, the case for reform of ASIO by the Labor government was incontrovertible on the ground that it was, almost alone among government bodies, operating without any real ministerial supervision, even in questions of long term policy. Isolated attempts to exercise ministerial control, such as Murphy's visit to the Melbourne headquarters, were unlikely to remedy this situation.

In fact, when made in so flamboyant a fashion, these attempts could only increase ASIO's immunity from control since the media coverage of that incident ensured that Murphy consequently could not afford to be seen exerting pressure on ASIO. And he was doubtless aware that if he did attempt to exert pressure, ASIO would arrange for the media (and the Prime Minister) to be swiftly informed. Whitlam's solution to this problem was the Royal Commission constituted by Mr Justice

Hope which was not set up until February 1975 and had not reported when the government was dismissed. For a government that was never more than six months from the possibility of an election and of losing office, it was hardly an adequate response to an institution as urgently in need of examination and reform as ASIO. And so the government finally departed having done nothing to bring some measure of accountability to ASIO.

It was ironic therefore that on 10 November — the day before the government was dismissed — a cable was sent to Canberra by ASIO's officer in the Australian Embassy in Washington that exemplified this absence of accountability. The cable related the concern of the CIA about references by Whitlam to its operations in Australia after it had been disclosed in the press that the Canberra house of Country Party Leader Doug Anthony had been rented to a CIA agent in 1966 and that CIA agents were operating out of the US Embassy in Canberra under the guise of US State and Defence Department posts. The Australian Defence Department had always been aware of these operations but had at first denied their existence to Whitlam. After referring to these disclosures the cable went on:

CIA is perplexed at the point as to what all this means.
Does this signify some change in our bilateral intelligence security related fields.
CIA can not see how this dialogue with continued reference to CIA can do other than blow the lid off those installations in Australia where the persons concerned have been working and which are vital to both of our services and countries particularly the installation at Alice Springs . . .
CIA can understand a statement made in political debate but constant further unravelling worries them.
Is there a change in the Prime Minister's attitude in Australian policy in this field.
This message should be regarded as an official demarche on a service to service link. (Emphasis added.)
It is a frank explanation of a problem seeking counsel on that problem. CIA feel that everything possible has been done on a diplomatic basis and now on an intelligence liaison link they feel that if this problem can not be solved they do not see how our mutually beneficial relationships are going to continue.
The CIA feels grave concern as to where this type of public discussion may lead.
The DG should be assured that CIA does not lightly adopt this attitude.
Your urgent advice would be appreciated as to the reply which should be made to CIA.

At the very end of the government's term, just as at the very beginning, ASIO was, as the term 'service to service' demonstrates, operating in some areas beyond the knowledge and control of the Australian government. Contrary to the intent of the sender of the cable, a copy was sent to Whitlam by Frank Mahony, a Deputy Secretary of the Attorney-General's Department who happened to be acting as Director-General of ASIO in the interim between Barbour's departure in September 1975 and the arrival of Barbour's replacement, Mr Justice Woodward, a federal judge appointed by Whitlam to head the organisation in October 1975.

The incident demonstrated how Labor was bedevilled right to the very end by its failures to exercise genuine control over the processes and apparatus of government. Murphy shared in these failures, just as he stood at the centre of most of the external and internal forces acting on the government. Yet the diversity of his talents had still enabled him by the end of 1974 to demonstrate as Attorney-General (and would enable him in the future to demonstrate on the High Court of Australia) that, of all the Sydney lawyers on both sides who were to play a part in the turbulent events of 1975, he was least inhibited by this background and had the best prospect of reconciling what has often appeared a basic incompatibility between the roles of reformer and lawyer.

5   An equation in hydro-carbons Rex Connor

Rex Connor's speech to the House of Representatives on 9 July 1975 was as informative about its maker as any single speech can ever be.

The special sitting of the House to debate the government's overseas loan raising activities had been convened after weeks of ceaseless and concentrated attack from both the Opposition and the media on Connor's involvement in the $4000 million loan effort. The confidence of many of Connor's own colleagues had been clearly shaken in the process yet he rose to speak with no apparent concern at this predicament.

Dressed as usual in a shapeless dark suit that recalled the 1940s, he turned his huge frame squarely toward the Opposition benches — a study in scorn and defiance. He began with the assertion that the minerals and energy reserves in Australia were worth, on current valuation, $5700 billion, against which the government's proposal to borrow $4 billion was 'peanuts'. The real question, as he put it, was 'Who will own Australia?' This would be one of the major issues on which the next federal election would be fought, despite the smears and sneers of an Opposition which had, he accused, through its actions when in government allowed the bulk of Australia's mineral and energy resources to pass into foreign ownership and control.

He described the journalists responsible for the spate of stories on overseas loans over the previous weeks as 'graduates from the same gutter'. He made the boast that 'throughout my two and a half years as a Minister of the Crown I have stood in the path of those who would have grabbed the minerals resources of Australia'. Looking straight at Country Party Leader Doug Anthony he added:

I fling in the face of the little men of the Opposition the words of an old Australian poem:

Give me men to match my mountains,
Give me men to match my plains,
Men with freedom in their vision,
And creation in their brains.

and as a final jibe:

I treat with contempt the allegations of the Opposition.

It was no rhetorical flourish, as it might have been from anyone else. Contempt was never far from Connor's thoughts — and it was not always reserved for the 'little men of the Opposition'. Yet he was the only person in the Parliament likely to have stated that life was an equation in hydrocarbons and to have expressed his own philosophy in late 1974 in these terms:

No man is complete who lacks a cosmogony, or who does not possess the knowledge that he is intermediate in stature between the atom and the star. Man is, in fact, the microcosm of the macrocosm, and is in a process of spiritual evolution, of which present world doubts and fears are the outward symbols. I have the firm belief that man is a moral being, and that he is, in fact, emerging slowly but certainly from an age of darkness where materialism and its mechanistic expressions are the symptoms of a deep, but definitely not fatal, spiritual crisis. Man, in fact, has yet to realise the significance of the inscription on the portals of Eleusis, 'Man, Know Thyself'. (O'Brien 1977)

Reginald Francis Xavier Connor was listed in the Parliamentary Handbook as being born in January 1908. Many people in the Labor Party added five or even ten years to the 67 years that the 1975 Handbook recognised. Connor's childhood was spent in Wollongong, the coal and steel city 50 miles south of Sydney. Connor qualified there as a lawyer while working for one of the town's solicitors, but he never practised law on his own account. Instead he set up a motor garage and later market gardens.

In the 1941 federal election he stood for the House of Representatives' division of Werriwa, which then extended to Wollongong, as a candidate for the NSW Branch of the ALP which had been suspended by the ALP's Federal Executive earlier that year in a fierce clash of factions. He was opposed by an official (federal) Labor candidate and also a Labor candidate running under the banner of former Labor Premier, Jack Lang. Out of this confusion, the official Labor candidate was elected and Connor was automatically expelled from the ALP under the rule which forbids any member from standing against an endorsed Labor candidate. He was re-admitted to the Party four years later after the NSW party split had been patched up.

In 1950 Connor's attention switched to State politics where he succeeded in defeating the local Labor member for party pre-selection and was easily elected to the State Legislative Assembly division of Wollongong-Kembla. Although Labor was in government in NSW at the time and was to remain so until 1965, he was continually passed over in a succession of Caucus elections for the ministry. He would not have disputed that many of those chosen had considerably less ability but, as he was unwilling to play by the rules of the club, he paid for his impatience and sharpness of tongue. In 1963 he departed from State parliament with little regret to enter the House of Representatives as the member for Cunningham, a rock-solid Labor seat centering on Wollongong.

The terminology of the 1960s would have put Connor on the left of the NSW Labor Party and Whitlam on the right of the federal Party but the two nevertheless formed a close relationship during the next few years of Opposition. Connor made an early and typically sweeping judgment that Whitlam was the only person in Parliament capable of leading Labor into government. What Whitlam admired even then about Connor, on the other hand, was that he was a dreamer, that he was never deterred by the fact that something had not been done before. When they had reached the goal of government, this characteristic was to appear even more attractive to Whitlam, who always considered many of his colleagues timid and unadventurous souls. It was Connor's scorn for cautious accountants that would play a major part in Whitlam's conflict with Treasury — that traditional Jeremiah for all governments whose thankless role is to put forward sound financial arguments why the schemes of ministers and departments are not feasible.

It would never be a popular role, and it was particularly unpalatable to Connor and to Whitlam, who once remarked in this context to a colleague that he wished he could launch a monumental project, something like Disraeli's Suez Canal, that would stand the test of centuries. Surrounded by people who stressed complexities and raised difficulties, whose tendency was to place every conceivable barrier in the way of action, Whitlam found Connor immensely refreshing as a man who could offer simple solutions — without ifs, buts or maybes.

In addition to the invaluable asset of the Prime Minister's confidence and support, Connor brought to bear on his Cabinet colleagues, as he did on the Opposition, a formidable style of debate. Any questioning of his proposals — in Cabinet or elsewhere — provoked a brutal and often effective tongue-lashing, particularly for anyone who strayed into his domain of natural resources policy. His response to the earnest and lucid arguments of backbencher Joe Berinson (later to become Minister for the Environment) at Labor's Federal Conference at Terrigal in February 1975 when Berinson raised the difficulty of insisting on 100 per cent Australian equity in all minerals and energy projects, was short but to the point:

> Don't give me this shandy-gaffe.

The concept of 100 per cent Australian ownership had always been one of his basic tenets and, towards the end of the 1960s, it began to acquire genuine electoral appeal for Australians.

Connor was to some degree responsible for this development in public awareness and when a number of his colleagues also took up the issue of foreign ownership and control in Australia, Labor began to emphasise it in the run-up to the 1972 election. For public purposes it was hardly necessary to go past the raw figures. The amounts of foreign capital entering Australia had increased steadily since the end of World War II, and then risen dramatically at the end of the 1960s. This escalating inflow had pushed the degree of foreign control to new levels in a number of sectors — 97 per cent in automobiles, 83 per cent in chemicals, 76 per cent in pharmaceuticals, and almost 60 per cent in the mining industry on which so much of the nation's development was dependent. To a large extent, foreign capital rushed in to fill a vacuum created by the inability of Australia's small population to raise the necessary investment funds. This situation was accentuated by the spectacle, transparently obvious to foreign investors, of State governments outbidding each other in an effort to attract projects to their own region by promises to accept any degree of foreign supervision and to demand only the most nominal royalties.

It was not a subject that had excited the concern of the federal Liberal government in the 1960s, with the single exception of Prime Minister John Gorton's impetuous prevention of the foreign takeover of one of Australia's largest life insurance companies in 1968. It was just this kind of action that led to Gorton's removal by his own Party in 1970.

Only in September 1972, just two months before the imminent election, did the Liberal government introduce legislation designed to place some limits on future foreign investment. It was hastily drawn up and a patent ploy to defuse as an electoral issue the question of 'Who owns Australia' which Labor had been steadily pushing for some time. In fact it was not even successful in doing that, as the issue was by then too firmly identified in the public's mind with Labor policy. Throughout that campaign the ALP continued to make the emotional pledge that Australia would no longer remain wide open to unquestioned exploitation by multinational corporations.

Once in government, as Minister for the newly-created portfolio of Minerals and Energy, Connor combined his distaste for foreign control over Australian development programs with a determination to initiate a series of massive natural resources projects during the 1970s — each in itself almost. worthy of Whitlam's 'Suez Canal' concept and based on his prescient determination to develop alternative sources of energy to oil. He planned a national pipeline grid to carry the vast reserves of natural gas between the North West Shelf, the Cooper Basin and Bass Strait, just one section being from the north west to the south east corner of the continent — almost 8000 miles of pipeline in total. He proposed enrichment plants to process the uranium deposits of the Northern Territory. He envisaged a complete updating of port facilities to handle the coal reserves of Queensland and NSW and the electrification of all rail facilities along the east coast. He was anxious to investigate the potential for solar energy as soon as possible.

In the absence of substantial foreign participation, he intended to use government agencies such as the Australian Industry Development Corporation (AIDC) and the Australian Atomic Energy Commission to manage these projects, and in addition two new agencies that were quickly established — the Pipelines Authority which was to administer the construction of the pipeline grid, and the Petroleum and Minerals Authority (PMA) which was to engage in all aspects of the production of oil, gas and minerals.

The PMA was one of the most ambitious ideas of those years. It was designed to be vertically integrated like a multinational mining corporation — it would find the minerals, mine them, process them and then market them, instead of having to hand raw materials over to foreign interests for the profitable stages of processing and marketing. In some cases private corporations, domestic and foreign, would be asked to join in the particular project, but never on the basis that they would call the shots. In the meantime, the PMA began to acquire substantial interests in projects started by private companies or consortiums. Without foreign funds the enormous sums required to undertake his programs would have to be found by the government.

In this cost squeeze lay the roots of the $4000 million loan, Connor's solution to the budgetary restraints on spending conventional economics imposed. To him $4000 million, while apparently a large sum, was insignificant in the long term and would generate its value many times over in the next two decades if applied to his grand designs for mineral and energy development. And for Whitlam it was further evidence of Connor's undeviating resolve to achieve some of Labor's long held goals in the face of bloody-minded obstruction.

The goal of government participation in natural resources development produced virulent opposition from both domestic and foreign mining companies. Their complaints aroused little sympathy from Connor, who had always believed that they had obtained access to Australia's mineral wealth far too cheaply in the 1950s and 1960s. His response was to set up an inquiry into the taxation advantages they had enjoyed under successive LCP governments, and when the inquiry found that over the last six years the Australian government had actually paid out more, directly or indirectly, to the mining industry than it had received in tax revenue, and recommended that a number of those concessions be removed, he ensured that the recommendations were followed up.

Mining company executives who attacked him in public were dismissed as 'hillbillies' with caustic reminders of their role in the speculative mineral share boom of the early 1970s and its subsequent crash. Ironically he was not, as often portrayed, anti-business. The truth of the matter was that he considered himself a businessman (as he had been before entering politics) and a better businessman than most of those he encountered in the mining industry. He found it hard to believe, for example, that businessmen would enter long term supply contracts with the Japanese without provision for re-negotiation of price and cost escalation before delivery some years in the future (particularly in the case of uranium where he was confident — and correct —

that the world price would continue to rise dramatically). As it was the nation's assets that were being sold he felt that he could not allow them to make the kind of bad bargain they were otherwise free to make in the conduct of their business. And unlike most of his colleagues, he had a constitutionally and administratively watertight method of enforcing his own opinion — the government's control over the export of any minerals in performance of those contracts. If the price or terms were unsatisfactory, no export authorisation would be granted. It was as simple as that.

His view of the business sense of the former LCP government was given — brutally as usual — in a speech to Parliament in April 1973:

> I found also that, so far from being a businessman's government, the former Government had not done its sums. In Japan we are dealing with one of the most numerate, sophisticated, literate and competent countries in the world, and we need to be just as well geared and just as well prepared for trade as Japan is. Instead of that, what did I find? I found no records at all. There was no idea of business competence on the part of the previous Government. No statistics were kept, beyond those of 1968 that I have just quoted. No records were kept of the export prices obtained. There was no idea whether we were getting world parity prices or somewhere at least close to it in respect of export contracts. No research had been done and no records kept as to what was the denomination of currency payable under export contracts and particularly how many of those contracts were denominated in United States dollars. There was no idea of the period of the contracts and no idea as to whether there were any protection clauses in respect of currency revaluations. This was from a so-called businessman's government. Australia is the twelfth trading nation of the world and I am ashamed that our dollar, which is a good and a strong currency, is not accepted in the bourses of the world. Again, that is due to the then subservient government which was tipped ignominiously and unceremoniously out of office.

It was essentially the introduction of this iron regime that produced the violent reaction of the mining companies and of the Queensland and Western Australian State governments. Yet as far as the mining companies were concerned, he was as determined upon development as they were. None of his development-oriented opponents could have attacked Environment Minister Moss Cass as savagely as he did in mid 1975 when Cass tried unsuccessfully to halt sand-mining on Queensland's Fraser Island until the effects had been subject to an environmental enquiry.

Connor's view of the role — or lack of it — for State governments in this area was indicated by a press statement in September 1974 reviewing his legislative program:

> A progressive program of legislation, designed to assert and secure the exercise of full National sovereignty over all energy resources has followed, to correct the failure of the preceding Government to act in terms of National sovereignty during its period of office from 1949 to 1972. The former Government had, in fact, permitted the usurpation by the constituent States of the Australian Federation, of the national functions in planning, development and export of energy resources.

By forcing the coal and iron ore producers to negotiate with the Japanese as a bloc to avoid being played off one against the other, or by negotiating directly with them himself, he did raise the export prices for these kinds of commodities. His judgment that world prices for minerals would rise much more steeply in the immediate future than the companies predicted proved out to be much more in line with market trends. All of which only reinforced his scorn for his critics.

His standard response to criticism inside the government had always been remarkably effective. It was one of ridicule, quickly replaced by threats of resignation if the challenge was serious enough. For the first two and a half years of his period as a minister it had been a potent mixture and it was solidly backed up at the administrative level by the head of his department, Sir Cyrus Lenox Hewitt.

Hewitt was himself a complex character, even in the byzantine world of the Canberra bureaucracy. Imperious and acid-tongued, a dedicated and meticulous worker, he was elevated from the relative obscurity of the Universities Commission to the head of the Prime Minister's Department by John Gorton in 1968, and had wielded enormous power in that position because of his close relationship with Gorton. Gorton's fall in 1970 deprived him of his patron and left him defenceless against his many bureaucratic and political enemies who had waited patiently for their chance to strike. He was banished from the Prime Minister's Department, which ranked first in the hierarchy of departments, to one that ranked last and dealt with miscellaneous leftovers ranging from the arts to war graves, to be replaced in the Prime Minister's Department by Sir John Bunting whom he had initially deposed from that position.

Labor took office in December 1972 and Hewitt again came in

Labor's Minister for Minerals and Energy, Rex Connor,
flanked by his permanent head Sir Lenox Hewitt and his
political protege Paul Keating, on one of the rare occasions
when he faced a press conference

from the cold when Connor chose him to head the new Department of Minerals and Energy. The importance of resources policy to the new government and the strength of Connor in Cabinet guaranteed Hewitt a solid power base. His comeback must have given him exquisite pleasure. He had always considered himself excluded from the clique of senior permanent heads who presided over the most powerful departments and settled particularly delicate problems over working lunches at Canberra's exclusive Commonwealth Club. His old rival, Sir John Bunting, had been until his appointment as High Commissioner to Britain in 1974, the unofficial convenor of this group which included Sir Frederick Wheeler, head of Treasury; Sir Arthur Tange, head of Foreign Affairs and later Defence; Alan Cooley, head of the Public Service Board; and Clarrie Harders, head of Attorney-General's.

In a rare public reference to his feeling of isolation Hewitt complained bitterly during his testimony before the Coombs Commission on Government Administration in 1974 that his Department of Minerals and Energy had been frustrated by the Public Service Board in its attempts to recruit adequate staff because it was not part of this network. His distrust of other departments, particularly Treasury of which he had himself been a Deputy Secretary, was to be an important element in the way the overseas loan negotiations were conducted and the damaging way they were finally disclosed. Realising that he was unable to rely on other departments he gave Connor undeviating loyalty and never lost Connor's trust — aware, of course, that this was the sole source of his own power.

In building that mutual loyalty, so much practised in Canberra's political world, no detail is too small to be overlooked. A few months before Labor's dismissal and soon after Hewitt had departed from Minerals and Energy to become Chairman of Qantas, a minister recently returned from overseas mentioned casually at a social function that he had lost his glasses on the return trip. Hewitt left the gathering to institute a search of all Qantas aircraft, and had a pair of glasses delivered to the minister's office the next day. The impression made on the minister was little diminished by the fact that the glasses found were not his.

Hewitt could be as caustic as his minister with those public servants, particularly from Treasury, whom he saw obstructing his minister's programs. Even Connor's Cabinet colleagues discovered that they could not expect from Hewitt the normal deference of a bureaucrat to a minister if disputes arose between their department and Minerals and Energy. The role of the Department of Minerals and Energy in the bureaucracy was almost a mirror image of Connor's role in the Cabinet. Neither minister nor Secretary tolerated the time-consuming consultation between departments which often enables radical proposals to be first delayed and then diluted. For the same reasons, they simply refused to supply their potential opponents in Treasury, or other areas, with information about their plans, reasoning correctly that it would be much harder for others to attack programs about which they had only the most elementary knowledge, if any at all. They warned off not only competing departments from Minerals and Energy territory but also resisted encroachment from outside the bureaucracy.

In September 1973 the government set up a Royal Commission into Petroleum, headed by Mr Justice Collins of the NSW Supreme Court and charged to investigate and report on all aspects of the refining and marketing of petroleum in Australia. It became one of the longest running shows of the Whitlam government and still had not finished its work when the government was dismissed despite lengthy hearings throughout Australia and a sojourn overseas. Connor became increasingly dubious about the Commission's activities and was in a position to take action as the Commission had intended to rely on the Department of Minerals and Energy to provide it with information and assistance through the counsel representing the Australian government. This would have entailed Minerals and Energy co-ordinating the views of various departments on areas for which more than one department was responsible. But Connor steadfastly refused to allow it to carry out this role, pleading lack of staff for even its existing activities.

In May 1975 matters came to a head when Richard McGarvie, QC, counsel assisting the Commission, complained that he had been unable to get access to Minerals and Energy files and that inquiries as to the government's future policy on the allocation of Australian crude oil had produced response from that department to the effect that the Commission should really mind its own business. After this blow-up, the Commission received a little more co-operation but it remained evident that Connor had no intention of assisting a free-wheeling body bent on intruding into his policy domain, even if it did have the status of a Royal Commission.

An acrimonious but illustrative clash between the Connor/Hewitt juggernaut and the forces of tradition entrenched in other departments followed the invalidation by the High Court in June 1975 of the legislation establishing the PMA. The court had not held the legislation to be beyond the government's powers but found that the legislation had not met the requirements of the Constitution for presentation to the Joint Sitting of Parliament which had followed the 1974 double dissolution. The legislation had been resisted at every opportunity by the Opposition in the Senate, having been rejected twice before the double dissolution and then defeated a third time after the May election. Its only chance to pass into law had been the Joint Sitting and, as soon as it had been approved by that body, the PMA was set up and began operating.

Conscious of the legal challenge, Connor arranged to have a

company incorporated in the ACT, without publicity, early in 1975 to take over the functions of the PMA if it became necessary. Called the Petroleum and Minerals Company of Australia Pty. Limited, it had two issued shares which were held in trust for the government by Hewitt and A. B. McFarlane, head of the PMA. Before its invalidation, the PMA had entered into a number of commitments to participate in development projects which would require outlays of funds for some time into the future, even if no further investments were made.

Two of these arrangements — for $560,000 towards a 50 per cent interest in the South Australian oil and gas interests of Delhi International Oil Corporation and $700,000 towards a 49 per cent interest in a coal mine owned by Wambo Mining Corporation Pty Ltd — had to be met by 30 June 1975. The PMA had been allocated $50 million in the previous Budget for these sorts of transactions but it was legally impossible for what remained of these funds to be used by the Petroleum and Minerals Company. On 27 June Connor wrote to Bill Hayden, as Treasurer, in the following terms:

> On Tuesday last the High Court declared the Petroleum and Minerals Authority Act 1973 invalid. As the Australian Government had been joined with the Authority as a party to the commitments entered into by the Authority, those commitments reside now with the Australian Government.
>
> One of these commitments is the purchase of 50 per cent of the oil and gas interests in South Australia of the Delhi International Oil Corporation. A quarterly purchase payment is due next Monday 30 June. It is for an amount of $560,000 depending on the current conversion rate. It is a contractual commitment and if not paid the Government will be in breach of contract.
>
> Another commitment was announced last November, viz the purchase of 49 per cent of the Wambo coal mine at Warkworth through an investment in the Wambo Mining Corporation Pty Ltd. The Wambo mine has reserves in the ground which, at today's prices, represent the equivalent of $5,400 million . . .
>
> There is a very pressing obligation to assist the Company by Monday 30 June with a further loan of $700,000 to enable it to continue its operations as a measure of security whilst our negotiations are finalised in the immediate future. This must be done to protect the Australian Government's overriding interest in a most valuable asset which had attracted the avid attention of the Australian Anglo American Corporation.
>
> You will have seen my own statement endorsed most strongly by the Prime Minister that we shall re-introduce legislation as soon as possible in the next session of the Parliament to re-establish the Authority.

For the purposes related to the acquisition from Delhi the Authority set up a Company in February incorporated in the Australian Capital Territory titled the Petroleum and Minerals Company of Australia Pty. Limited. You will have seen my announcement, and that of the Prime Minister that the Government will make use of this Company to honour the Government's commitments to other parties, and you will no doubt have also seen the Prime Minister's public endorsement of the use of the Company to enable the Government's policies to be continued . . .

Before the High Court decision of last Tuesday, the Authority had 69 proposals, large and small, under consideration in almost all states of the country and in the Northern Territory. It is through the Company that these proposals will be processed in pursuance of our commitment to the policy of promoting Australian ownership and control of our natural resources and direct Government participation in oil and mineral search and development throughout Australia and its offshore territories.

I am advised by the Attorney-General that the best method of meeting the obligations and commitments of the Government is through the Company being provided with funds from the Treasurer's advance. I estimate that approximately $12 million will be required until the end of October 1975. By this time the new legislation will have been introduced and dealt with by the Parliament . . .

I must emphasise that of the $12 million which I am requesting, $560,000 is required for payment to the Delhi International Oil Corporation under our contract of purchase with that Corporation, on Monday 30 June. Otherwise the Australian Government will be in default and in dishonour.

In these circumstances Connor's proposal was therefore that the Company be granted funds from the Treasurer's Advance for the payment due immediately and a further $11 million for payments over the next three to four months — the Treasurer's Advance being an amount put aside in the annual Appropriation Acts to cover unforeseen contingencies of a minor nature, such as unexpected wage rises to government employees. Both Treasury and the Attorney-General's Department objected to the use of what they regarded as an emergency fund for regular financing of Minerals and Energy programs. Attorney-General's was also concerned that the government might appear to be getting around the High Court's decision on the PMA and bypassing the Parliament by a back-door exercise. Connor and Hewitt viewed these objections as typically obstructionist.

Strictly there was no legal barrier to the use of the Treasurer's Advance in the fashion proposed and, as far as they were concerned, no conventions to the contrary were as important as carrying out the work that the PMA had already begun. If the High Court decision — which itself relied on a legalistic approach — could be circumvented by the purely legal manoeuvre of setting up a company, then there should be no concern. As for the argument about bypassing Parliament, the Opposition had shown its total objection to the concept of the PMA by using the Senate to block the legislation on three occasions so it was pointless to re-submit it.

Connor put the whole issue on the basis that he was trying to carry out the government's policies in the face of opposition. He expected that opposition. However, the last thing he would tolerate was obstruction from within the government itself. He put this view flatly in a follow-up letter to Hayden in July 1975 saying:

> We are in the aftermath of a High Court decision which required an immediate and forceful demonstration of our resolve. There can be no frustration of it . . .

Soon after, he accused Treasury of 'interrogating' his departmental officers when Hayden, on Treasury advice, provided the funds necessary to meet the Delhi and Wambo commitments on 30 June (with payment going straight from the government to the companies involved, and not through the Petroleum and Minerals Company) but refused the additional $11 million until the legal situation was further considered.

At the same time there was a second major confrontation with Treasury over the payment of staff recruited to the now-defunct PMA. Treasury insisted that the staff could be paid only if they were put on the rolls of one of the public service departments. Connor's response was that they had chosen to work for an independent statutory body and that they should now work for and be paid as employees of the Petroleum and Minerals Company. He argued that he had promised the PMA's staff that they would be able to continue working for an independent organisation dedicated to the principles of Australian ownership, and he viewed 'that commitment to this dedicated group of people — as a commitment of honour'.

Hewitt followed up with a stinging letter to Attorney-General's, who had raised legal difficulties concerning the payment of the salaries, describing the issue as one 'on which there appears to have been much obfuscation'. It was not the usual language of interdepartmental correspondence.

Contrasting styles: South Australian Premier Don Dunstan,
Rex Connor, and ACTU President Bob Hawke, lead a trade
union march in Adelaide

Connor seldom hesitated to use the personal power his role in
the government had gained for him. His response was usually
swift, often savage. In early 1975 he focused on Alan Renouf,
Secretary of the Department of Foreign Affairs. Renouf had
been one of the party accompanying Whitlam on his overseas
travels and late in the trip he had given an in-flight background
briefing to several of the journalists travelling with Whitlam. It
was highly critical of Connor's policies on natural resources and
the effect of these policies on Australia's relations with other
nations, particularly Japan, who wished to purchase Australian
minerals for their own needs.

The briefing was given on the basis — quite common — that it
would be attributed to 'government sources' but not to Renouf
himself. The story was run in Australian newspapers as a Con-
nor-Whitlam split on resources policy and Connor immediately
demanded to know who was responsible. Those members of the
press party present at the background briefing observed the

agreement on attribution, but the story was picked up by a journalist who was not present and who did not consider himself bound by the arrangement to protect Renouf as the source. When Renouf was named, Connor let it be known to the press that he expected Renouf to appear in his office in Parliament House on his return to explain his comments at the briefing. Renouf received no support from either his own minister, Senator Don Willesee who had not been aware of the briefing, or from Whitlam who had been responsible for Renouf's initial appointment. After Renouf had seen Connor and Hewitt, he had to put up with press reports originating from Connor's office to the effect that he had been forced to apologise although Renouf later denied that this was so. It was an impressive demonstration of Connor's unassailable position in the government at that time. The incident was also a reminder to bureaucrats, ministers and backbenchers alike that Connor was someone to be challenged only with extreme caution.

Although there were many, even in the government, who had substantial reservations about Connor's policies and tactics, particularly his fixation with gaining Australian equity in natural resource projects — at whatever cost — as the only means of control over foreign investors, few were prepared to deny his legacy to resources policy in Australia. The Opposition was forced to take up the issues of control over foreign investment and Australian participation in development projects because Connor had made them national issues. While a Liberal government would never adopt some of Connor's policies — such as *public* enterprise participation — their policy shift after 1972 was dramatic, at least on the face of it. The investment guidelines, announced in April 1976 by the Treasurer in the first Fraser government, Phillip Lynch, required 50 per cent Australian equity in all projects and a 75 per cent equity in uranium development. Even though it became obvious that these would not be strictly enforced, it was evident that the completely open door of the 1950s and 1960s could never recur.

Within the context of this shift in Liberal policies lies also the most bizarre quality of the loans affair, a quality chiefly attributable to Connor's consistent refusal to take others into his confidence. Handled differently, the $4000 million might have been portrayed as the fulfilment of Connor's dream of self-reliance, with the Australian people as the principal shareholders in the projects it would fund. This would not have saved the exercise from the basic criticism made of it in terms of the economic situation in late 1974 — that if such a sum, or even any part of it, had been brought into the country and spent by the government on development projects or anything else, it would have driven up an inflation rate that was already running at over 16 per cent largely because of government spending in 1973/74 that had not been funded from taxation but from increases in the money supply. If on the other hand, it was not intended to bring the money into the country, there was no point in borrowing it all at once only to invest it overseas at approximately the same rate at which it was borrowed. According to Connor at least $750 million was destined for neither of these categories, but was to be used to purchase a full year's imports of Arab oil which would have been left in the Middle East in case of another oil embargo. Whatever the economics of the proposal, this argument alone could not have brought down a government.

As on other occasions the government did not present its case to the public until too late, until the Opposition had already established the climate for the debate by constant references to the issue in its own terms. This time most members of the government could do little about this as they also were ignorant of the proposal. In the government's increasing struggle to implement its policies over the resistance of its opponents, there was something exhilarating about Connor's determination to drive irresistibly towards his goals despite the reservations of the Senate, the bureaucracy or his own colleagues. But the core of the Connor vision was that it always remained an essentially private one. When the storm broke in mid 1975, that vision might continue to sustain his personal faith but it would not save him or the government from its public consequences.

6 Room at the top John Kerr

'I give your Government style' was Sir John Kerr's reply to one of Whitlam's ministers in late 1974 when told light-heartedly what a splendid figure he made in his vice-regal garb and decorations.

It was not just the decorations. Tall, expansive in physique, with patrician features and a mass of silver hair, Kerr made a striking impression in his navy blue suits or black frock coats set off only by a white kerchief or, on formal occasions, by the gold and silver of imperial medals and the rainbow flashes of their ribbons. Less than a year later, however, he was to give the minister and his government not style, but a coup de grace that reduced Labor to its smallest representation in federal Parliament since federation. Yet Labor had been Kerr's party for some years in an earlier part of his life — and the only political party to which he had ever belonged.

It is one of the most striking aspects of Australian Labor history that some of the worst wounds have been inflicted on the Party not by its political opponents but by those from within its own ranks. There is an obvious distinction in this sense between Kerr and the parliamentarians who changed sides, like Hughes or Lyons, and who had their positions only because of the Labor ticket they held. When Kerr became Governor-General, he had not held a ticket for almost 20 years. But he had once held one — and that meant that the dismissal of the Whitlam government, like so many of Labor's other defeats, could not be attributed solely to forces outside the Party. Over the years, Labor has spawned too many potential destroyers not to raise the question of why so many of its favoured sons have turned so violently on the movement.

'A man in the plenitude of his powers' was Whitlam's description of Kerr when he announcing his appointment as Governor-General on 27 February 1974. It was a fair comment to make about a man not yet 60, who had been Chief Justice of NSW for less than two years, after an illustrious career at the Bar and on the federal Bench. It was also a reference to the fact that for most, if not all, of Kerr's predecessors in the office of Governor-General, their tenure of that position had been the gilded twilight to a military or political career that had drawn to an effective close some time before. In the case of his immediate predecessor, Paul Hasluck, the appointment was Prime Minister John Gorton's precise means of ensuring that Hasluck, then Foreign Minister and a possible threat to Gorton's leadership, did indeed close his political career. Hasluck's period of office was archetypal. He toured the nation incessantly, performing countless openings of conferences and buildings, delivering a multitude of vague homilies on the need for decency, industry and unselfishness. Once every year, like a headmaster on speech night, he gave one of these homilies over national television — the Governor-General's Australia Day Message. It probably distracted the populace very little from the long weekend.

The role was, in short, the antithesis of the Labor tradition. It represented those values of mundane paternalism and social pretentiousness that Labor had, rightly or wrongly, always identified in its opponents. Moreover, it symbolised for many Labor men a system of government — the constitutional monarchy — which they considered anti-democratic in its very basis. Why then should a Labor Prime Minister seek to enhance it by the appointment of a man in the plenitude of his powers, a man whose career for the last decade had been one of advancement by Labor's opponents and a man who, somewhat puzzlingly in view of his age and present position, wanted to have the post? The appointment can be viewed as the culmination of almost a century's inferiority complex on the part of the Labor Party.

The anti-Labor forces had always been able to convey the impression to some sections of the community that there was something inherently less respectable and less responsible about Labor and its supporters. So effective had this approach been, that the feeling had existed inside Labor's own ranks also. In making appointments to the Bench, to statutory boards, to community bodies, Labor governments have often sought the candidate who will reassure their opponents. And how better to reassure them than by appointing someone they might have ap-

pointed themselves? What history demonstrates, however, is that
Labor's opponents are never reassured by such gestures. What
reassurance could possibly have been offered to such opponents?
What the appointment of John Kerr did offer them, ultimately,
was the means of bringing to fruition their refusal to recognise
the legitimacy of the government elected in 1972 and 1974.

Born into a Balmain boilermaker's family in 1914, John Kerr
attended the academically illustrious Fort Street High School
and later Sydney University Law School where he graduated
first in his class. At the age of 24 he was a settled man,
established as a barrister in Martin Place chambers, and married
the same year. But the year was 1938, and everyone's plans were
to be altered by the approaching conflagration of World War II.

He continued at the Bar until 1941 when he entered the services as a Lieutenant in the Army's Directorate of Research in
Civil Affairs. The Directorate was at that time a rather nebulous
group with no clear publicly-acknowledged functions. While it
was basically engaged in information-gathering activities, its particular task was to provide information and formulate policy for
the new Commander-in-Chief, Sir Thomas Blamey, himself a
skilled political operator who had already demonstrated an
ability to secure most of what he wanted from the Cabinet. It was
natural for Blamey, the politician as well as the soldier, to be
seeking information well beyond the technically military. Kerr
himself categorised the unit as 'existing for the purposes of the
Commander-in-Chief's relations with the Army's relations of a
slightly unorthodox character with outside institutions in the
country and abroad'.

The Directorate's head was Colonel Alf Conlon who appears
to have made a spectacular impression on most of those who
came in contact with him over those years. He was later
described by Kerr in words that may reveal his own standards of
excellence:

> It has to be appreciated that Alf was a master of talking to people in
> their own language, and he was in those days a very skilled political
> realist. He was able to deal with actualities of power and position,
> and it was quite possible for him at the same time to convince the
> Minister for Territories that he was mainly concerned, in the exer-
> cise of army power, to ensure that a proper policy in relation to New
> Guinea affairs was evolved and, if possible, begun in army days,
> whilst at the same time being able to persuade General Blamey that
> the army wouldn't suffer by any steps that were taken, but on the

contrary would profit, and so would his reputation in the eyes of history. (Sugerman 1963)

And his own approach to his career:

> Alf had the skill of being able to knock on the doors of the great, and of course in this country if you do that you're generally invited in (it's a small provincial society, after all) and once inside he could sell an idea.

Other members of the group included James Plimsoll, who was later to head the Department of External Affairs, and post-war academic and literary identities — James McAuley, John Legge, Julius Stone, R.D. 'Panzee' Wright and Wal Stammer. Despite this competition, Kerr became Conlon's Deputy Director, at the same time rising in rank from Lieutenant to Captain, to Major, to Lieutenant-Colonel. He spent considerable periods of time out of Australia, chiefly in England and in New Guinea.

It was at this time that Kerr acquired what was to be a life-long interest in Australia's role in the Pacific region in general and its role in the future of New Guinea in particular. Towards the end of the war he took charge of a section of the Directorate established to train personnel for work in New Guinea after hostilities ceased. This section continued its operations after the war ended and in 1946 was converted to the Australian School of Pacific Administration in Sydney. Kerr became the school's first Principal and in 1947 was a member of the Australian delegation, led by External Affairs Minister Evatt, to the United Nations Session where he provided advice on the Pacific area. He was also one of the persons responsible at this time for the creation of the South Pacific Commission which was to be a body representing all the colonial powers with an interest in that region. When the commission got off the ground he acted as Secretary-General, pending a full-time appointment. He decided not to take it. He made overtures to Sydney Law School where a vacant professorial chair was about to be filled. The chair was given to someone else and so in 1949 he returned to the Sydney Bar. In 1949 Labor had just lost office but it seemed that it must return in three years or at the most six and John Kerr, living in Lindfield on Sydney's north shore, was a member of the Gordon branch of the ALP.

Out of the busy practice which he quickly developed at the Bar, one case had particular significance — his involvement in the protracted struggle to remove the communist-led faction from control of the Federated Ironworkers and to substitute the group led by the present federal secretary, Laurie Short. The path a barrister's career takes is very often dictated by chance. One lengthy case in a particular jurisdiction can lead to more briefs on the same subject and, before long, a reputation as a specialist in the area.

Nowhere was specialisation more pronounced at this time than in the field of industrial law. Most major cases were (and still are) handled by a small group of solicitors acting either for employees or unions, but rarely both, and a second group of barristers habitually briefed by those firms. For those barristers, the ultimate crown was a place on the federal Bench, either the Conciliation and Arbitration Commission or the Australian Industrial Court. Because appointments to those positions in the 1950s and 1960s were made exclusively from that clique of barristers, many of them could expect a judgeship in the natural progression, unless they flaunted political views opposed to the government of the day.

Notwithstanding the substantial element of chance in the direction any career takes at the Bar, Kerr's gravitation to the industrial field was an interesting one. As he himself was to say later:

> Law is so intimately connected with the distribution exercise and control of political power in every field. (Kerr 1964)

But questions of power were closer to the surface in industrial law than they were in many other jurisdictions. The intricate maze of statute and case law in the industrial area tends to mask with a legal veneer the bitter disputes between employers and the union movement over the distribution of the nation's economic product, and the equally bitter disputes between competing union factions for control of their organisations. The control of individual unions also represents proportionate influence in the Australian Council of Trade Unions and its State Trades Hall branches. It leads ultimately, through union representation at State conferences, to control of State branches of the ALP.

All these elements were involved in the lengthy battle for control of the Federated Ironworkers, with the final result being the transfer in 1952 of the resources of a key union away from prominent members of the CPA to the Short faction which had close links with the Industrial Groups. Similar battles were fought and won in the Clerk's Union, the Transport Workers'

Union and the Australian Railways Union.

Kerr's work in these cases does not seem to have entailed any ideological commitment to the Industrial Groups. His instructing solicitor was James McClelland who would later become a Labor Senator in the 1960s. In these complex internecine struggles within the union movement, power rather than ideological commitment was more likely to be the motivating factor. Evatt himself had a close working association at this time with some of the most prominent Groupers, including B. A. Santamaria, even though he was to fall out with them violently a few years later. Kerr's approach is probably best reflected in his triumphant comment to Short at the end of the Ironworkers' case when judgment was handed down:

> You've won a union today, Laurie, but I've won an empire.

It seems clear that the question of Kerr's seeking preselection was raised in Labor circles in the early 1950s, most particularly in relation to the House of Representatives seat of Lowe in Sydney at the time of the 1951 double dissolution forced suddenly by Menzies. What is not clear is how seriously Kerr sought the opportunity. Lowe was contested for Labor in 1951 by John Burton, Evatt's former Private Secretary and his department head at External Affairs, who spectacularly resigned his post as Australia's High Commissioner to Ceylon to return for the poll. Burton lost to William McMahon who had won the seat for the Liberals when it was created in 1949. Although Lowe is still held by McMahon as a safe Liberal seat, its future could not have been obvious in 1951 when there was only a single contest to gauge by — and that in what was then considered a vintage Liberal year. Yet Kerr does not appear to have made any real effort in the crucial period immediately preceding the preselection and his interest at this time must be doubted.

In fact his political activities did not consume very much of his time. He attended branch meetings but held no office in his branch or in the Party and did not attend State conferences. He was, however, spending a great deal of time on his practice at the Bar. Some counsel are best suited to pleading in court, some to writing opinions in chambers, some to negotiations in conferences. Kerr was able at all three but was most at home in court, on his feet — striking in appearance, lucid and forceful in argument. His practice continued to have its basis in industrial disputes and took him constantly before the NSW and Com-

monwealth industrial courts and occasionally before the High
Court on junior briefs. But the appearances as a junior ended in
1953. That year he took silk, confident that he would be able to
retain his clients despite the much increased fees they would
have to pay to command his services as a Queen's Counsel. He
retained them and by 1955 he was one of the dominant figures at
the Sydney Bar.

1955 was the year of the split. Although the fissures in the
Labor Party were not as visible in NSW as in Victoria they still
ran right through its ranks, from top to bottom. Kerr was approached by the nascent NSW Democratic Labor Party to take a
titular post that would have diluted, at a public level, its essentially Catholic content. Perceiving its limited role as a sectarian
minority group, he refused. Yet he also dropped out of the Labor
Party, sending to the secretary of the Gordon Branch a short letter of resignation without any reasons. It may well be that, more
prescient or more calculating than his Labor colleagues, he
foresaw how destructive Evatt's leadership would be, how effectively the spectre of communism would be used against Labor
in the next decade of the Cold War, and how long it would take
the Party to come within striking distance of power again. At 41
years of age, even one decade in such a wilderness would have
seemed an intolerable waste of his considerable talents over what
should be a person's most creative years.

In the next few years there was a noticeable shift in his clients
— away from the unions of the early 1950s to employers and
federal government agencies — the West Australian Colliery
owners, Commonwealth Steamships, Qantas, the Australian
Stevedoring Industry Authority. Yet he still felt strongly enough
about the issue of union control to write an article in 1960 entitled 'The Struggle against Communism in the Trade Unions'
which set out a blueprint for challenging communist-led union
executives. He explained why the role of the lawyer was vital:

> success will also depend upon the team availing itself of every op-
> portunity at law to hem in and constrain the Communist opponent
> and to keep him within the rules and the law. This is where legal ac-
> tions come into the picture. They have the additional advantage of
> enabling Communist dishonesty and trickery, tyranny, railroading
> and violence to be exposed in the full light of publicity. (Kerr 1960)

He now saw the development of Santamaria's Industrial Groups
as a product of a 'failure of leadership' on the part of the ALP —
an unmistakeable indictment of his former mentor Evatt. Yet the

solution lay not in re-establishing the Groups but in:

> making the ALP into a Party which, however left-wing or militant it may be, believes that it and not the Communist Party is the true representative of the Australian working people for both industrial and political purposes. (Kerr 1960)

In 1958 Kerr had been elected to the Executive of the Australian Association for Cultural Freedom. The association was a national body concerned with domestic and international issues of civil liberties and freedom of expression. In 1958 its President was Sir John Latham, former Chief Justice of the High Court and UAP Attorney-General in the early 1930s.

The association's tenor was anti-communist and anti-Soviet — a popular stance in the days of the Cold War just two years after the Hungarian uprising. That same year it sponsored the visit to Australia of Tibor Meray, a prominent Hungarian emigre who engaged in a lecture tour of the eastern states. It published a monthly magazine *The Free Spirit* and was closely associated with the quarterly *Quadrant* whose editor, James McAuley, was an ex officio member of its executive. The association was affiliated with a US parent body, the Congress for Cultural Freedom, which pursued similar policies on an international level and was revealed later to be substantially funded by the US Central Intelligence Agency.

Shortly before his election to the executive of the association, there had been published in *The Free Spirit* under the names of J. R. Kerr QC and J. H. Wooten, his colleague at the Sydney Bar, an opinion on the celebrated Orr Case (Kerr 1958). Sydney Sparkes Orr, Professor of Philosophy at the University of Tasmania, had been dismissed by the University in 1956 for misconduct in allegedly sleeping with a female student. The case aroused violent feelings in Hobart between supporters of the University and those who argued that Orr had been victimised for his earlier confrontations with the administration and the Vice-Chancellor over reforms within the University. Protracted litigation by Orr and his supporters failed to have him re-instated but demands were still being made at this time that the case be re-opened. In their lengthy opinion, Kerr and Wootten argued that no legal ground existed to justify re-opening the matter. Moreover they suggested that 'public confidence in one of our Universities and in our judicial system has been undermined dishonestly or irresponsibly' and that 'those who have done so are themselves guilty of a grave offence against public morality'.

The case was a difficult one as there was little evidence on either side except for the contradictory statements of Orr and the student. This, however, was exactly what Orr's supporters were complaining about. They argued that this evidence would have been insufficient to gain a conviction in a criminal trial but had resulted in Orr suffering just as drastic a penalty as he had lost his livelihood, being now barred from any other university in the British Commonwealth. Kerr and Wootten had clearly concluded that Orr was being used in an effort to undermine the institutions of academe and the judiciary. Their opinion provoked its own violent reaction, including the following one in the columns of the *Observer* by its editor, Donald Horne, himself to join the Executive of the Association for Cultural Freedom in 1961:

> we consider the Kerr-Wootten article in *The Free Spirit* to be a dangerous misrepresentation of what is worth talking about in the Orr case and to be prejudiced, selective and narrow in its approach. A strictly courtroom approach to questions that go far beyond the limitations of legal procedures reduces any discussion to idiocy and can be used — as the Kerr-Wootten article has been used — by the University of Tasmania in an intellectually dishonest way. (*Observer* 23 Aug 1958)

In the event, the case was never re-opened.

Kerr continued on the Executive of the Association until 1961 when Latham stepped down from the Presidency. He stood for that position but was defeated by Lloyd Ross of the Australian Railways Union. Soon afterwards he resigned from the Executive and ceased to play any further part in the Association's activities. If this entailed a judgment that the Association would have better prospered under his own leadership, he was possibly correct. It declined over the next decade and never really re-emerged into public view. He himself, however, prospered both in legal and social terms in the early 1960s. The two spheres are in fact closely intertwined and he gained election at this time to a number of positions that normally herald an appointment to the Bench. Between 1960 and 1966 he was at one time or another a Member and late Vice-President of the NSW Bar Council, President of the NSW and then the Australian Industrial Relations Society, Member of the NSW Medical Board, President of the NSW Marriage Guidance Council, Member of the Council on New Guinea Affairs,

President of the Law Association for Asia and the Western Pacific, and Vice-President and later President of the Law Council of Australia. He had in fact been suggested as Chief Justice of NSW in 1960 when the post fell vacant. Ironically it was filled by Evatt who had retired, broken and spent, from politics.

In those years Kerr continued to dominate the industrial Bar as the chief representative of the employer side. His clients did not appeal to all his old friends. When he appeared for the Northern Territory pastoralists to argue against the principle of equal pay for Aboriginal stockmen (who were then paid £2.8.3 a week plus fifteen shillings for clothing), his wartime colleague Conlon told him to his face: 'Rather than think you saw any merit in the case, John, your friends would prefer to believe that you are doing it just for the money'. That was the end of their relationship.

It was during this period also that he sounded out William McMahon with the suggestion that he was prepared to enter politics but would need to be assured of preselection for a safe Liberal seat and a rapid transition to the ministry such as Sir Garfield Barwick QC had experienced in 1958. When this was relayed to the Prime Minister, Menzies remarked dryly that no doubt a seat could be found but that promotion to the Cabinet would require some evidence of political expertise over a few years on the backbenches. They were, it seemed, years that Kerr was unwilling to give.

In 1965 and 1966 he represented the federal government before the Conciliation and Arbitration Commission in the National Wage Cases. In 1965 he argued that price stability was too important to be jeopardised by increases in wage levels — in fact, any increase at all in the basic wage was fraught with danger. In 1966 he submitted to the Commission:

> In general, therefore, the Commonwealth would prefer not to see any strong and sudden lift in demand and it would accordingly be apprehensive of the effects that other than a moderate wage increase could have. There is certainly a clear risk that a large wage increase would upset the balance which has more or less been reached in our overall economic situation.
> . . . However important the interests of wage earners may be, they most certainly cannot be put above the interests of society as a whole.
> (Basic Wage Cases 1966)

He had therefore become the government's in-house industrial lawyer and the logical choice for the next vacancy on the industrial Bench. He was appointed in late 1966 to the Industrial Court and at the same time to the Supreme Court of the ACT, and the Trade Practices Tribunal.

Over the next six years he lived the comfortable and prestigious, but normally unpublicised, life of a federal judge. There were two exceptions to this rule of tranquility. In May 1969, sitting as a Judge of the Industrial Court, he committed Clarrie O'Shea, Victorian Secretary of the Motor Omnibus and Tramways Employees Association, to gaol for contempt of court. O'Shea, spearheading a trade union attack on the penal clauses of the Conciliation and Arbitration Act which had caused the imposition of more than $250,000 in fines on unions for strikes, had refused to pay his association's fines and had refused to present evidence on the whereabouts of the union's bank funds or books.

The issue had simmered throughout the 1960s and O'Shea's gaoling sparked off a major confrontation between the government and the union movement. More than one million employees stopped work and a series of demonstrations swept the major cities. The turmoil ended abruptly when a lottery winner paid the association's fines, although there was considerable speculation that he had not provided the funds himself. The unions took the view that Kerr had no option except to commit O'Shea to prison but objected to his comment from the Bench that:

> Union officials do not enjoy any exemption under the law. People who choose today what is fashionably called civil disobedience must take the consequences. (Lloyd and Clark 1976)

It was also an unmistakeable jibe at the anti-Vietnam protests which had become a regular feature of Australian politics since the commitment of Australian troops to Vietnam in 1965.

In fact, the result of O'Shea's stand was that no further attempts were made by the government to collect the outstanding fines. Less dramatically, Kerr headed an inquiry in 1970 into the pay and conditions of members of the armed forces, and then in 1971 into those of federal parliamentarians. The latter exercise was essentially an attempt by members of Parliament to obtain salary increases without the public opprobium and press assaults which had followed previous votes in the House to accept increases, and Kerr's comprehensive research cushioned the impact of the increases he recommended by providing supporting evidence from a non-parliamentary source.

When Kerr was appointed a federal judge he had been promised a place on the proposed Superior Court of Australia. The Superior Court never eventuated and he soon cast about for new worlds to conquer. There could be no better world than the Chief Justiceship of NSW that he had almost had a decade ago, and when it became vacant in 1972, Kerr was appointed Chief Justice by the Askin Liberal government. It had been a forceful exercise in lobbying and self-promotion, directed chiefly at the establishments of the Sydney Bench and Bar. Not that this approach is at all extraordinary for it is how judges (and most public office-holders) normally gain appointment. It was, however, the nation's second legal prize (after the Chief Justiceship of Australia) and the competition was intense. Some long standing contacts in the Liberal Party finally convinced Premier Robin Askin and former Party Secretary Senator John Carrick of Kerr's suitability for the post.

As Chief Justice he built a reputation as an administrator rather than a lawyer. In fact he was never, like many of his colleagues at the Bar, a lawyer's lawyer and appeared to relish the broader managerial role. Yet despite this seemingly inevitable progression towards public life, it is difficult in his extensive published writing and speeches to discover any germ of a political philosophy. Notwithstanding his membership of the Labor Party, which he terminated, and his later association with the Liberal Party, which he never joined, his comments on Australian affairs have been almost uniformly episodic — such as his attacks on those subverting the trade unions and the universities — and lacking any broad proposals for the society around him. It is interesting to contrast this output with that of his immediate contemporary Whitlam, who began to formulate his comprehensive plans for the Australian community in the mid 1950s.

Yet there is no doubt he was fascinated with the question of power. He himself had exercised power as a soldier, as a judge, as head of professional bodies — but never the direct power of a minister or a Prime Minister. He conceded that Whitlam had his position because of his complete dedication to parliamentary politics as a career and his willingness to spend 20 tedious, single-minded years on the Opposition benches to achieve his goal. But he always felt that he could have, perhaps should have, got there — if he had not wanted to do other things; if, as he remarked even in 1975, he had been prepared to risk all on one throw and opt for a lifetime of politics as Whitlam had done in the early 1950s.

His own writings in the 1950s and 1960s refer constantly to the location of power in any given situation. In an article on the future of Papua New Guinea in 1971, discussing the role of the titular head under any new Constitution, he posed the questions:

1. Do we want the Administrator stripped of real *power* and converted into a kind of Governor-General or do we want him to retain full executive *power* and become a kind of *powerful* President?
2. Do we want a *powerful* Administrator-President elected or appointed for a fixed term irrespective of what the House thinks of him? Do we want such a President to be outside the House with a Government of Ministers picked by him from outside the House? Do we want the Ministers to be *completely under the President's direction and control* and to hold office at his will?
3. Or do we want the Administrator converted, not into a *powerful* President but into a weak Governor-General who must take the advice of a Prime Minister and Cabinet, working as a committee, all elected from and remaining members of the House? Do we want such a Ministerial system on the basis that the Government must resign if it loses the confidence of the House or must obtain a dissolution of the House and a new election if the House cannot agree on another Government which a majority will support?
4. Do we want a complete separation of *powers* between the President and the House with each staying in office for its fixed term even though the President and the House are at odds? (Kerr 1971, emphasis added)

In every question the focus is on precisely where power will lie — including the power of any Governor-General.

It was not observed at the time of his appointment as Governor-General that his long-held interest in Papua New Guinea had led him to consider in detail the nature of the constitution an independent Papua New Guinea might adopt, and that this in turn involved an analysis of the power possessed by a Governor-General under the Westminster system in order to establish whether these powers ought to be altered in any way for the Governor-General or Head of State who would come with independence.

As part of this inquiry he wrote in 1969:

These are important and difficult questions. If a modified Presidential system were adopted there would be no need to codify in the con-

stitution the difficult conventional rules about the power of a Westminster style Governor-President *to dismiss a Prime Minister who has
lost the confidence of the legislature and to commission a new Prime
Minister or to grant or to order a dissolution of the legislature.* Nor
would it be necessary to decide and to record in the constitution the
rules for *balancing the power of the Governor-President and the Prime
Minister* but there would be need to specify the rules for balancing
the power of the President and the legislature in the case of conflict
on policy. (Kerr 1969, emphasis added)

He was, therefore, even in 1969 closely considering the extent
of the powers he would himself exercise as Governor-General in
1975. The reference to a Prime Minister 'who had lost the confidence of the legislature' is interesting as it was to be his contention in November 1975 that Whitlam had lost the confidence
of Parliament if either of its Houses obstructed the processes of
government. In addition to reflecting his usual preoccupation
with the distribution of power, the notion of 'balancing the
power of the Governor-President and the Prime Minister' was
also a striking reference. It clearly entailed the view that the
Governor-General had sufficient powers to require balancing
against those of the Prime Minister. It was an idea that simply
had never occurred to Whitlam. It had occurred to Kerr. The
same theme was emphasised in his discussion of the merits of
codifying these powers:

If, on the other hand, the Westminster system is to be persisted with,
then before even the early stages of self-government under that
system are reached the difficult task of setting out in written constitutional form *the unwritten British conventions for regulating
relations between the Governor-President and the Prime Minister* must
be undertaken. In the constitutions of the older Dominions it was
not necessary to do this, certainly not in detail, because the conventions were inherited and understood as, for example, in the case
of the Australian constitutions, both federal and state. But in the new
Commonwealth countries codification of most if not all of these conventions has been necessary and the solutions adopted have varied.
Where there is a strong nationalist movement and a single dominant
nationalist party there could be resistance to the entrenching in the
constitution of rules *settling the power relationship of Governor-
President and Prime Minister,* on the ground that it is insulting to im-
ply that the classic conventions cannot be understood or will not be
honestly worked in such conditions. However, generally speaking,
the attempt has been made mainly because the conventions,
necessary for the proper working of the Westminster system, are not
native to the country concerned and need to be written down to be
properly appreciated and understood. (Kerr 1969, emphasis added)

Perhaps the most specific precursor of November 1975, however, came in his consideration of whether

> the Westminster system or some modification of it is the best one for New Guinea. If it is to be persisted with in the evolution of a New Guinea constitution then one of the difficult problems requiring careful and continuous discussion will be the expression in the Constitution of the rules for selecting the Governor-President and the statement of his powers in respect of the dissolution of the House, the obtaining of alternative governments in some circumstances on the defeat in Parliament of a government in office, and *the dismissing of a Prime Minister either because of loss of confidence in the legislature or because the machinery of parliamentary government is threatened with disruption by the Prime Minister's improper conduct.* (Kerr 1969, emphasis added)

The idea that a Prime Minister could be dismissed because a Governor-General had formed the view that the machinery of government was threatened with disruption by his improper conduct was a novel one which had no precedents in modern constitutional law. Yet Kerr had given notice six years before November 1975 that his conception of the office of Governor-General extended to such a judgment on a Prime Minister's actions. Elsewhere in the same article he noted that

> the Westminster system . . . normally envisages a strong Prime Minister and a relatively weak Governor or President.

Yet he added a comment that again calls to mind his relationship with Whitlam, referring to the risk of 'what might be done to the classic Westminster model by a strong authoritarian single party headed perhaps by a leader who managed to combine both the offices of Governor-President and Prime Minister in his own person'.

He was, therefore, something of a constitutional theorist — but a theorist who was to be given the most dramatic crisis in Australian political history as a means of testing his ideas in practice.

This, then, was the man approached by Whitlam for whom he was no more than an acquaintance in late 1973 to succeed Hasluck as Governor-General. He was a man who had moved in both sides of politics but settled for neither, who had developed constitutional theories but had had no experience of government, who had been obsessed by the exercise of power but never the purposes for which it could be employed. It would have been a dangerous appointment for any political party to make, for Kerr was a genuine cynic, an ideological soldier of fortune with no preconceived notion of the political process, a man who believed in nothing — except himself. As his friend from pre-war days, Francis James, remarked later: 'God Save the Queen! Honestly, John, it's a bit much when you believe in neither God nor the Queen'.

Ultimately, Labor would have fared better under a genuine conservative like Hasluck whose basic approach to the Senate's blocking of the Budget would probably have been to try to preserve the status quo — which until 1975 had entailed, in all Westminster countries, the supremacy of the Lower House in the formation and maintenance of governments. Instead it had placed its fate in the hands of a man whose motivations were as unpredictable as they were personal.

When the appointment was announced it was acclaimed by Bill Snedden, then Leader of the Opposition. In April, legislation went through Parliament increasing the Governor-General's salary from $20,000 to $30,000 and providing a pension of 60 per cent of the salary of the Chief Justice of Australia. Kerr's other condition of acceptance had been appointment for ten years instead of the normal term of five years. Whitlam agreed and, as no term is fixed but only observed by convention, approached Snedden to ask what his attitude would be on a change of government sometime in the future. Snedden said that he would be happy to keep Kerr if it was his decision. On 11 July, Sir John Kerr KCMG formally assumed the office of Governor-General of Australia.

His first twelve months as Governor-General convinced him that he had been right to take the job, despite a growing sense of frustration. As Head of State and Commander-in-Chief of the armed forces he instantly became privy to the innermost workings and secrets of the political, military, diplomatic and bureaucratic worlds. In addition to daily briefings from generals, ambassadors and permanent heads, the great proportion of government actions were formalised by the Executive Council in meetings, normally at Yarralumla or in Admiralty House in Sydney or in the federal parliamentary offices in Melbourne, often with only Whitlam and one other minister present to make up the minimum attendance.

In two areas in particular he was able to indulge without inhibition in the attributes of vice-regal office. One was his role in foreign affairs. In early 1975 he visited several central Asian countries after attending the coronation in Katmandu of the King of Nepal. Travelling as a Head of State he was received, in terms of protocol, as Australia's most important personage and was given audiences with their presidents and kings, often the possessors of great power in substance as well as in form, who corresponded to his own position. The other was in his social activities at home. He entertained frequently and opulently at Yarralumla, invited a more disparate group than his predecessors while still confining himself to persons of position or distinction in their field. Yarralumla itself is part of this world — a mansion set in spacious grounds which take in the shores of Canberra's Lake Burley Griffin, with 60 rooms and the services of a butler, valet, housemaids, kitchen staff, laundresses, cook, footmen, chauffeurs and gardeners. He was in a unique situation to observe and to impress his ideas on the Australian social elite — but increasingly as his own man, not as a mere extension of the Labor government to which few of his guests would have been naturally sympathetic.

Other factors were working to increase his distance from the Labor government. On the one hand it was impossible not to feel the exhilaration of being at the very centre of decision-making and of national events but, on the other hand, he was constantly aware of Whitlam's belief that a Governor-General was irrevocably bound to follow the advice and opinions of the Prime Minister of the day. And few Prime Ministers can have held such strong opinions, or expressed them so forcefully, as Whitlam. In this situation lay the seeds of Kerr's frustration. He was now in a unique position to observe the exercise of national power and he believed that he was capable of making a contribution. Yet he was forced to work with a Prime Minister of unusual authority and flair who insisted that his role was essentially formal — 'My Viceroy', as Whitlam once remarked. There was nothing personal in Whitlam's patronising of Kerr — it was merely that in Whitlam's comprehension of the Australian political system any Governor-General was a decorative symbol, a figure of style but not of substance.

By the end of the first year, Kerr's distaste for Whitlam's approach was well-defined if well-disguised. Too well-disguised for Whitlam, who would never realise its extent until their confrontation on 11 November 1975.

7 State of siege
Reform and reaction

John Kerr's proclamation dissolving the 29th Parliament on 11 November 1975 would list 21 Bills which met the literal terms of section 57 of the Constitution. Section 57 provides for a dissolution of both Houses if even one Bill has been rejected by the Senate after passage through the House of Representatives and then rejected again after an interval of three months and a second passage through the House. Each of those 21 Bills had been rejected. In view of the role played by the Senate in finally forcing the election of 1975 and in blunting Labor's thrust during its three years of government, it was singularly appropriate that the proclamation which terminated the Labor governments should reflect the most frustrating aspect of its period in office.

In a very real sense, Labor had never been in power. It had merely been in office. Certainly there was no period when it was in a position to decide on a policy in the knowledge that its implementation rested simply on the preparation of legislation and the establishment of an administrative apparatus to carry out that policy. Its successors, in contrast, had that ability from their first day in government.

The anti-Labor forces in the Senate — a majority constructed through an amalgamation of Liberal, Country Party, DLP and Independent Senators — had demonstrated their resolve to the infant Labor government at the earliest opportunity. In February 1973, the Opposition amended the Address-in-Reply to the speech of the Governor-General opening the 28th Parliament to insert a condemnation of the two-month old government. It was the opening shot in a three-year war of attrition.

At that stage most Labor members were unaware of its significance. In the first flush of victory after 23 years in Opposition it was not difficult for the members of the new government to assume that they would be able to govern as a succession of LCP governments had done — untroubled by the most strident complaints of the Opposition, despite its majority in the Upper House, based upon Senate elections held in 1967 and 1970. Some time during that first year they realised that it was not going to be like that — the old order had changed. Exhilaration turned to bewilderment, assurance to disillusionment, as the feeling of living on borrowed time and the ever-present sense of uncertainty and unpredictability ate into the resolve of the government.

It was this atmosphere of impermanence that sapped its collective will to undertake the sheer drudgery involved in long-term detailed planning, for there could be no guarantee that measures could ever become law — or even that the government would be in office six months hence and thus in a position to follow projects through. It is impossible to overestimate the destabilising effect of this phenomenon on Labor's three-year government.

Integral programs were abandoned in expectation of their certain defeat, while others were accelerated from fear of an early election. The disorientation ultimately permeated the day-to-day workings of government and there were months when the most important administrative resources of the government were directed almost exclusively to the question of the government's survival, when policy formulation and implementation were completely paralysed.

The spearhead of the attack on Labor's ability to govern was always to remain in the Senate. It was, however, merely the most public aspect of a coherent campaign to prevent Labor putting its programs into effect. The pattern of resistance was reinforced by the efforts of the non-Labor State governments, within whose borders federal Labor measures had to be carried out, and by private groups upon whom particular measures impinged. Thus Medibank, having escaped extinction only by means of the 1974 Joint Sitting of Parliament which followed the May double dissolution, remained under siege, running the gauntlet of the non-Labor State governments and the organised medical profession. This kind of triple alliance operated also against federal legal aid where the Victorian government encouraged the challenge to the ALAO prepared by the Victorian Law Institute, and enabled the proceedings to be brought before the High Court of Australia.

The use of the courts to challenge Labor programs was to become an important aspect of its opponents' strategy. By 1975, the High Court list was cluttered with cases initiated by State governments, private groups, or both, seeking the invalidation of various Australian government measures. The Petroleum and Minerals Authority Act was successfully challenged, although not on the ground that the establishment of the PMA was unconstitutional but because the Act had not met the requirements to qualify it for the Joint Sitting where it had been finally passed — after three rejections in the Senate. Challenges to the granting of Senate representation to the ACT and the Northern Territory, to the Australian Assistance Plan, and to the declaration of Australian government sovereignty over the off-shore waters and the continental shelf, all failed although the first two only by a 4-3 vote of the seven member High Court. Writs were also taken out against the ALAO, the Regional Employment Development Scheme, and the National Parks and Wildlife Conservation Act, but these actions had not come before the High Court for hearing by the time of the government's dismissal. All these actions were commenced originally by one of the non-Labor State governments. In most cases, the other non-Labor State governments intervened to support the challenge.

It has been explained that in the case of the Australian Assistance Plan, the Regional Employment Development Scheme and the ALAO, no statute to establish the programs existed. There was, therefore, no legislation that could be struck down to invalidate the programs and the only parliamentary reference to their existence occurred in one or two lines of the Budget's Appropriation Acts. The drafting of guidelines for expenditure of the funds appropriated and the setting up of administrative machinery to implement the schemes was then done, not by statute, but by the relevant government departments. This approach, rather than detailed legislation, could be used to minimise the Senate's opportunity of rejecting the legislation and thus preventing the programs from coming into operation.

It was symptomatic of the way in which ministers were driven to complex and unprecedented administrative arrangements in an effort to get their programs off the ground. The only difficulty was that, deprived of an opportunity to defeat these measures in Parliament, the government's opponents were quick to seek the same result in the High Court. One body to escape legal challenge was the Australian Purchasing Commission. When the legislation establishing the commission, which would have co-ordinated all departmental purchases, was rejected by the Senate in August 1975, the commission was simply maintained as an administrative unit of the Department of the Special Minister of State and carried out all of the functions envisaged by the rejected legislation. The commission was difficult to attack in the courts as its functions were clearly within the powers of the Australian government. When the Senate Opposition also rejected the proposed Overseas Trading Commission, which would have conducted exporting transactions for Australian businesses, a similar arrangement was suggested but had not been implemented by the time the government was dismissed.

During the period of the Whitlam government the Opposition Senators had a number of options open to them in respect of a Bill. The first step was to reject the Bill outright. In its first eighteen months of government, with 26 Senators out of 60, Labor could be defeated in the Senate at any time by a combination of the LCP and DLP Senators.

After the May 1974 double dissolution at which the ALP returned 29 Senators and the LCP 29, with two Independents, neither side could be absolutely guaranteed a majority. But the Tasmanian Liberal Party rapidly came to an agreement with the Independent Liberal Michael Townley. The Opposition was then certain of 30 votes, and sometimes had 31 when the South Australian Liberal Movement Leader, Steele Hall, voted with them. But even with 30 votes, the Opposition numbers were adequate, as the Senate Standing Orders provide that if a vote is tied, the motion is defeated. The tactic of outright rejection was used frequently, both in the first eighteen months and later, with the support of Townley. This tactic accounted for the defeat of 93 Bills in the government's 35 months of office. In the previous 75 *years* of the Senate's history, it had rejected outright a total of only 68 Bills.

Among those Bills rejected was all the legislation establishing Medibank — rejected by the Senate in 1973 and early 1974. Only the passage of the most crucial Bills at the Joint Sitting allowed the program to go ahead. The other legislation to go through the Joint Sitting, after being twice rejected by the Senate, provided for the election of Senators from the ACT and the Northern Territory, the establishment of the PMA, and reform of the electoral laws. Only the first endured. The PMA was invalidated in the High Court on the technical ground already referred to, and the additional legislation necessary to implement a redistribution of electorates was defeated by the new Senate in 1974 and 1975. Although the 1975 election was conducted on electoral boundaries devised in 1968 (on the basis of the 1966 Census) and so took no account of the increases and shifts of population since then, Labor's electoral legislation was probably the measure most fiercely resisted by the Opposition for the reduction it would have made in Country Party representation in the House of Representatives (even though the Liberals would have gained increased representation along with Labor). Every Bill dealing with the redistribution of the 1968 boundaries was defeated in the Senate over Labor's two terms of office.

All significant measures relating to control of natural resources, with the exception of the Pipeline Authority, were defeated. In addition to the PMA, the Senate rejected legislation aimed at regulating offshore and continental shelf mining and the establishment of a National Investment Fund to finance the activities of the AIDC. In the economic area, it turned down the establishment of the AGIC, the creation of the Australian Purchasing Commission, an expansion of functions for the AIDC, and attempts to stabilise land prices in the Northern Territory. In the legal area it quashed the Superior Court of Australia and also a bid to abolish remaining appeals from Australian Courts to the Privy Council. All measures providing for referenda to amend the Constitution were defeated or deferred indefinitely. Among these had been proposals to ensure that elections for both Houses were held simultaneously, to allow the Australian and State governments to exchange powers, and to enable the Australian government to make grants direct to local government bodies. In terms of legislation simply rejected, as opposed to being prevented from coming into operation, the Senate's reaction to Labor's second victory at the polls in May 1974 was to throw out in the following eighteen months almost exactly double the number of Bills rejected in the government's first eighteen months.

The Opposition's second option was to attempt amendment of a Bill to the point of emasculation to substantially defeat its purpose. This tactic required 31 votes out of 60 as a tied vote could only block but not pass a motion. Before the 1974 election this was not a problem. After that poll, with the 29 Senators the Opposition had returned and the support of Townley, they needed also to win the support of Steele Hall or, after Murphy's elevation to the High Court in February 1975, the support of Cleaver Bunton, the 'political neuter' chosen by NSW Liberal Premier Tom Lewis to replace Murphy. On over 50 pieces of legislation as diverse as the Racial Discrimination Act, the National Parks and Wildlife Conservation Act, the Financial Corporations Act, the Fisheries Act, and the National Roads Act, the Opposition gained the support of one or other of these and was able to force amendments which very often defeated key provisions of the Bills in question.

The third option was to have a Bill referred to a Standing or Select Committee of the Senate, or of both Houses, for examination and suggested amendment. This manoeuvre which had the advantage of sounding considerably more constructive was guaranteed to bury any Bill for at least twelve months, probably longer. The National Compensation Bill and the Corporations and Securities Bill suffered this fate. The former spent nine months before the Senate Standing Committee on Constitutional and Legal Affairs and the latter had still not emerged from six months before a Senate Select Committee when the government was dismissed. This was obviously a useful tactic when the measure in question was an electorally popular one and one which it would therefore be dangerous to oppose outright no matter how unpalatable it was to the Opposition. Designated for this strategy was the Legal Aid Bill, which would have given legislative backing to the ALAO. The Opposition gave notice in the House of Representatives in October 1975 that it would move in the Senate for the Bill to be referred to a Select Committee of both Houses. But the Bill reached the Senate only shortly before the government was deposed.

For almost three years, therefore, the Opposition in the Senate attempted to exercise the functions of government without any requirement to assume responsibility for the success or failure of the government's policies. Its Deputy Leader, Ivor Greenwood, gave an unconscious glimpse of the Opposition's view during one of the Joint Sitting debates, when he protested that, but for the Senate, Labor would be able to achieve its aims 'simply by the passing of Bills through the numbers which it possesses in the House of Representatives and there would be no means whereby the people of Australia could be prevented from suffering the excesses of that authoritarianism'. Clearly Greenwood's view was that gaining those numbers at elections was not enough. Consequently electoral defeat did not in any way mean this Opposition accepted the government's right to govern.

The most damaging power open to the Opposition Senators was refusal of supply. Yet even its use to ultimately destroy the government does not suggest its full effect on Labor's two terms of office. It was essentially a power whose use could be threatened every six months — in October when the Appropriation Bills connected with the August Budget reached the Senate, or in April when supplementary Supply Bills are introduced to cover the financial interregnum until the Budget is passed.

The possibility of cutting off the government's funds and thereby forcing it to an early election was first raised in October 1973, when the Whitlam administration was less than a year old. Opposition Senate Leader Reg Withers supplied Liberal Leader Bill Snedden with draft motions for the deferral of the Budget. It was a step no Senate had taken in Australian parliamentary history, despite the fact that there have frequently been periods during which the Senate was in control of a party or coalition different from the party commanding a majority in the House of Representatives. As it turned out, no move was made in 1973 but in April 1974, using the motions drafted by Withers six months before, the Opposition (with the support of the DLP) voted to hold up supply in an attempt to precipitate the election for both Houses which Whitlam, in fact, called. Undeterred by its failure at the polls in this election the Opposition seriously discussed the issue in October 1974 and again in early 1975.

On the second occasion only the removal of Snedden by Fraser made an early election impractical for the Opposition. Fraser then played a waiting game with the government, never actually saying he would let the Budget pass until, after months of speculation, the Budget was blocked in October 1975. This meant that every six months after its first six months in government, Labor faced the threat of being forced to the polls.

How close the threat of the Senate cutting off its funds always was to the government's consciousness can be illustrated by the fact that in January 1975, less than a month after the Darwin cyclone disaster of Christmas Day 1974, Whitlam raised the possibility of using the relief grants that would have to be made to Darwin to ensure the passage of the April Supply Bills through the Senate. The essence of the scheme was that the relief funds would be included in those Supply Bills. The Opposition

in the Senate would clearly be reluctant to reject any legislation providing for the assistance of Darwin. If it tried to detach the Darwin appropriations from the rest of the supply legislation, the government would argue that this was an attempt by the Senate to amend a money Bill which was in violation of section 53 of the Constitution.

In any event the Opposition had then only 30 Senators out of 60 and without the support of Steele Hall they would not be able to force such an amendment. Their only practical choice would therefore be to vote for the legislation, giving the government supply for another six months. Whitlam asked Solicitor-General Byers whether the scheme was feasible. Byers replied that the relief funds could probably be included in the normal Supply Bills but pointed out that if the Senate did amend the Bills to detach those funds it almost certainly could not be challenged in the courts. If it could not raise the numbers to amend, however, it would have to reject outright or let the Bills pass. The deposing of Snedden by Fraser removed any need for the scheme in April and, of course, the Darwin factor was no longer available in October. It was a graphic example of the government's siege mentality.

Earlier in 1974 Whitlam had also canvassed the possibility of two year's supply being included in one year's Budget legislation so that the government would face no threat in 1975 if it survived in 1974. He was told that the scheme was legally feasible but that such legislation could be amended by the Senate to split the two years up — so no escape again.

It was not only the feeling of futility injected into day-to-day administration by this consciousness of borrowed time that affected the development of policy and programs. Equally debilitating were the months spent unproductively, and ultimately unsuccessfully, on basic political survival. This involved both planning for and striving to avoid an election simultaneously, and resulted in substantial neglect of routine administration. This syndrome reached its peak in the last three months of the government's life when senior ministers, their staff, and many senior departmental officers spent the majority of their time dealing with the problems of the passage of the

Opposite: A jovial Reg Withers, Opposition Senate leader and a key figure in Malcolm Fraser's capture of the Prime Ministership

Budget, the provision of alternative funds, and the likely requirements of an election campaign.

What is quite clear is that the federal Opposition, the non-Labor State governments, and some major interest groups, never accepted the legitimacy of the Labor government. Even after May 1974, they continued to regard the Whitlam government as an aberration, destined to disappear quickly into the mists of history. Never was this attitude better illustrated than in Melbourne in the last week of September 1975.

At the Hotel Windsor, the second session of the Australian Constitutional Convention was in progress. The Convention, originally canvassed by Victorian Liberal Premier, Sir Henry Bolte, had been established in 1973 to consider ways of adapting Australia's turn-of-the century Constitution to the political and social realities of the 1970s — a long overdue exercise from any political viewpoint. The federal Parliament and all the State Parliaments sent delegations to the 1973 session of the Convention, with members coming from both government and Opposition parties. At this second session, however, only the South Australian and Tasmanian delegations were representative of all parties. Elsewhere, LCP members had boycotted the Convention which had originally been scheduled to meet in the Victorian Parliament building — directly across the road from the Windsor Hotel which later became the venue. But the new Victorian Liberal Premier, Rupert Hamer, had withdrawn that long-standing arrangement a week before the Convention was to meet.

Yet in Hamer's offices, next to the Victorian Parliament, federal Opposition Leader Malcolm Fraser and his shadow ministers were meeting the Premiers of the non-Labor states to discuss the new Liberal policy on 'federalism' — the same subject being discussed a few hundred yards away at the Windsor under another name. Fraser advised the State Premiers that there was a good chance he would be Prime Minister by the end of the year and thus be able to implement the policy he was outlining to them. The non-Labor Premiers, for their part, were happy to treat Fraser as de facto Prime Minister — it was in keeping with the campaign they had been mounting for more than two and a half years against a government they regarded as invalid and transitory. Their judgment as to transit may well have been justified. It was the reservations as to legitimacy, however, that lay at the heart of the farce of the dual conventions held in Melbourne that week. The government's tenure was precarious precisely because it was clear that powerful sections of the community did not consider it a legitimate administration, but rather one they were entitled to fight with what had in Australia previously been considered illegitimate means. In a comment that recalled the New Guard of the 1930s, Tasmanian Liberal Senator Peter Rae said of this period in May 1976:

> Throughout 1974 and 1975, Australians saw a threat to their way of life. They demanded strong anti-socialist leadership. From Mt Isa to Bunbury I found small numbers of people talking about the prospect of armed rebellion. (Rae 1976)

Perhaps Rae has a vivid imagination but what is significant is that he believed it and considered it understandable.

Immediately after the aborted Constitutional Convention, Fraser aired his horrified vision of a Labor government able to pass any legislation into law. Commenting on the possibility of Labor gaining temporary control of the Senate at a half-Senate poll he said 'They would only need control for one day and it would utterly distort the future of Australia'.

This, then, was the spirit of the opposition to Labor. But the actual campaigns of its opponents — those interlocking forces of resistance made up of the federal parliamentary Opposition, the non-Labor State governments, the private interest groups affected by legislation, and the judicial system they employed — bear closer examination. Three such campaigns against Labor government initiatives may give some idea of how these forces functioned to make the implementation of policies — very often policies given considerable exposure in election campaigns and by implication accepted by the electorate — tediously difficult, if not finally impossible. One of these campaigns — the campaign against Medibank — failed at that time. The other two — against the establishment of the AGIC and the development of the ALAO — were successful.

MEDIBANK

Medibank — more than any other of Labor's programs — was fought ferociously by the Opposition inside the Parliament, and at the same time by the organised medical profession and the health funds throughout the country. It was also frustrated with varying degrees of persistence by non-Labor State governments. The campaign against Medibank can be taken as the most extensive and protracted example of resistance to a government program in Labor's period of office.

In view of the two and a half year struggle to introduce Medibank it is extraordinary to recall what the scheme entailed. In essence it was a health insurance program designed to provide complete cover to patients against the costs of standard ward hospital treatment and a constant level of cover against medical expenses. The basic principle behind the medical benefits side was that the benefit for each service would be at least 85 per cent of the doctor's fee for that service but in no case would the gap between the scheduled fee and the benefit for any service exceed $5. On the hospital side, agreements would be made with State governments so that hospital care, including medical treatment, was provided without charge in standard wards of public hospitals. The net operating costs of public hospitals would be shared equally by the Australian and State governments. Medibank was, therefore, nothing more than a system of universal health insurance under which funds raised by taxation would be used to enable all persons in the community to use the existing health services.

It was not a program in any way similar to the British National Health Scheme. The much greater problem of improving the quality of health services was to be tackled as a separate long-term objective. The concept of health insurance itself was hardly new, as the various private medical and hospital benefits schemes had been in operation for many years. Medibank's advantage over these would be its coverage of *all* persons, including those one million unable to afford private insurance, and its rationalisation of a multiplicity of funds which varied in resources, coverage and efficiency. It was envisaged that these funds would continue in existence (as they did) and provide supplementary insurance for persons who wished to be covered for additional medical services and for accommodation in hospital rooms other than standard wards.

In November 1973 legislation to establish Medibank was introduced by the government. The Health Insurance Bill authorised the payment of medical benefits and the negotiation of hospital agreements with the States. The Health Insurance Commission Bill established the administrative structure of Medibank. After passage through the House of Representatives both Bills were defeated in the Senate in December. In April 1974 both Bills passed the House of Representatives again and were again rejected by the Senate a week later. The Bills formed two of the six Bills relied on by Whitlam to secure a double dissolution in April 1974. After victory at the subsequent election, the two Bills were introduced into the House in July and were defeated in the Senate later the same month. They were passed by the Joint Sitting held in August 1974 — with the Opposition voting against them for the seventh time — and finally became law on 8 August 1974. They were sufficient to get Medibank off the ground.

Despite this, further legislation to facilitate its introduction was rejected in August 1974 by the Senate and was still being rejected in April 1975. This legislation included Bills to arrange an orderly changeover when Medibank actually came into operation on 1 July 1975, to enable private health insurance organisations to be supervised in their contributors' interests, and to finance the program by a levy which would be additional to income tax. Ironically, the Opposition's rejection of the levy principle was a major factor in public acceptance of Medibank as the government then had no alternative but to present it as a 'free' scheme.

The Opposition's resistance to Medibank inside Parliament was the vanguard for a number of private groups who were fiercely opposed to its introduction. After the basic legislation passed the Joint Sitting, the participation of these groups in the campaign against Medibank became more desperate and it was portrayed as the first stage in the nationalisation of health and medical care in Australia.

While the campaign against Medibank took the basic form of other campaigns opposing government initiatives, it was on a larger scale and over a longer period than any other. Behind the scenes it involved representations to the Minister for Social Security, representations to his department, and lobbying of individual government MPs. Lobbying of Opposition MPs was hardly necessary but supplying them with ammunition for statements in parliament and the press was a major exercise. Petitions, public letters and media advertising were employed in the next stage. There was also the opportunity to distribute printed material in doctors' surgeries and in the offices of the health funds through which large numbers of the public passed. In addition all the major private bodies opposed to Medibank were themselves engaged in the provision of health services and could therefore offer resistance at a working level also.

The most obvious group to be in the forefront of the opposition was the private health insurance funds. Although these were to remain in existence they reacted violently to the prospect of a possible loss of business. The attitude of the funds was that, although their existence and growth was due in large part to the subsidisation of their activities by a succession of federal governments, those governments had no business interfering in the area of health insurance. It was of no concern to them that the taxes of persons unable to afford private health contributed to that subsidisation. The funds waged a constant public relations and advertising campaign against Medibank — all of it paid for by contributors' money.

The relationship between the funds and the medical profession was a particularly close one. The Medical Benefits Fund of Australia, for example, had been essentially set up by the Australian Medical Association and medical members of the Fund were the only members entitled to vote for the governing council. Contributors were entitled neither to vote, nor to attend, nor to be notified of the general meetings of the council. The opposition of the medical profession to Medibank was as virulent as that of the funds: in June 1973 the AMA described it as

> a cleverly devised plan for the ultimate nationalisation of all medical and hospital services, and a first major step to achieve socialisation of the Australian community in accordance with the socialist objectives of the Australian Labor Party.

The General Practitioners' Society urged members to send letters to their patients and suggested, as a guide to the contents, that the following be included

> the control of our country has fallen in the hands of socialists . . . socialism was the brain-child of Karl Marx, a bitter man and a strange mixture of semi-scientist and half-baked philosopher. Lenin accepted the teachings of Marx, fomented a revolution in Russia, exterminated millions of ordinary decent people and enslaved the rest . . . the fight that the General Practitioners' Society in Australia is spearheading is basically a fight for freedom — not just freedom for doctors — but freedom for you, for your children, and for all people in the country.

The AMA set up a 'fighting fund' to raise $2 million and conducted an extensive advertising campaign, much of it in the form of printed material directed at the captive audience of patients waiting in their surgeries. Like the health insurance funds the doctors considered their activities no business of the government, despite the fact that approximately two thirds of their earnings were indirectly paid out of taxation revenue by the government through medical benefits. In particular the doctors attacked the proposed practice of 'bulk billing' whereby doctors would simply bill the government for consultations instead of patients paying and claiming rebates from Medibank later. This was one of the profession's real fears about Medibank — not that it would result in any direct loss of income but that it would create a system under which accurate records could be kept for the first time on the level of doctors' fees and incomes. Although a 'common fee' was established in 1970, charges in excess of that fee were frequent. Under a system of bulk billing it would become apparent what the *average* fee was as opposed to the *common* fee. Doctors, of course, always had one of the most effective and inexpensive methods of warning the public about the dangers of Medibank — the quiet chat with a patient during a consultation. Although a Doctors' Reform Society was established by doctors who supported Medibank and actually achieved some media coverage, its membership remained small.

The private hospitals, whether religious, charitable or profit-making, were the third interest group to actively oppose the introduction of Medibank. They claimed that they would be forced out of business, although the planners of the program had envisaged that private hospitals would continue to exist and had stated that the government would meet the full cost of treatment for standard ward patients in private as well as public hospitals. Private hospitals were, moreover, to retain the right to appoint their own boards of management and to maintain their own admission policies, and the overall hospital system in a State would continue to be administered by the State authorities and not by the federal government.

A final but thorny source of opposition to the implementation of Medibank was that of the non-Labor State governments. It was necessary to negotiate agreements with all State governments concerning the hospital side of Medibank since they, not the federal government, ran the hospitals. They did, however, want money to run those hospitals. Again their attitude, like that of the health funds and the doctors, was that the government should pay out for, but otherwise not intrude upon, their activities in the field of health care. Queensland's hospital system already met the Medibank requirements and its resistance had no basis but political action. It only ended when Premier Joh Bjelke-Petersen was overruled by his own Cabinet led by the Deputy Premier, Sir Gordon Chalk, who argued that the State could not afford to forego the financial advantages involved for it. The remaining three non-Labor States came into the hospital agreements either just before or soon after 1 July 1975 when it became clear that, in addition to the financial incentive, the electoral consequences of staying out were too dangerous. That was after a year of negotiations during most of which these States had suggested that they would never agree to the federal government's proposals.

In the case of Medibank, therefore, the campaign to prevent its coming into existence failed, although only the chance occurrence of the Joint Sitting allowed the government to overcome the Senate and make the first essential steps feasible. Even then it was not to endure for long as its basic structure was dismantled during 1976, the first year of the Fraser government.

THE AUSTRALIAN GOVERNMENT
INSURANCE CORPORATION

The campaign to prevent the establishment of AGIC involved a combination of the parliamentary Opposition and the interest group affected, the insurance industry. The AGIC Bill had to pass the Senate to become law. Therefore it could be defeated by use of the Opposition's numbers in that House. It was defeated — after one of the most concentrated and sophisticated applications of pressure ever seen in Australia, despite the fact that it was never demonstrated what threat the establishment of the AGIC would have posed to the insurance industry.

The industry was expecting trouble from the government and was only too ready to find a threat in the AGIC proposals. It was hardly a secret that Labor was not as sympathetic to it as the previous government had been, and the reduction in the taxation advantage provided by life insurance policies in the 1974 Budget was tangible evidence of Labor's reservations about the industry's contribution to society. A National Compensation Scheme had already been drafted and the Bill had been introduced into Parliament. A national superannuation scheme was being considered for the immediate future. Both would have a certain, if yet incalculable, effect on insurers by making some aspects of their business redundant.

The AGIC was designed as a commercial enterprise which would operate in competition with existing insurance companies. Under the legislation establishing it, the AGIC would have been authorised to undertake all forms of insurance, both general and life, including superannuation business and also re-insurance, much of which currently has to be taken out overseas by Australian companies. In addition it would have covered an area not handled by existing companies — natural disasters insurance, particularly losses of crops and livestock from those disasters. It was not intended that the AGIC should have any advantage over its private competitors, being liable to all federal and State taxes and required to invest its reserves in the interests of its policy holders. State government insurance offices had operated in this fashion for many years but the coverage offered by them varied. Only in NSW and Queensland were all types of insurance available and even these offices did not offer natural disasters insurance.

In two respects the AGIC could pursue its operations in a way designed to draw attention to what the government considered socially unproductive aspects of the insurance industry. One was to compete by means of the premiums offered to customers rather than by the use of agents, so that the customer received a saving instead of the agent receiving a commission. The other was to invest reserves as far as possible in housing loans to individuals rather than in office buildings and development projects.

It would probably not have unduly concerned Labor ministers if the AGIC had bitten deeply into the business of the industry, as they considered that much of the industry's growth to its present colossus level was due to the taxation incentives which had persuaded its clients to take out life insurance. After receiving so much benefit through government policies over the years the industry should not, they felt, begrudge the government the opportunity to enter the same field. There was no expectation that the AGIC would have a significant effect on the economic well-being of the industry. Nevertheless, in its nervous frame of mind the industry was determined to fight it as the vanguard of nationalisation and to fight it with all its resources.

Operating through two public relations firms, Eric White, and International Public Relations, representatives of the various sections of the industry lobbied on two fronts. The government, through Social Security Minister John Wheeldon, and Treasurer Jim Cairns, was pressed for an assurance that the AGIC would not proceed. The election of Malcolm Fraser as Opposition Leader in March actually intensified the lobbying of government sources, as Fraser's first statements made after gaining the leadership suggested that he would change Snedden's strategy and allow government legislation to pass through the Senate unless it was totally unacceptable to the Opposition. In these circumstances the obvious tactic was for the campaign to go public. The industry had to persuade either the government or Malcolm Fraser that the AGIC should be dropped, as either had the power to abort it. A public campaign could, if it took off, force the government to back down or alternatively convince Fraser of the electoral mileage to be gained by coming out against the AGIC.

In the second week of April, $150,000 worth of advertisements were screened in prime television time in all capitals. The advertisements pushed two lines — that everyone's taxes would be used to subsidise another inefficient government enterprise and that it was a first step towards the nationalisation that Labor's platform still espoused. They concluded with the suggestion that there was more to the government's proposal than met the eye. It was a campaign pitched squarely at that dark corner of the Australian psyche which still recalled the battle over bank nationalisation in the late 1940s.

When Wheeldon announced on 15 April that the government intended to proceed with the AGIC, its usefulness was already an issue in newspaper editorials and letters columns. In the month to come, although his confrontation with the industry was to become increasingly acrimonious, Wheeldon never succeeded in crystallising for the public the reasons why the AGIC should exist. The government began on the defensive and never gained the initiative. Ironically, one of the main reasons for going ahead with the Bill was so that it would be available as an election issue if the Opposition forced a poll through refusal of supply — yet another example of how this consideration was ever-present in the minds of government members and distorted their priorities.

After the introduction of the AGIC Bill in the House of Representatives on 23 April, the industry's public campaign was stepped up while at the same time spokesmen for the industry proposed meeting with ministers and officials and submitted amendments that would have the effect of neutralising the thrust of the Bill — an approach very similar to that employed by the legal profession with respect to the Legal Aid Bill later in the year. On the public side, staff from insurance offices were assembled for well-reported protest demonstrations in the capitals and public meetings were held around the country. Opposition members were invited to attend and to speak. At these meetings, they were able to draw the clear inference that the industry could marshal hundreds of bodies for voluntary work in any electorate during an election campaign if it were so minded. The industry employs more than 50,000 persons and employees were given time off to attend demonstrations and to arrange meetings of the Insurance Staffs Federation in an effort to force the federation to come out against the Bill. Staff were also used to collect signatures for petitions to be presented to the Senate, and 50,000 signatures were obtained. Not all staff members were willing conscripts into the anti-government crusade. An example of the direct pressure exerted on staff members came with the public disclosure of an office memo circulated with a petition in the Manufacturers Mutual Insurance Company. The memo warned that while staff could not be directed to sign the petition

> it is to be brought to the notice of a staff member who refuses to sign that should the legislation be enacted their future employment would be far from assured. (Edwards 1975)

That was clear enough for most employees, presumably.

Meanwhile, the most crucial time for the industry was approaching. The Bill passed the House in May and went to the Senate on 26 May. Wheeldon was still prepared to consider amendments put up by the industry so it obliged, submitting further amendments it believed would be unacceptable, thus gaining valuable time. During that period, the pressure on the Opposition and the public was maintained. In early June, the Opposition used its majority in the Senate to have the Bill deferred until the Budget sitting in August. Fraser seems to have realised quite early that he would be able to extract a high price in terms of electoral effort from the industry for the exercise of his powers to extinguish the AGIC. Soon after the deferral, the various branches of the industry formed the *Life and General Insurance Committee* to co-ordinate the campaign. It operated out of a Canberra office and was staffed full-time by two insurance executives, maintaining branches in each State capital and regional committees throughout the States. During the parliamentary recess of June and July, full-page advertisements, letters to the editor, petitions, meetings and personal approaches to Opposition members kept up the pressure. The advertisements appeared in strategic newspapers during the Bass by-election campaign in late June and during the South Australian State election campaign in June and early July.

Parliament resumed on 19 August and the Bill was voted on in the Senate two days later. It was defeated. Whether or not the Bill would have been rejected by the Senate without the expensive public campaign will never be known. Given the Opposition's use of its Senate majority during that period, it is difficult to accept that the Bill was anything other than doomed from the start. The insurance industry, it seems, was the one of the few groups to take seriously Fraser's early statements on the role of the Senate. But the industry was not prepared to gamble and its campaign left nothing to chance. For Fraser it had been a profitable exercise. In addition to its efforts in the Bass by-election, the industry set up an election headquarters during the 1975 federal election in the AMP Building in Melbourne, and made salaried staff available to work in marginal electorates in support of Liberal candidates. In view of the innocuous import of the Bill, it was not clear what the industry gained from the use of all its time and money except for some sort of psychological satisfaction. It was certainly a question insurance policy holders, who had financed the campaign without being consulted, could have asked themselves.

THE AUSTRALIAN LEGAL AID OFFICE

The campaign against the ALAO employed the combined efforts of the parliamentary Opposition, the non-Labor State governments, and the legal profession. The battle was complicated by the fact that, unlike the AGIC, the ALAO was established initially without Parliament's approval and in the early stages presented itself to this array of opponents as a *fait accompli*.

Set up as an administrative entity by Murphy in July 1973 it had, by mid 1975, 30 offices across the country providing legal assistance in areas arising under federal law such as family law, and to persons for whom the Australian government had special constitutional responsibility such as migrants, Aboriginals, pensioners and ex-servicemen. Eligibility for assistance was determined according to a means and needs test which took into ac-

count the resources of the applicant and the nature of the case.
Taking the nature of the case into account allowed assistance to
be given to bodies such as environmental and civil liberties
groups where a case was too costly for any one person or group
of persons, no matter what their personal resources. With
lawyers employed by the ALAO interviewing 15,000 people a
month throughout Australia it had become, for a large part of the
electorate, a fact of life and this also influenced the strategy of its
opponents.

At a parliamentary level, the Opposition was not required to
declare itself until June 1975, when the government introduced
the Legal Aid Bill into the House of Representatives. The purpose of the Bill was to put the ALAO on a statutory basis, to
define its powers and functions and to provide for a board of
management. Although the absence of any statute authorising
the ALAO's activities had been one of the Opposition's main
criticisms of the Office's operation in its first two years, its
solution was the removal of the Office by preventing its enabling
legislation. Some members of the Opposition were dubious
about rejecting the Legal Aid Bill in the Senate, as they foresaw
that such a move could be treated by the media and the public as
a vote against the *concept* of legal aid. Ivor Greenwood, as
shadow Attorney-General, recognised the problem but insisted
that the Bill could not be allowed to pass into law. He had
suggested using the numbers in the Senate to refer the Bill to a
Select Committee of both Houses. This would avoid the odium
of rejection but ensure that the Bill was long delayed and finally
gutted. The Law Council of Australia had already put its lengthy
submission to Attorney-General Kep Enderby, the import of
which was that the ALAO should become a mere cipher, referring
all cases immediately to private solicitors. In Greenwood's mind,
this proposal also could be pursued in the Select Committee
hearings. As an alternative, however, he offered a series of
eviscerating amendments. These were set out in his review of the
Opposition's options, prepared for the shadow Attorney-
General's committee of the Parliamentary Liberal Party:

The courses open to be adopted by the Opposition Parties:

1. *To support the Bill in its entirety*
   This course is not recommended. The arguments against the Bill
   which have been already canvassed have weight. Moreover there

are strong grounds for the contention that the Commonwealth Parliament lacks constitutional power to enact the Bill.

2. *To oppose the Bill*
    The risk of opposing the Bill outright — which, nevertheless, is the logical consequence of the arguments raised — is that we would be castigated as opposed to legal aid. The truth of our opposition would be lost in the welter of publicised condemnation of 'voting against legal aid'.

3. *To amend to give effect to our position*
    This is a feasible course. It may be expressed as alternatives — the first alternative is to move to have the Bill withdrawn with a view to a new Bill being introduced to give effect to legal aid on different — but stated — principles; and the second alternative is to give effect to textual amendments in the committee stages of the Bill — after supporting the second reading speech.
    The proposed line of amendments — consistent with the proposed policy statement attached hereto — would be as follows—

    (i)   to make the Legal Aid Commission the central body the Bill establishes
    (ii)   Not to establish the Legal Aid Office
    (iii)   To retain the consultative committees — but with the function of advising the Commission and existing legal aid agencies
    (iv)   to provide for State grants to be made by the Commission to the States on agreed terms and conditions — such conditions to relate to the functioning of State legal aid schemes in which the profession has a predominant voice, to the provision of referral centres, duty solicitors and adequate staff responsible to the State legal aid Committee
    (v)   For State representation on the Legal Aid Commission.

When the Bill was debated in the House of Representatives in October, the Opposition gave notice of its plan to move for a Select Committee when the Bill reached the Senate. The Bill passed through the House and went to the Senate but did not come up for debate before 11 November.

While it was always probable that the government's efforts to put the ALAO on a firm statutory basis would founder in the Senate, the non-Labor states and the legal profession were equally concerned about its already existing operations. The States were concerned, as ever, with the territorial imperative. Although their own legal aid schemes had received $5 million from the Labor government, as opposed to nothing from previous LCP governments, the ALAO represented an intrusion on their long-held if lightly-tilled domain. The Victorian Attorney-General Vernon Wilcox was the most vociferous of the

State Attorneys and in July 1975 wrote to Greenwood, urging that the Legal Aid Bill be 'vigorously' opposed and expressing the hope that the Senate 'will prevent this Bill coming into operation'.

The legal profession's opposition to the ALAO was motivated by a mixture of economic and territorial considerations. The ALAO was not affecting the incomes of private practitioners, as studies had shown that most people who found their way to an ALAO office would never have approached a solicitor on the same matter — either because they were intimidated by the law in general or because they were apprehensive of the likely cost of legal representation. The clients of the ALAO represented a previously untapped source of business, rather than a group of paying customers culled from the profession's existing clientele.

Many practitioners were in fact supplementing their incomes from the ALAO, which was forced by the number of people entering its doors to farm out the bulk of its cases to private solicitors. Of approximately $13 million allocated for legal aid in the 1975 Budget, only $6 million was for the running of the ALAO and the remaining $7 million was to go to practitioners in legal fees. But the objection of the legal profession was that it did not have a major influence in the operation of the ALAO, whereas at the State level the private profession dominated all legal aid schemes. It could exercise no control, therefore, over the future operation of the ALAO, which might pose a significant economic threat to private solicitors even though this was not the case to date. There was also hostility towards the creation of a class of lawyers who were staffing ALAO offices. They would be outside the jurisdiction of the various State law societies who exercised firm control over all practising lawyers through the power to remove the right to practise, and thus the livelihood, of any offenders against their rules.

In its submission to Enderby, the Law Council of Australia had no reservations about the Australian government funding legal aid in Australia on a large scale. It did, however, protest at the government's intention to take a major role in the activities on which its funds were expended. The Council suggested that the administration of the ALAO should be left to 'eminent' members of the legal profession. Early in 1975, the Victorian government and a reluctant Law Institute of Victoria combined in a challenge to the existing operations of the ALAO. A group of Victorian solicitors had long urged the Victorian Institute to take proceedings before the High Court on the constitutionality of the ALAO. This group convened an extraordinary general meeting of the Institute for 20 February 1975 to consider the challenge and to debate a general motion that:

> The Council of the Law Institute be instructed to resist Governmental nationalisation of the profession at all costs, being destructive of an independent legal profession and as being likely to cause that profession to become no less than an arm of Government.

As in the case of the campaigns of the insurance industry against the AGIC and the health funds against Medibank, the spectre of nationalisation was raised to oppose a government instrumentality that would do no more than supplement the work of the existing private profession and, in the case of the ALAO, would operate in a narrower range of matters and deal with a section of the public not even catered for by the private profession.

The governing council of the Institute was at this time not enthusiastic about the challenge. Whatever their philosophical objections to the Australian government's entry into the legal aid area, they did not want to alienate a government that had just given $307,000 to the Victorian Legal Aid Committee in which the Institute played a large role. That committee had received only $77,000 from the Victorian Liberal government in the period 1970-5. The council, therefore, recommended against a challenge while realising that the members would take the final decision.

The Institute also had the technical problem of gaining a hearing before the High Court — it did not have the standing to take the action of its own right as it was not considered at law to be adversely affected by the existence of the ALAO. The solution to this problem was to have the State Attorney-General, who had the required standing at law, issue his fiat to enable the Institute to get before the court in a case brought nominally by the Attorney-General. Normally an Attorney-General's part in such an action would be purely formal, extending only to the lending of his title. But Victoria's Vernon Wilcox became personally involved. On 19 February — the day before the Institute's general meeting — he wrote to the director of the Institute encouraging the idea of a challenge to the ALAO by the Institute and more or less guaranteeing his fiat if it was undertaken:

19 February 1975

Mr Gordon Lewis,
Executive Director,
The Law Institute of Victoria,
465 Little Bourke Street,
MELBOURNE 3000.

Dear Mr Lewis,

I note that the Institute is to hold a general meeting on Thursday next, 20 February, to consider motions submitted in relation to the organisation known as the Australian Legal Aid Office.

In a number of areas the Government has been disturbed at the apparent acceptance of the principle that the Commonwealth Government might acquire practically limitless power by the simple expenditure of funds without legislative authority or control; indeed, based solely upon an item in the Appropriation Act.

I would expect that this principle, which has been employed in the establishment of the Australian Legal Aid Office, would be of real concern to the legal profession. In addition to this important constitutional aspect, I am concerned about the whole scheme in relation to the independence of the legal profession — a vital matter. As I have said on a number of occasions, 'if the profession loses its independence who stands between the citizen and the almighty state?'

I have also noted the view expressed by Mr Richard Searby QC, that the Australian Legal Aid Office is operating outside the limits imposed by the Constitution. In addition, Mr Searby has expressed doubts whether the Law Institute or individual practitioners would, without my fiat, have locus standi to institute proceedings to curtail the activities of that organisation.

If an application for my fiat was made, the decision as to whether it ought to be granted or not must depend upon a proper consideration of all the circumstances surrounding the application. However, upon what has emerged and having regard to previous experience there would at present appear to be sound grounds for a fiat to be allowed.

In view of the importance of the matters, I thought I should convey my views to you.

Yours sincerely,

V. F. Wilcox
Attorney-General.

The letter was of great tactical advantage to the anti-ALAO forces. Not only would those attending the meeting be in no doubt as to the prospects of getting the challenge off the ground, but they also would be in no doubt as to the Victorian Attorney-General's stand on the issues. A group of Victorian lawyers who accepted the need for a body to handle low-income cases organised against the anti-ALAO group and managed to prevent them getting the necessary 75 per cent majority required at the general meeting of 20 February. But in a postal referendum of the Institute's members following the meeting, the tables were turned and the opponents of the ALAO succeeded in gaining the simple majority that a plebiscite required. (The motion calling on the Institute's council to resist nationalisation of the profession was passed by 1396 votes to 548 in this referendum.) Wilcox then granted his fiat, adding an assurance that the Victorian government would meet all costs of the action.

Even while this action was pending, another assault was mounted on the ALAO from a different direction. The Law Society of the ACT initiated a challenge in the ACT Supreme Court to the right of ALAO lawyers to represent their clients in the ACT courts. The Supreme Court upheld the challenge on the grounds that a public service lawyer could not devote himself exclusively to the interests of his client because of his duty to his department. It was possible to overcome this problem through legislation in the ACT, where the federal government's powers are plenary. But it would not have been possible to completely negate the ruling if it were used as precedent in the States, where the federal government lacked the power to legislate the problem away. From that time on, therefore, the ALAO's position was precarious: until the Legal Aid Bill became law, the ALAO faced the problem of having its lawyers unable to represent their clients. And there was the Catch 22 — the Opposition in the Senate was not likely to pass the Bill without emasculating amendments. Even if the Victorian Law Institute's High Court challenge failed, the government was probably precluded from continuing the ALAO in its non-statutory form and it did not have the numbers to ensure the continued existence of the ALAO in statutory form.

It was a potent example of the tenacity and resourcefulness of the forces opposed to the Labor government. And while these forces did not halt the operation of the ALAO, they had ensured that it was not so firmly established as to be able to survive under a less sympathetic regime — that regime of their own which had been watching and waiting throughout Labor's time in office.

These detailed examples of opposition to Labor's programs — Medibank, the AGIC and the ALAO — were no more than examples of an overall pattern of obstruction.

In retrospect the most effective feature of this opposition, which was always fierce and persistent, was the way in which the familiar trilogy — Senate, State governments, private interest groups — meshed together to form a web from which few major initiatives emerged intact. There is no doubt that the Senate was the fulcrum of this campaign and that the attitude of the LCP Opposition in the Parliament — that Labor was not a valid or legitimate government — encouraged other groups in the community to adopt this view. When it found itself unable to implement its programs, the government became increasingly frustrated and desperate to find a way around the impasse. Moreover the Senate's ever-present ability to block supply led to regular periods of administrative paralysis and political neurosis inside the government. As the government began to disintegrate in 1975, in large measure due to this campaign of obstruction and destabilisation, it made it even easier to argue that Labor had had no right to hold office at any time.

8   The paper chase
The loans affair

On 13 December 1974 it was still more than six months before the full impact of the loans affair would strike the government. As that night demonstrated, the loans affair had its origins in the forces outside and inside the government which had bedevilled it for two years. On the one hand it was an attempt to bypass a hostile Senate and State governments by going outside Parliament and the Loan Council. On the other, it represented in part the product of intense rivalry between sections of the bureaucracy, in which ministers themselves became embroiled.

But if the loans affair arose out of these kinds of forces it was also to intensify them seriously during 1975. For a government that faced the possibility of an election every six months, the affair provided a climate where the blocking of supply to force such an election was given political feasibility — and then it provided, though hardly necessary, a final triggering of the Opposition's resolve. For a party thrust into an election campaign, the affair proved to be a damaging liability by itself, an image that reinforced the Opposition's other allegations, and ultimately a debilitating and divisive legacy within the party's own ranks for at least two years afterwards. These were the external consequences.

Within the government it removed much of 1975 from the area of administration to that of survival. For weeks and then months at a stretch after May that year, ministers, staff and senior bureaucrats in key departments devoted most of their time to propping up the government's crumbling credibility, only to find, often within a matter of days, that all their efforts had been eroded anew. In this atmosphere, the formulation of policy and the implementation of long term programs was abandoned and finally took on an air of futility as an election became more likely. At the height of the storm, in June and July, even the most basic day-to-day administrative tasks were delayed until columns of urgent files climbed towards the ceiling in ministerial offices and unanswered correspondence spilled out of in-trays.

These political events had their origin in a chain of bizarre personalities which in late 1974 stretched between London and Canberra. On one side this chain ran through Gerry Karidis, an Adelaide builder and businessman; to Tibor Shelly, an Adelaide opal exporter; to a Hong Kong import and export firm, Thomas Yu and Associates; to Theodor Cranendonk, a Dutch commodities dealer; and finally to Tirath Khemlani, Pakistani national and manager of Dalamal and Sons (Commodities) Limited of Eaton Place, London. On the other side it ran to Clyde Cameron, then Minister for Labor and an acquaintance of Karidis to Rex Connor and then to Gough Whitlam and the Lodge in Canberra on 13 December 1974.

On 11 November 1974 Khemlani had arrived at Parliament House in Canberra, having travelled this human chain from London. He was introduced to Cameron by Karidis and to Connor by Cameron. The possibility of the Australian government's borrowing large sums from Arab sources was discussed. The figure mentioned was US$4000 million — to be obtained in blocks of US$500 million repayable at the end of 20 years. Armed with a letter signed by Hewitt stating that the government was 'interested' in such an amount, Khemlani left Australia next day. Over the next month he kept in close contact with Connor's Parliament House office by telex and assured him that the first US$500 million would be delivered before 9 December — five days before Whitlam was scheduled to leave Australia on a six-week overseas trip.

Khemlani arrived back in Sydney on 7 December with Cranendonk, to be met by Hewitt and Karidis and taken to Connor in the Australian government offices in Chifley Square. With Connor was Dennis Rose of the Attorney-General's Department. Hewitt had asked Harders the day before to supply a financial lawyer and Harders had sent Rose, probably the best mind in the department and the person who advised Treasury on all legal questions relating to overseas loans. On the preceding day Hewitt had canvassed the possibility of a substantial sum being borrowed either by the government itself or on the government's behalf by a statutory corporation such as the PMA, the Pipeline Authority, the Atomic Energy Commission, the Reserve Bank, or the Commonwealth Trading Bank (CTB). Rose put his view on both occasions that all of these involved legal problems, most particularly in relation to the bypassing of the Loan Council where the approval of a number of States would be required. Connor replied brusquely that the loan was to be obtained without the involvement of the States or the parliament and that it could be done by the Reserve Bank.

Next day, Sunday, the meeting continued with discussion centering on Khemlani's claim to a 2.5 per cent commission on the loan. At Harders' instigation, Solicitor-General Maurice Byers was consulted. He supported Rose's view that borrowing by the Reserve Bank would have to be subject to Loan Council approval. On Monday morning the negotiations had shifted to Canberra. Everyone assembled in Whitlam's office — Whitlam, Connor, Murphy, Cairns, Byers, Hewitt, Harders, Rose — to resolve the deadlock. Harders maintained that it was impossible to proceed without information on Loan Council practice from Treasury and the Reserve Bank. They were not to be brought in, replied Whitlam, with the comment that:

> Minerals and Energy are the only people who can keep a secret these days.

By lunchtime, however, he had capitulated. That afternoon Wheeler attended, with the Governor of the Reserve Bank, Sir John Phillips, and the Chairman of the CTB and former head of Treasury, Sir Roland Wilson. When they departed there seemed to be tentative agreement that the loan could be made to the CTB with the States being informed soon afterwards in the hope that none would challenge the exercise. Two days later, after a meeting of the CTB Board, Wilson wrote to Whitlam expressing serious doubts about this plan.

Meanwhile, Khemlani and Cranendonk remained in Canberra at the Lakeside Hotel. Conscious of their presence and now aware of Wilson's reservations, Connor changed tack and on the Thursday — 12 December — informed the Chairman of the AEC, Bob Boswell, that the Commission would take the loan and that the documents would be finalised the following day. Early on the Friday morning — 13 December — an alarmed Boswell contacted Harders who quickly collected Byers, Rose, Menadue and Wheeler in his office. After this meeting Harders and Rose went to Murphy's office in Parliament House where they explained that in addition to the question of any Loan Council approval, there was some doubt that the AEC was authorised by its own charter to borrow a large sum that it had no intention of using itself.

Murphy's response was that as the money was to be used by the Australian government and not the CTB or the AEC, it should be borrowed directly by the government, adding that Loan Council approval was not necessary because there was no requirement for approval under the Commonwealth-States Financial Agreement where the borrowing was 'for temporary purposes'. At this proposition Harders looked very uncomfortable and Rose expressed flat disagreement. In this state of division, they set off through the corridors of Parliament House to Whitlam's office on the other side of the building where they were to spend the whole of the afternoon together with Connor, Hewitt, Wheeler, Menadue, Byers and Phillips. Hewitt still favoured a borrowing by the AEC as, unlike a borrowing by the Australian government, this would not have to be disbursed by means of parliamentary appropriations but could simply be left on deposit with the Reserve Bank for lending to other bodies like the PMA.

Byers supported Murphy's argument that it would be more realistic if the loan were made directly to the Australian government. There was no doubt, in his view, that the government had the power to borrow the money. It would be an exercise of its executive power — the same advice that he had given that very week with respect to a proposal that the government guarantee the repayment of a loan to the failing construction firm, Mainline Corporation. He was not nearly so confident that such a loan would be 'for temporary purposes' and thus not require Loan Council approval. The term 'temporary purposes', he felt, probably referred to short term loans and, while Murphy's view was arguable, it was a 'long bow'. Might not, Harders had suggested as a solution, the States be persuaded to accept the arrangement by some additional financial assistance from the commonwealth in the immediate future?

Not necessary, Murphy insisted — the real purposes of the loan were temporary — to meet the immediate economic crisis that would be evidenced by unemployment reaching 500,000 in the first six months of 1975 — even though the money would be borrowed for 20 years and used for long-term resource projects. Such a sum could not, he argued, as a matter of international

financial practice, be borrowed for a short period even if that were desirable. In fact Murphy's advice was probably unnecessary. Even if the loan were not for temporary purposes the government did not require the prior approval of the Loan Council to arrange the loan. The Loan Council could have vetoed the actual borrowing later but the votes of the federal government together with the South Australian and Tasmanian State Labor governments would have been sufficient to have had it approved anyway. At this stage, Whitlam halted discussion to announce that the money would be borrowed by the Australian government directly and that a Loan Council meeting would be held early in February 1975 on his return from overseas to ratify the transaction.

Wheeler continued to raise objections. At the end of his patience, Connor explained: 'I am a minister of the Crown'. 'Yes, Minister, and I am a permanent head,' replied Wheeler. Connor responded with terms such as 'temporising' and 'prevarications'. But it was Whitlam who cut Wheeler off with the remark: 'Fred, you are on the skids'.

One question still remained in dispute — the payment of Khemlani's commission. Khemlani was not authorised to conduct any negotiations on behalf of the government, merely to discover available funds, but he was nevertheless seeking a 2.5 per cent commission. This could not be paid directly by the government if parliamentary appropriations were to be avoided. Nor could it be paid, Khemlani was adamant, by the unnamed Arab lenders as he did not want them to know the size of his commission. The result was a compromise in which the commission would be deducted by lenders but Khemlani was not named as intermediary in the documents. It should be noted that, while no parliamentary appropriations are necessary to obtain a loan, they are necessary to spend the money. There was no possibility, therefore, of using loan funds to get around a blocking of supply by the Senate even if they were obtained.

Murphy told Rose to have documents prepared by 9 pm for an Executive Council Meeting which would authorise the loan later that night at the Lodge. After insisting that Harders confirm

Opposite: Sir Frederick Wheeler, permanent head of the Treasury 1971-79, on his way up the front steps of Parliament House, Canberra

Murphy's orders, Rose returned to the Attorney-General's Department at 7 pm to prepare the material, together with Byers, Harders, Wheeler and officers of Treasury and Minerals and Energy. Not until 11 pm did they appear at the Lodge to join Whitlam, Connor, Murphy, Hewitt and Menadue in the dining room. After more than an hour's discussion, much of it acrimonious as Wheeler insisted that Connor and not Cairns, who was still at the ALP National Executive Meeting a few rooms away, be the minister authorised to raise the loan. Finally an Executive Council minute authorising the loan and specifying Connor as the relevant minister was signed by Whitlam, Connor, Murphy, and finally by Cairns who appeared at the very end of proceedings. Around 1 am, the ministers returned to socialise with the National Executive delegates and the officials drove off into Canberra's suburbs.

Next morning, while Sir John Kerr was adding his signature of approval to the minute at Admiralty House in Sydney, Whitlam flew out of Australia with a large party that included Hewitt. Khemlani left for London on 16 December. For the rest of that week in Canberra, Karidis and Cranendonk attended meetings with Attorney-General's, Treasury, and Minerals and Energy. Khemlani had promised that the funds would be available through the Union Bank of Switzerland, and Attorney-General's engaged lawyers in Zurich, where the Union Bank was located, to advise on the documentation. A set of steps to conclude the deal had actually been prepared on the assumption that the funds would be available on 16 December.

The program provided for Connor to sign the loan agreements on 16 December and for an acceptance and promissory note to be telexed the same day to the Union Bank. By 18 December the Union Bank should have notified Connor that the money was available and could be transferred to a nominated account. It was then necessary that by 25 December the Federal Reserve Bank of New York approve the transaction, because of its implications for the Australian Reserve Bank's holdings there, and that an authorised Australian official, probably the Australian Ambassador to Switzerland, sign the promissory note for a draft drawn by the Swiss National Bank on the Federal Reserve Bank of New York. That draft would finally be exchanged for a transfer by telex of the funds from the Union Bank to the Federal Reserve Bank of New York.

By the middle of the week, the simmering dispute between

Treasury and Minerals and Energy had erupted anew, and
Treasury was excluded from all discussions on Connor's orders.
He was incensed at its attempts to frustrate the deal but
Treasury's objections were inevitable. They had two chief
grounds — first, that overseas loan raising had always been an
exclusive function of Treasury and this area of territorial
supremacy was now being undermined and, second, that the use
of Khemlani would expose Australia, and Treasury as its usual
loan negotiator, to ridicule in the world of international finance.

Connor now discovered that with Whitlam absent and Cairns
Acting Prime Minister, Wheeler was in a new position of
strength. He convinced Cairns of the need for a general meeting
to resolve these disputes and this was set down for 8.30 am on
Saturday 21 December 1974 at the Reserve Bank offices in
Canberra. In addition to Cairns and Wheeler from Treasury,
Connor, Murphy, Menadue, Phillips, Rose and a number of
Minerals and Energy officials attended. At the outset, Connor
explained that the previous night he had communicated with the
Union Bank but it had disclaimed any knowledge of Khemlani
and expressed amazement at the proposed transaction. Cairns'
response was to direct that all dealings with Khemlani cease and
that Whitlam be informed in London. Connor agreed without
argument and allowed a telex to be sent that day to Khemlani in
his name stating that the loan would not be pursued further.
Treasury followed up this success by drafting, for Cairns'
signature, an Executive Council minute revoking Connor's
authorisation of 13 December. This revocation was approved by
the Executive Council on 7 January 1975.

That day Khemlani was meeting Hewitt in Paris at the Hotel
Crillon and explaining that the funds were lying in another
Zurich Bank and two New York banks. Connor had telephoned
Khemlani on 22 December to tell him that the loan was still
wanted and he had also arranged the meeting in Paris.
Throughout January the telex in Connor's Parliament House
office clattered out messages to and from Khemlani. Karidis, and
some of Connor's staff, often slept fitfully on couches in the
office, waiting all night for a message and leaving exhausted in
the morning as most other staff were arriving at work. Khemlani
himself arrived in Canberra on 29 January and with Connor and
Hewitt waited by the telex machine until 4.30 am for news of the
availability of the funds — without result. In anticipation of this
visit definitely producing the money, Connor's authorisation of

13 December had been re-issued on 28 January by an Executive
Council consisting of Kerr, Connor, and Murphy, in exactly the
same terms except that the amount specified was not US$4000
million but US$2000 million.

A few weeks earlier Khemlani had suggested a solution to the
deadlock caused on one side by the government's refusal to
commit itself until it was assured that funds were available and
on the other, according to Khemlani, by the unnamed lenders'
refusal to deposit any funds until the government agreed to
accept the loan. His proposal was that both the lenders and the
borrowers appoint a bank to act as trustee for them in the loan
arrangements. The bank acting as trustee for the Australian
government would then ascertain the existence of the loan funds
and manage their transfer to a nominated account. Khemlani
stated that the Moscow Narodny Bank of London was prepared
to act as trustee for the Australian government in this matter.
And in anticipation of dividing the spoils, he and Cranendonk
had drawn up an agreement in Amsterdam allocating the
expected US$40 million commission among ten people. Of the
US$40 million, Dalamal and Sons were to receive US$7.5
million, Karidis and Cranendonk US$7 million each, and Shelley
US$3 million.

Khemlani returned to London on 30 January but was back in
Canberra for one day on 7 February and for a week towards the
end of that month. The First National Bank of Seattle in Zurich
was now proposed as the place where the funds were to be
assembled, with the Moscow Narodny Bank still acting as
trustee. In March Khemlani made three visits to Australia, and
the Overseas Development Bank of Geneva replaced the Seattle
Bank in the scheme. He was now also talking about US$8000
million without any dissent from Connor.

During this period the negotiations seemed a well kept secret
— from most persons inside the government, let alone outside.
But there had been a sole warning that the Opposition had access
to at least some information from one of the departments
involved. On 13 February shadow Treasurer Phillip Lynch had
asked Connor at Question Time:

> Is the Government engaged in seeking massive overseas loan funds
> from the Middle East? If so, will he make a full explanation to the
> House?

And in the Senate shadow Minister for Manufacturing Industry,

Bob Cotton, had asked government Leader, Ken Wriedt:

> Is it a fact that the Australian Government is negotiating to borrow
> up to $A2000m from the Arab countries of the Middle East? Is it
> also a fact that in these negotiations the Russian Moscow Narodny
> Bank Ltd is the intermediary?

Matters relating to the currency could not be discussed, Connor
replied and sat down. Wriedt, a quietly-spoken Tasmanian who
had succeeded Murphy as Senate Leader and held the post of
Primary Industry Minister, was able to express simple
ignorance. Not until 23 April would the Opposition raise the
matter again.

In the first week of April Treasury made another effort to halt
the negotiations. They were provided with concrete evidence of
their continuation in the shape of a cable from the Australian
Ambassador to Switzerland, Keith Brennan, who had been
approached by Khemlani using Connor's name and had called
Connor to verify the relationship. On 3 April he reported to the
head of Foreign Affairs in Canberra, Alan Renouf:

> Since my 0.10344 the Minister for Minerals and Energy has spoken
> to me on the telephone. Apparently Khemlani is an agent of the
> lenders not of the Australian Government. He will arrange funds
> and Mr Connor will actually sign the Loan Agreement next week in
> London. I have asked the Minister to telegraph to me the text of the
> letter that I am to send. Please ensure that whatever instructions I
> receive have all the approval needed. The amount of the loan is four
> billion United States dollars.

Apart from Renouf, only Hewitt and Menadue were on the
distribution list for the cable but Treasury obtained a copy and
persuaded Cairns who was in Melbourne to send the following
telex to Connor in Canberra that evening.

> I was notified this evening (3 April) of receipt of two telegrams from
> our Ambassador in Switzerland . . . Informed of the previous
> decision that documentations relating to this borrowing proposal was
> to be examined by Treasury Reserve Bank Attorney-General's
> Department and Department of Minerals and Energy before any
> arrangements were entered into. I strongly suggest that before any
> further action is taken, including despatch of any letter by
> Ambassador Brennan, matter should be discussed by the Prime
> Minister you and me plus appropriate officials.
> I am sending a similar message to the Prime Minister.

Both Connor and Whitlam disregarded the suggestions.
Treasury had failed again.

The telexes continued to flow between Connor's office in Parliament House and Dalamal and Sons in Eaton Place, London. By the end of April, Khemlani's proposal was for the Bank of America in San Francisco to transfer funds in its Luxembourg branch to the Deutsche-Iranian Handelsbank in Hamburg where they would be available to the Australian government, presumably after examination by the Overseas Development Bank of Zurich.

It was at this time, that the information dam began to crack. On 23 April Lynch asked Connor at Question Time:

> Did the Minister for Minerals and Energy receive authority from the Executive Council to borrow up to $4,000m overseas? Was the borrowing limit subsequently reduced to $2,000m by decision of the Executive Council signed by the Governor-General and the Minister himself? Why has this unprecedented authority been given to the Minister for Minerals and Energy? Finally, is it a fact that senior Treasury officials have been urging the Government to rescind this authority?

The Opposition had obviously obtained at least one reliable source within Treasury and on 13 May Cotton asked Senator Wriedt:

> My question is addressed to the Minister representing the Treasurer. Is it a fact that the Australian Government, through the Minister for Minerals and Energy, Mr Connor, is seeking to negotiate an overseas loan of $2,000m? If that is the case, is not such a loan in breach of the financial agreement between the Commonwealth and the States as it appears to be something to finance a deficit?

All that was conceded in the answers to these questions was that Connor was authorised to raise the loan. Accordingly Fraser asked Whitlam on 20 May:

> I ask the Prime Minister: Can he inform the House whether the proposed $2 billion borrowing by the Minister for Minerals and Energy has the approval of the Australian Loan Council? If not, when will the Government seek approval of the Loan Council? What is the purpose of the loan?

And received the answer:

> The answer to the first question is no; to the second, if and when the loan is made; to the third, for matters related to energy.

The next day Fraser asked whether the energy purpose was a uranium enrichment plant. Whitlam replied in one line:

> The authority has been revoked.

And it had been revoked — at an Executive Council meeting the previous evening after Treasury had pointed out that the government was to borrow US$100 million in New York through regular channels in the next few weeks and US law required it to have no other loan proposals outstanding at the same time. The reason was a formal one only and Connor had certainly not abandoned the venture. Question Time next day — 24 May — marked the start of the public debate. The Opposition was clearly aware of Khemlani's existence and his use of the 13 December documents. Over the next week he appeared in the press as the mysterious Pakistani money broker, and the London correspondents of the major Australian newspapers haunted his Eaton Place office in an effort to question him.

It became apparent on 28 May that the Opposition's access to Treasury was not simply good but in some respects better than the government's. Lynch asked Whitlam if he was aware that some time ago the Treasury representative in London had obtained a report on Khemlani from Scotland Yard. Whitlam expressed ignorance but when he checked with Wheeler after Question Time discovered that Lynch was correct. The incident provoked him into one of the several attempts made to dislodge Wheeler at about this time. Aware that the Public Service Act makes no real provision for the removal of permanent heads, he sought Harders' advice on the possibility of compulsory retirement for Wheeler, who was 61. Harders advised that the Act did provide for compulsory retirement for persons over 60 but only on the recommendation of the Public Service Board, not the minister. There was a more drastic course of action available — Treasury could simply be abolished and instantly re-established under another name, say the Department of Economic Affairs, with all employees except Wheeler transferred to the new department — but it was evidently too drastic for Whitlam and he abandoned the idea, at least temporarily.

Two weeks later on 12 June, Wheeler again came under pressure when Labour Minister James McClelland produced in the Senate a minute from a Minerals and Energy officer to Hewitt in which it was alleged that Wheeler had obtained the Scotland Yard report in December 1974 and deliberately concealed it from ministers. On the other hand, McClelland said cynically, Treasury material regularly found its way into the hands of the Opposition. To have a senior minister try to

Sir Clarence Harders, permanent head of the Attorney-General's Department 1970- , walking from his office to Parliament House

discredit a permanent head in the parliament with material provided by another department was certainly an extraordinary way of effecting personnel changes in the public service. It was also quite ineffective. Wheeler sat tight and survived.

What was demonstrated by this incident — and was generally not appreciated by those who attempted to cut Treasury off from all information relating to the loan negotiations — was that it had its own information network in the world's financial capitals and this made it almost impossible to shut Treasury out. Early in May, for example, the Paris Branch of the Bank of Montreal was approached in relation to the Connor loan by a French merchant bank. The Paris branch passed this material on to its London Branch which in turn sent it to the Reserve Bank's London Office. From there the information went straight to the Treasury representative in London and on to head office in Canberra. In addition to illustrating the extent of Treasury's resources, the exercise also indicates the attitude of Treasury and its official bank contacts to fringe financial operators like Khemlani, as captured in one of those communications:

Bank of Montreal
47 Threadneedle Street
London
EC2D 8AM

H.N. Little
Regional Vice-President Operations
Europe, Middle East and
Amca Division

May 15th, 1975

Dear Mr Forsyth,
Referring to our conversation on the telephone on Tuesday, I enclose for your ever-growing file all the various pieces of paper which came to hand from our Representative in Paris. Happily I had already expressed the view to him that it was nonsense so no action is called for anywhere — I hope.

Yours sincerely,

H.N. Little.

R.A.J. Forsyth, Esq.,
Chief Representative in London,
Reserve Bank of Australia,
10 Old Jewry,
London, EC2R 8DT.

It was also Treasury's foreign service which provided the material for Cairns' dismissal from the ministry. On 6 June Cairns had lost the Treasury and become Minister for the Environment. Two days before, in the House, he had tabled letters that he had given to George Harris but denied in answer to Opposition questions that there was another letter containing a reference to a 2.5 per cent commission on any loan funds taken up by the Australian government. On 9 June, in Washington DC, Treasury's representative in that city was given a copy of the 2.5 per cent letter by the Vice-President of a New York banking firm which had been approached by Harris in March when he was in the US. The text of the letter was cabled to Canberra the same day and gave Whitlam a traditional reason for removing Cairns as a minister — that Cairns had misled Parliament — to supplement his personal concern at Cairn's presence in the Cabinet and at the business activities of Cairn's stepson who was also his Private Secretary. Cairns did not appear to regard the incident or the threat of dismissal as serious, suggesting that he had signed the letter but had not read it. The result was that when Whitlam announced his decision on 2 July, Cairns refused to accept it. Whitlam's response was to drive out to the Governor-General's residence at Yarralumla at 8 pm that evening and have Kerr withdraw Cairns' commission as a minister of the Crown. In the Caucus meeting that followed, Cairns retained some of his old support but not enough. Whitlam's decision was ratified and Crean replaced Cairns as Deputy Prime Minister.

This was a week from which the government would never recover. Beginning on 1 July, Cairns and Connor loan stories alternated on the front pages of the nation's press. The flood of material, true and false, was led by the Melbourne *Age* and its coverage for that week gave some indication of why opinion polls later recorded the government's support during this period at an all-time low of 33 per cent. On 1 July the *Age* headlined Phillip Cairns' involvement in Arab loan negotiations to finance land development in Melbourne's western suburbs. The next day it led with telexes that referred to a US$600,000 commission for Phillip Cairns, and introduced an exotic cast of characters that included Eric Farnborough Sear Cowls, self-described bullfighter, CIA agent and management consultant, and 'Uncle

Harry' Gilham who ran a one-man finance organisation out of Bulldog Drummond's London address. It was this material that had been the subject of a wild auction conducted in London between the representatives of the *Age* and the *Australian* to be finally knocked down to the *Age* for £5000. The crowded front page also carried a 'Please Explain' letter from Whitlam to Cairns concerning the 2.5 per cent Harris letter. On 3 July it was 'WHITLAM SACKS CAIRNS'. The admission of Sear Cowls that he had fabricated his account of Phillip Cairns' US$600,000 commission was lost in the welter of surrounding sensations.

On 4 July Connor's $4000 million loan took over in the headlines with allegations of a US$180 million commission, an early telex from Connor to Khemlani, and copies of five cheques, each made out to 'Bearer' for US$20 million and drawn on the London branch of the First National City Bank, which had been sent by Khemlani to a Zurich financier on the basis that they would be cashed when the loan came through. The front page of the following day carried a story from London of an offer of $A2 million from an undisclosed Australian source for other loan documents. There was also a report of alleged discussions — never substantiated — by Cairns in the Philippines in April relating to a US$9 million reclamation scheme for the city of Manila by a Sear Cowls company. By 8 July the Connor loan had taken over again and the front page reproduced Hewitt's letter to Khemlani of 3 December 1974.

Unable to dispel with denials either the aura of impropriety created by these real and imaginary transactions or the impression of instability conveyed by Cairns' removal, Whitlam reacted on Friday 4 July with a gambler's last throw — a special sitting of the House of Representatives the next week, on 9 July — where he would be on his home ground, the floor of Parliament, for an all-out effort to restore the government's credibility. Parliament had adjourned on 12 June until 19 August for the winter recess and it had originally appeared that this would provide a period, free from the daily pressure of Question Time, to defuse the loans issue.

At Menadue's direction a small group in the Prime Minister's Department made efforts to obtain a comprehensive set of loans material from Connor and his department so that it could be examined for its legal implications by Attorney-General's. Even this exercise was unsuccessful as they were unable to obtain much of the documentation. It was still a strategy based on secrecy and therefore destined, despite its aim, to maximise the damaging quality of information as it filtered slowly but surely to the Opposition and into the press. This clandestine atmosphere ensured that the legal implications of any documents published were politically irrelevant and indeed made their very existence and the means by which they had been obtained the issue of credibility.

Menadue had one incidental motive in this approach. He had always had reservations about Connor, whose presence in the ministry he saw as one of the government's central problems, and he had attempted to quietly gain for his own department an input into the formulation process for minerals and energy policy. Up to that time he had made little impact on the formidable Connor/Hewitt machine and a frontal assault on their position appeared too dangerous until some time later. He did, however, at this time ask both Hayden and Enderby to demand further information on the loan negotiations from Connor in the hope that he would respond, as he often had in the past when pressed, by offering to resign if he was not given a free hand. Menadue hoped to arrange that, on this occasion, Connor's bluff would be called and his resignation accepted. Summing up the situation, Connor for once employed every tactic but a threat of resignation.

With Cairns' removal from the Cabinet, any assault on Connor's position became dangerous to the government as it could scarcely afford the dismissal or resignation of another senior minister within a matter of days or weeks. In preparing the government's case for the special sitting on 9 July this realisation led to the brutal conclusion that Cairns, already politically dead, should not be defended at all but that Connor's position had to be preserved at all cost. As the day of the sitting approached, it became apparent that part of the cost might well be that not even those inside the government would be aware of all Connor's dealings with Khemlani and that therefore the possibility would remain of further damaging disclosures at a later date.

There was even at this stage some consideration of the Opposition's proposal that a Royal Commission be set up to inquire into the loans. Some ministers supported the idea and Attorney-General's prepared a list of the arguments for and against for Menadue:

Points for Setting up a Royal Commission

1. The Opposition would find it more difficult to use the loan controversy as the reason for refusing Supply — especially if the Budget itself is difficult to oppose.
2. To set up a Royal Commission would be a responsible step.
3. Publicly, the heat would be taken out of the controversy for the time being.
4. In Parliament, the controversy would be put aside, for the time being — provided that there is no disputation about the terms of reference.
5. If a Royal Commission is not set up the Senate may be recalled, and the Opposition might now be ready to support Senator Steele Hall in setting up a Senate Select Committee.
6. While a Senate Committee could not compel a member of the House of Representatives to appear before it, the Solicitor-General, Heads of Departments and other Departmental officers could be summoned. Difficult legal and political questions could arise regarding their attendance, their compellability to answer questions and to produce documents.
7. If there were to be a change of Government the new Government might pursue the matter to the point of setting up a Royal Commission, even at that stage.
8. Generally, the pressure from the Opposition and the press may be very difficult to resist. If there is to be a Commission, the sooner it is established the better.
9. If there is to be no Commission, some alternative course of action would have to be sought that would satisfy the public and the Opposition.

Points against Setting up a Royal Commission

1. To agree to a Commission would be to bow to pressure from the Opposition — but this cannot be decisive.
2. The terms of reference would have to be reasonably acceptable to the Opposition.
3. It seems very difficult to formulate terms of reference that make the matter a suitable one for enquiry by a Royal Commission of Judges.
4. It would be one thing to have terms of reference relating to illegal action and breaches of the law — but this is not the nub of the matter because it seems highly unlikely that Ministers at least have been involved in breaches of the law. What is really involved is the method employed by Ministers in seeking to negotiate loans. This is a political matter and the appropriate forum for consideration of it is the Parliament.
5. A Royal Commission would require the attendance of the Prime Minister and other Ministers.
6. A Commission might find itself examining the correctness of the decision to remove Dr. Cairns from his position as a Minister.

7. The Khemlani matter would have to be included in the terms of
    reference (but this is not a decisive consideration because, if
    there is no Royal Commission, the Khemlani matter will
    undoubtedly be pursued in the Parliament, including pursuit by
    a Senate Select Committee).

8. Is there any alternative — consider having a full-scale and
    comprehensive debate in Parliament, including the production
    of documents — but consider also whether there would be any
    risk of Government members crossing the floor or of absenting
    themselves, thereby leading to the defeat of the Government in
    the House.

9. A Royal Commission would result in headlines week after week
    while the Commission was hearing evidence. This could have
    an adverse effect on the functioning of Parliament.

10. If the Government were to set up a Royal Commission it could
    scarcely claim privilege in respect either of documents or of oral
    evidence. Departmental files could not be refused and officers
    would have to be free to give evidence of all relevant matters.

Whitlam had the last word:

> It will run for months and we will never be off the front pages.

So it was to be Parliament on 9 July.

In the four days available for preparing its case, Whitlam's
office worked around the clock, assisted by advisers to other
ministers and key officials in Prime Minister's, Treasury and
Attorney-General's, who scrutinised every available document
prepared in connection with the loans and every reference
already made to them in Hansard. Although Whitlam had told
Connor to turn over all his files, Harders' concern at the absence
of all relevant information can be gauged from his minute to
Prime Minister's on the morning of 9 July, only hours before the
House was scheduled to assemble at 2pm, in which he referred to
a fresh set of documents produced by Connor the previous
evening:

> I refer to your letter dated 8 July 1975 in which you sought advice
> whether further documents received from the Minister (Financial)
> London, and from the Minister for Minerals and Energy involve any
> commitment to any person on the part of the Australian
> Government.
> As I have mentioned to you orally (last night and this morning) the
> further documentation refers to still other documents that we have
> not seen, opens up new areas and may possibly affect aspects of the

matters that we have previously considered. As I have said to you it is not possible to give advice in these circumstances. It is not possible to advise whether any person would have a claim against the Government . . .

I find the situation so confused as to make it impossible to give a clearance for the purposes of the Prime Minister's speech that the arrangements for the borrowing fulfilled all legal requirements. There may well be a satisfactory explanation that the Minister could provide and that would satisfy the legal requirements but the fact remains that there is still a lack of complete documentation and of any relevant oral communications.

Harders was not alone in his concern. At midday, Treasurer Hayden was still refusing to speak in the debate on the grounds that he did not have sufficient information.

But at 2.55 pm Whitlam strode to the bar table of the House to speak. The members on both sides were tense, in contrast to the usual lethargy of parliamentary debate, and every corner of the press and public galleries was crammed with spectators, many of whom found their gaze wandering from the centre of the House to the last row of backbench seats on the government side where Cairns now sat. It was an aggressive speech by Whitlam with alliterative attacks on the press for their use of 'purchased or purloined documents', and on Treasury, the source of 'leaks from the disaffected or the disloyal', and a spirited defence of Connor's loan raising as an attempt to increase Australia's control over its own resources in the face of the determination of foreign corporations, abetted by the Opposition, to take them out of Australian hands. Six months earlier the theme of 'Who owns Australia' might have taken off, but the issue was now that of the internal workings of the government and even Whitlam's formidable oratory could not disguise the disarray at its very heart.

In keeping with the strategy of treating Cairns as politically deceased, Whitlam had made a cursory reference to his dismissal at the beginning of his speech and simply tabled all documents relating to his departure from the Ministry. After Whitlam, Fraser seemed anti-climactic. He was not a powerful speaker and his allegations of illegality and impropriety were predictable. But the galleries remained crowded, waiting for Connor who tabled some documents relating to the negotiations — although none later than 27 January 1975 — and gave the speech that was so accurately caught in its finale:

I treat with contempt the allegations of the Opposition.

After that, people began to drift away, although many returned for Cairns' almost incoherent complaint at his dismissal, heard by both sides of the House in embarrassed silence. Several speakers followed on each side, including Hayden who discussed the economic affects of long term loans and pointedly avoided the Connor negotiations, until 10 pm when the House adjourned for the rest of the interrupted winter recess.

Meanwhile the Senate had also re-convened that afternoon. Whitlam had wanted only the House of Representatives to sit but the Opposition naturally had the chamber in which they had a majority recalled as well. Without spending time on debate, Opposition Senate Leader Reg Withers proposed that unless a Royal Commission was established by the government, the Senate would call before it for questioning on 16 July, Byers, Wheeler, Hewitt and Harders together with seven other departmental officers who had been involved in meetings with ministers relating to loan negotiations. When this proposal was pushed through by the Opposition majority, the Senate adjourned until a week later — 16 July.

Over the next week a major debate took place inside the government as to whether the summoned public servants should be directed not to even attend on 16 July for questioning. The gist of the debate is caught by a table of the arguments for and against supplied to Menadue by Harders on 13 July, the more important of which were:

ATTENDANCE OF WITNESSES

PROS AND CONS

PROS

It is difficult to see any *legal* grounds on which it could be claimed that the summons is contrary to law in so far as it merely requires attendance. The officers concerned are Commonwealth officers and have been served within the jurisdiction and are at present within the jurisdiction.

To instruct officers not to attend would be likely to turn the issue into one of major confrontation between a House of the legislature and the Executive. In such a situation, the Government could be seen to be obstructing ordinary constitutional process on a basis that was (with one distinguishable exception) novel.

If the Senate moved to take action for contempt against any of the non-attending officers, the situation could deteriorate because the Executive may instruct the Police not to enforce the Senate's warrant. This would be likely to cause a major nationwide outcry and do considerable damage to the Government.

Certainly, it can be expected that one or more of the officers will attend and the difficulties of claiming privilege will therefore have to be faced in any event in relation to that officer or officers.

It is a contempt of the Parliament to prevent a witness duly summoned to attend before a House of the Parliament from so attending. Strictly, therefore, any obstruction or attempt to influence a proposed witness could itself be the subject of action by the Senate.

CONS

There is a strong argument that, because of the nature of the inquiry on which the Senate seeks to embark, the Senate is unable to force from officers what it is unable to compel Ministers to produce or reveal.

In particular, the deliberations of the Executive Council are secret and this secrecy must extend, by necessary implications, to deliberations and advice that led up to the recommendations placed before the Executive Council.

As officers could, and would, be instructed to claim privilege, there is no real distinction between permitting them to attend and claim privilege at once and instructing them not to attend with an explanation being sent by the Prime Minister to the President of the Senate.

Politically, the Opposition would place itself in a difficult position if it sought to take punitive action against officers who acted in accordance with the Government's directions. It is more likely that action would be taken by way of resolution of the Senate condemning the Government and claiming that its obstruction confirmed the Opposition's allegations.

Once a witness is before the Senate, it will be difficult to control what the Senate does and, despite all valid objections, claims of privilege in relation to particular questions or matters may be overruled and the officers put in an untenable position.

The ultimate objection to attendance of officers for a purpose such as that in question is that no Government would be workable if an Opposition in the Senate is to be able by its mere numbers to delve into the innermost secrets of the Government by the device of calling officers who are placed in the dilemma of revealing those secrets which they know to be wrong or facing disciplinary action by the Senate in the face of which they are powerless.

Again, the ultimate decision was Whitlam's and, influenced by Harders' own emphasis on the political dangers of a struggle over the use of the ACT Police and his warning that at least one of the officers summoned would refuse a direction not to attend, he ordered that they all appear but then refuse to answer any

questions on loan negotiations, relying on a written direction
from their own minister that would assert, on behalf of the
Crown, the confidentiality of conversations between ministers
and officials advising them. Byers, who as Solicitor-General was
not a public servant, would have to make this argument on his
own behalf. With his essentially traditionalist approach to
government administration and his lack of appreciation for the
Opposition mentality, Whitlam was genuinely concerned in
taking this stand to maintain the existing relationship between
ministers and officials and was outraged that this might be
affected by the Opposition's desire to obtain a short term
political advantage, particularly as he knew that they would
themselves prefer the existing system to survive in the long term
for when they returned to office.

The result on 16 July was a fiasco. Surprised by the claim of
privilege — for once there had been no leak of the government's
tactics — and unable to prise more than their name and position
from Byers and the various permanent heads and other officials
who had each been escorted to a small table with a single chair on
the floor of the Senate by the Usher of the Black Rod, the
Opposition backed away from citing them with contempt. Before
adjourning next day, they agreed to a proposal by Liberal
Movement Senator Steele Hall that Karidis, who would have no
Crown privilege to rely on, be called before the Senate in another
week's time. Karidis did appear then but his combination of
halting English, vague memory and shrewd sense of when to
object to a question, ensured that the cross-examining
Opposition lawyers — Ivor Greenwood and Reg Wright — spent
a frustrating afternoon before abandoning the exercise.

There the loans affair lay at rest, without a single mention
until Question Time in the House of Representatives on
Wednesday 9 October, when Fraser asked Whitlam a strange
question. He asked simply whether Whitlam would re-affirm his
confidence in Connor's administration of his portfolio. Slightly
puzzled, Whitlam said he would — the only possible answer.
Government members did not realise the question was the
opening bid in a game in which Fraser was already holding an
unbeatable hand. The same day, Fraser placed on the Notice
Paper eight questions concerning loan negotiations. That
afternoon, the Melbourne *Herald* carried across its front page the
first of a series of articles based on lengthy interviews with
Khemlani, having taken elaborate precautions in the preceding

weeks to ensure that no news of the intention to publish the articles leaked to the government. In the interview Khemlani insisted that contact with Connor had not ceased in May and that, in fact, he still had Connor's authority to seek a loan. All this was embellished with details of Khemlani's exotic lifestyle and the bizarre code names used in telexes to cloak the parties involved, such as 'The Father' for Whitlam and 'Rock Phosphate' for Connor.

With the Senate vote on the Budget due the next week, Connor was pursuaded to go on the offensive at once in an effort to kill the issue before it took off again. After a visit from Hayden and Menadue he appeared that night on all national television current affairs programs from a bed in the Canberra Hospital where he was recovering from serious influenza, dismissing Khemlani's story and announcing the institution of defamation proceedings against the *Herald*. Over the next few days the furore died down. Back from the brink yet again, but only until the next Monday — 14 October — when the *Herald* administered the *coup de grace* to Connor's career with a reprint of an otherwise innocuous telex from him to Khemlani on 23 May 1975 that read:

> Attention Mr T. H. Khemlani: Response your telex of 0310 of today. I await further specific communication from your principals for consideration. From RFX Connor.

Five days earlier, in an answer to a Question on Notice, Whitlam had told Lynch that 'all communications of substance' between Connor and Khemlani had been tabled on 9 July. As this telex had not been tabled Whitlam was obliged, by his stand on Cairns' answer to another Lynch question, to say that Connor had caused parliament to be misled. But Connor, like Cairns, felt that he should not have been sacrificed on such technical grounds, indeed would not have been sacrificed had there not been other reasons. He refused to agree to resign on the Monday evening and when, at 9.30 am Tuesday morning, he walked into the Caucus meeting, he simply threw down two envelopes with the words:

> Those are my resignation letters to the Governor-General and the Prime Minister, mates. If you're prepared to accept them I'll have to put them in today.

With Whitlam silent, this appeal had an instant effect on Caucus and proposals were made that the resignations not be accepted.

Ultimately they were accepted 'with regret' by an emotional meeting with 24 members still voting for him to continue in office.

So ended the basic record of the loans affair. Next day the Opposition would announce its decision to block the Budget — a decision possibly precipitated by these final events. But that would not be the end of the loans affair for Labor. It would continue to taint the government in the mind of Sir John Kerr who would soon have to decide the government's fate. It would continue to haunt the former government in the election campaign that followed his decision. And it would even continue to affect the Party in its role as the Opposition for some years afterwards.

9 Treason of the clerks?
Labor and the bureaucracy

Two basic administrative problems face any government assuming office — how to secure meaningful control of the machinery of government, and how to direct that machinery effectively towards its own priorities. At the end of 1974, after two years in office, the Whitlam government had largely failed to carry out either of these operations. The difficulty of the task should not be underestimated. The government inherited an unyielding bureaucratic structure which has the one quality that all governments lack — permanency — and consequently has enduring interests, both of policy and procedure, that will be vigorously pursued at all times unless exposed to strong countervailing forces. Labor confronted these competing centres of power on isolated occasions but overall it failed to come to grips with them. It is important therefore, to appreciate how, and why, the government's problems of policy were in fact more often than not problems of administration.

It is possible to get an overview of bureaucratic style, and to consider at the same time the government's only serious effort at administrative reform, by examining briefly the Department of the Prime Minister and Cabinet, that apex of the bureaucratic pyramid.

The Department of the Prime Minister and Cabinet was lodged at this time in an old brick building called West Block immediately behind Parliament House. It had traditionally had two basic functions — to advise the Prime Minister, and to service the Cabinet. But because these functions lacked clear delineation in comparison with those of other departments of state, the department had tended to become the bureaucratic embodiment of each individual Prime Minister's administrative and political methods.

During Menzies' long reign, the two permanent heads (first Sir Alan Brown and then Sir John Bunting) were responsible for drafting and circulating Cabinet agendas, and also for recording and interpreting Cabinet's decisions. The latter task was an important one, for it was not the Menzies' Cabinet's practice to vote on questions put before it. Rather, the Cabinet 'arrived at a consensus' after discussion of the issues. It was up to the permanent head, who attended its meetings as secretary to the Cabinet, to assess the nuances of the consensus.

In keeping with the style of Menzies, Bunting, who succeeded Brown in 1959, was a master of means rather than ends, of procedure rather than policy. What supervision there existed over the activities of other departments was frequently exercised through informal channels, for example the extensive personal contacts in the senior ranks of the public service that Bunting had always maintained. Although the Prime Minister's Department possessed the very important right to chair, and therefore to influence significantly, the work of every inter-departmental committee (IDC), it lacked personnel skilled in particular policy areas such as economics or industrial relations. In practice, therefore, its influence on IDC meetings was often insubstantial, particularly when the IDC was facing internal differences on these kinds of issues.

When John Gorton became Prime Minister in early 1968, he attempted to expand the role of his department. To spearhead this development he appointed Lenox Hewitt as his permanent head, although the price for securing this appointment was the splitting of the department into two — a Department of the Prime Minister under Hewitt, which comprised almost all of the old department, and a 12 man splinter department of the Cabinet Office under Bunting, which was a convenience designed by the Public Service Board and imposed on Gorton to spare Bunting the indignity of total dispossession. Hewitt had been a Deputy Secretary of the Treasury until his appointment in 1966 as head of the Universities Commission, and in his new role at Prime Minister's he installed Treasury men at the number two and three positions.

The department gained further expertise in the key areas of defence and social welfare through recruitment from other departments but its policy capacity still remained limited. Its real influence rested on the vulnerable base of Hewitt's close relationship with Gorton. When Gorton was deposed as Prime

Minister in 1970 and replaced by McMahon, Hewitt was an early casualty — rusticated to the bureaucratic wilderness as head of the lowest department in the hierarchy. Bunting was again appointed to preside over a fused Department of the Prime Minister and Cabinet where the embryonic policy units remained but were not encouraged to intervene in the affairs of other departments.

It was at this stage that Labor and Whitlam came to government. From the beginning, the policy divisions of the department were strengthened and their influence increased principally through intervention in IDCs as member or chairman. But it was the co-ordinating role of the department that assumed major importance in the first two years of the Labor government. The Cabinet branch, with the assistance of relevant policy sections, made an assessment of Cabinet submissions from all other departments in the light of government policy and associated projects. The significance of the assessment lay in its transmission to the Prime Minister as a recommendation as to whether or not the submission should be included on the Cabinet agenda. This role, while a product of Whitlam's heavy administrative demands, was basically inimical to Bunting's idea of how the department should work, and tension between Whitlam and Bunting, and Whitlam's office and Bunting, became evident. Whitlam's long-delayed solution to the problem was the appointment in November 1974 of John Menadue as permanent head to replace Bunting who became the Australian High Commissioner to London.

Menadue's appointment was the culmination of a long association with Whitlam. He was an Adelaide economist who had worked in the Treasury in Canberra from 1953 until 1960, when he joined Whitlam's staff as Private Secretary after Whitlam became Deputy Leader of the Opposition. He stayed seven years with Whitlam and, in those years that were often of seeming hopelessness in Labor's long struggle towards government, he became Whitlam's closest confidant as the ALP suffered a series of electoral disasters and Whitlam endured the personal frustration of struggling to impose his ideas on suspicious colleagues in and out of Parliament. In the 1966 House of Representatives election — Labor's worst result of all in this period — Menadue stood unsuccessfully as the ALP candidate for the NSW seat of Hume. Soon afterwards he left Whitlam to join Rupert Murdoch's News Ltd in Sydney where he rose quickly to the position of General Manager. And from News Ltd Menadue came, at the age of 40, to head the Department of the Prime Minister and Cabinet.

It was not the background of most of Canberra's permanent heads, and the appointment drew the traditional criticism that it aimed to politicise the public service. All of this could have been a severe handicap in dealing with older and more experienced counterparts in other departments but Menadue had a number of natural advantages. Firstly, he had established a significant reputation in business. Secondly, he had a relationship with Whitlam so close that it assured him the opportunity of carrying out his designs. Thirdly, he was determined to go about this task through traditional public service channels. His access to the Prime Minister alone would have guaranteed him respect, even as an outsider, by his public service colleagues who all appreciated just what a unique source of power that was. But the style in which he let it be known he would exercise that power won the co-operation of, and ultimately acceptance by, the mandarins who under other circumstances could have obstructed him almost indefinitely. An important element of this style was, from the beginning, to discourage the use by the government of outside advisers and consultants and, in his own dealings with the Prime Minister, to bypass Whitlam's staff wherever possible. The stormy public departure of Whitlam's adviser on Women's Affairs, Elizabeth Reid, in 1975 was a victory, if a rather bloody one, for Menadue in his efforts to have her policy function based entirely in the department, in the newly-established Women's Affairs Section.

Using the engaging charm and the reassuring conservatism he brought from the business world, Menadue approached the government as he would have a huge commercial enterprise badly in need of co-ordination and rationalisation. Nowhere was the need for co-ordination more urgent than in the area of government expenditures, and in early 1975 the Cabinet Expenditure Review Committee (CERC) was established, comprised of the most senior ministers and supported by a group of officials who were charged with examining all proposed expenditures for the 1975/76 Budget and suggesting where substantial cuts could be made. This group, headed by Eddie Visbord, formerly of Treasury but then of Prime Minister's, was kept in existence and continued its work after the Budget, examining all Cabinet submissions involving future expenditure with a view to keeping the financial proposals of 36 departments under some kind of continuous budgetary supervision. An alliance between Treasury and the Department of the Prime Minister became evident in the CERC officials' group, as it did in the group headed by Ian Castles who had also gone from Treasury to Prime Minister's to draw up the new personal tax scales for the 1975/76 Budget and then turned his attention to producing a plan for guaranteed minimum income levels.

With the success of these groups, a similar structure was used to break Rex Connor's grip on natural resources policy. The device employed was the Resources Committee of Cabinet which was set up in mid 1975 to oversee minerals and energy policy. It was to be supported by an officials' committee made up of the permanent heads of departments with an interest in resources policy, and therefore represented by ministers on the Cabinet committee — Prime Minister's, Treasury, Minerals and Energy, and Foreign Affairs. This committee was chaired by Menadue, who had always had serious reservations about Connor's policies, and was serviced by groups from the various departments. Although Connor was a member of the Resources Committee, the very establishment of this structure meant he could no longer make decisions unchallenged by other departments. Moreover it soon became obvious, particularly to Connor, that the point of the exercise was to achieve an about-face on several of his long-held policies.

A new approach to foreign investment, recognising that 100 per cent Australian-owned enterprise was an unrealistic goal, was one of a number of 'deConnorisations' steered through by Menadue. Soon afterwards, Deputy Prime Minister Frank Crean said publicly that the ban on immediate export sales of uranium — instituted by Connor to drive up the eventual price — was 'a bit silly'. A prerequisite to these developments was the departure of Lenox Hewitt as permanent head of the Department of Minerals and Energy. Hewitt would have bitterly resisted any power-sharing arrangement but, shortly before the Resources Committee was formed, he was appointed Chairman of Qantas Airways and his place at the head of Minerals and Energy was taken by the more conciliatory Jim Scully, formerly Deputy Secretary of the Department of Overseas Trade.

Menadue's most ambitious attempt at turning Prime Minister's into an overall co-ordinating body was the establishment of the Policy Co-ordination Unit (PCU). The aim was to

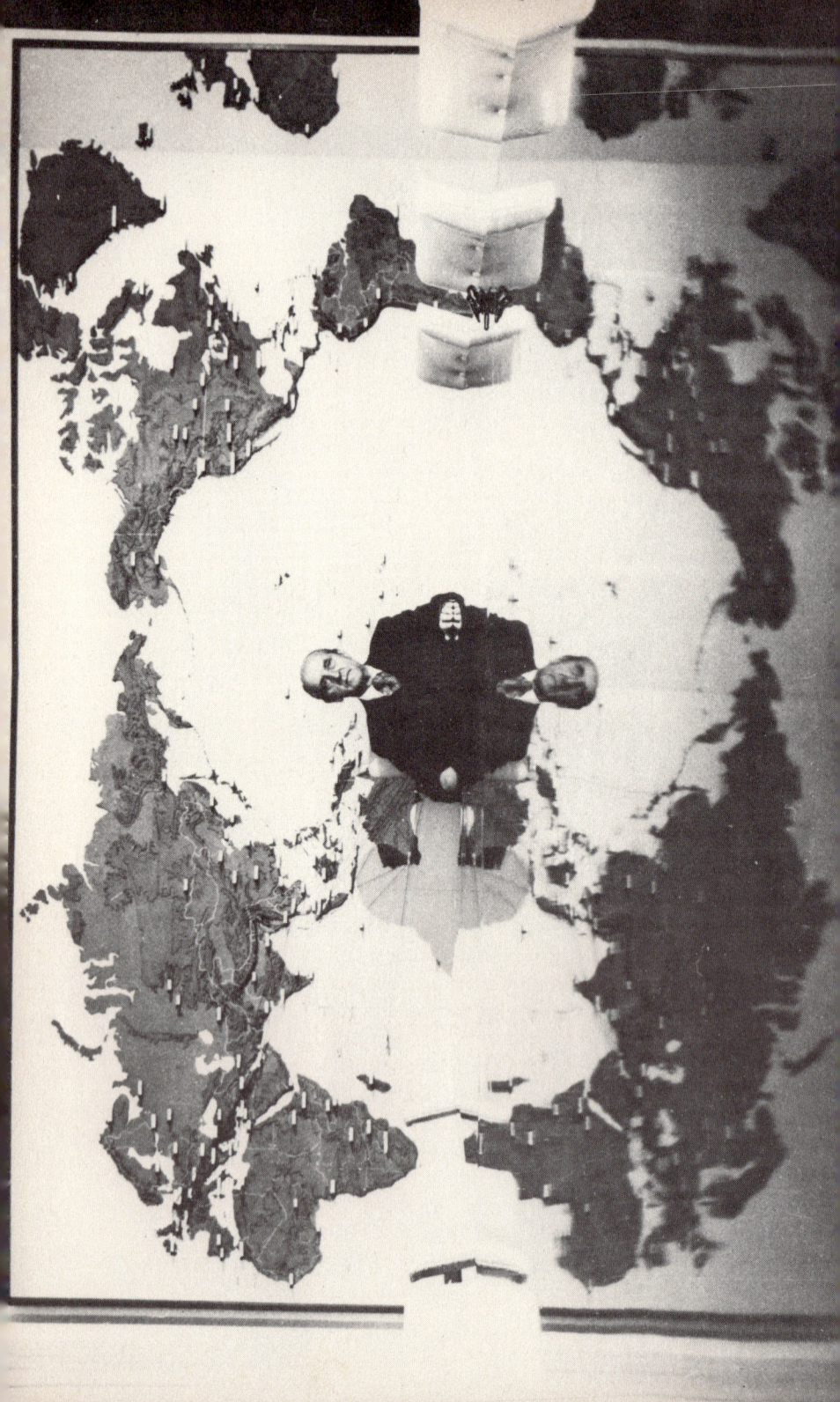

strengthen the department's existing practice of examining all Cabinet submissions by other departments in order to evaluate the arguments advanced and to assess their relation to the policy of the government as a whole. It was headed by John Enfield of Prime Minister's and included two outsiders, Brian Johns, former political correspondent of the *Sydney Morning Herald* who was to tackle the problem of federal/State relations, and Gregory Clark, former Foreign Affairs officer and Tokyo correspondent for the *Australian* who was to work on economic questions, particularly in the natural resources area. In addition it could refer questions to other sections of the department or to private consultants. Yet the PCU was still limited by an overall lack of expertise, given the wide range of subjects it would have to cover. To build such expertise would obviously be a lengthy process if public service recruitment procedures were generally observed. It was therefore impossible for Menadue to quickly convert the department's significant but essentially negative and restrictive effect on policy formulation into a dominating positive influence.

One aspect of administration in which Prime Minister's did become completely dominant under Menadue's direction was that of organising the day-to-day political protection — or sheer survival as it was finally to become — of the government. This meant providing Whitlam with everything necessary to defend the government both inside and outside Parliament and to counter, or where possible to forestall, Opposition offensives on any issue involving the Prime Minister personally or the government's performance generally. On one afternoon in October 1975, for example, it was rumored that the Opposition would move a no-confidence motion in parliament next day criticising the size of the Budget deficit and advocating a 12 per cent cut in government spending. Notes on the consequences of such a 12 per cent cut on existing services, such as welfare and education, were obtained from every department overnight and were processed and ready for use by Whitlam by 10 am the following morning. As it turned out, the motion did not eventuate, but such furious exercises in information retrieval and back-up,

Opposite: Sir Lenox Hewitt, ex-permanent head of the Department of Minerals and Energy, soon after becoming chairman of Qantas Airways

often managed by Geoff Yeend as Deputy Secretary of the department and a former private secretary to Menzies, demonstrated the extent to which the department had become involved in day-to-day questions of political strategy.

Menadue also used Treasury and Attorney-General's extensively for economic and legal contributions to these efforts. It was typical of his style that Hayden as Treasurer and Enderby as Attorney-General were often by-passed and the permanent head approached directly. But the daily pressures of mounting this kind of survival operation during the recurrent crises of the loans affair and then during the blocking of the Budget in October/November 1975 were enormous, particularly in the loans attacks where Whitlam, not Connor or Cairns, was always the Opposition's real target, and in neither of these major exercises was Prime Minister's really successful. The attempt to suppress the loans affair — of which it had been aware from its very beginning — led to the details emerging a morsel at a time in the press, and contributed heavily to the lurid quality that the saga took on. A total disclosure early in 1975 would have been embarrassing but preferable to the death by a thousand cuts that occurred later.

Similarly, the proposal in October to devise alternative arrangements by which the government could continue to pay employees and suppliers after its funds were exhausted was a tactical failure. It actually decreased the pressure on Opposition Senators who were concerned at the prospect of the money running out and also provoked widespread allegations of unconstitutional conduct.

Despite these tactical failures the administrative development of Prime Minister's under Menadue was considerable and the groundwork was laid for the even greater role the department would assume under the Fraser government. Yet at the time of the government's dismissal it was far from performing the comprehensive co-ordinating role that Menadue envisaged for it and that the government so obviously needed in numerous policy areas.

One of the most dramatic manifestations of this problem was the tendency for ministers to act in the vacuum of their own departmental responsibilities without attempting to relate those actions to the overall priorities of the government. Cabinet meetings were themselves studies in this phenomenon with many ministers appearing as delegates from their department, rather than as members of a political executive, and fighting desperately for the extension of departmental power or funds without regard to the relative merits of the issue or its likely effect on the government's fortunes. That few ministers had any notion of fitting their own proposals into a long term government strategy was most strikingly demonstrated during the Cabinet's annual deliberations on the Budget when expenditure for the next year was allocated between the various departments. Most fought tenaciously for their own department's estimates, irrespective of content, and some of these took the view that any criticism of other estimates was imprudent as it invited retaliation when their own submission was considered.

Even at the most elementary levels this approach continued to prevail. Of the multitude of boards, commissions, councils and committees to which a government is required to make appointments some, like the Federal Potato Advisory Committee or the Northern Territory Dental Board, have little political importance while others, like the Reserve Bank Board or the Universities Commission, are significant policy bodies. For none of these was there any attempt to maintain an index of persons qualified for such positions and sympathetic to the government's aims who could be considered when a vacancy arose. The result was that when vacancies did occur a minister's department would advise him of a suitable appointment — one much more likely to reflect its own interests and preferences than the government's — and this advice tended to be taken unless the minister had a particular person in mind himself. When the appointment was mentioned in Cabinet, as most had to be, ministerial colleagues would normally acquiesce, if only on the basis that they did not want their own appointments challenged in the future. This process meant that, even when Labor had an opportunity to replace 23 years of accumulated office-holders with neutral appointees or its own supporters, it often failed to take advantage of the opportunity. It certainly left no similar accumulation for its successors. Not until four months before the government fell was a decision taken to establish a 'talent bank' of suitable appointees for boards, commissions and committees in the Prime Minister's office. Even then the exercise was not given a high priority and, as a system that can only have a significant effect over a period of years as offices fall vacant, it had no impact whatsoever before the government departed.

Perhaps one reason for the inability of ministers to stand back from their department's view and act as a Cabinet instead of a disparate collection of individuals was that overall priorities and long term goals were never discussed in the Cabinet room. Like a computer with 27 programmers, Cabinet produced thousands of unrelated decisions on specific submissions but seldom considered their implications for the government electorally or how they interacted within its long term policies. Although Cabinet was stated in the Caucus rules to be the Executive of the Parliamentary Labor Party, the first meeting of Cabinet at which questions of political strategy were exclusively discussed took place only three weeks before the government fell, during the supply crisis. Into this vacuum flowed the ideas of the Kitchen Cabinet, the four or five ministers chosen by Whitlam to discuss strategy questions with him on a regular basis. At times the Kitchen Cabinet achieved a semi-formal status and some major decisions were taken in these meetings. Yet the frequency of meetings fluctuated widely, as did the membership, with particular ministers going in and out of favour with Whitlam. It was not a situation calculated to develop any sense of collective Cabinet responsibility among those who were never invited, or invited only to be later excluded.

In theory a detailed system of participation by Cabinet and Caucus members existed to overcome problems of communication within the government. A proposal for legislation was supposed to go from the relevant minister (having been prepared by his department) to one of the ten standing committees of Caucus which considered proposals according to subject matter. From these committees, whose membership could range from ten to 30 or 40, the legislation was forwarded, with the consent of the Prime Minister, to the standing Cabinet committee which had responsibility for that area (although any minister could attend) and then to full Cabinet. The Cabinet committee's recommendation was treated as the decision of the Cabinet unless challenged at the full Cabinet meeting. Finally, the legislative proposal went back to a full Caucus meeting for approval before being introduced as legislation into the parliament. Disapproval at any stage in this process meant revising the proposal or appealing directly to the full Caucus. This was the theory.

But after May 1974, none of Cabinet's standing committees — Economics, Welfare, Urban and Regional Development, Foreign Affairs and Defence, or Legislation — met regularly.

They were not disbanded but were replaced for the most part by a multitude of ad hoc committees established to consider a particular proposal. These had the advantage, so far as Whitlam was concerned, of not being open — as standing committees were — to any minister who wished to attend. Given the pressures of time, especially when parliament was sitting, it was therefore possible for a project to escape full scrutiny at any stage of this process. Certainly its relation to the rest of the government's program could be glossed over quickly and problems of implementation or acceptance by the electorate treated too cursorily.

The diversity of advice the government received helped compound this problem. The plethora of departments and statutory bodies with an input into economic policy have already been discussed. Social welfare was another field cluttered with inquiry bodies whose findings were central to the government's welfare policies but whose work was unco-ordinated and, in some cases, at cross-purposes. In addition to the Department of Social Security and the Social Welfare Commission — a statutory body established in 1973 to advise the government on the effectiveness of programs in the welfare field and to recommend new policy proposals — there existed at the beginning of 1974:

- Commission of Inquiry into Poverty
- National Superannuation Committee of Inquiry
- National Committee of Inquiry on Compensation and Rehabilitation in Australia
- Commission on Repatriation
- Taxation Review Committee
- Australian Labour Market Trading Inquiry
- Working Party on Social Welfare Manpower

All these had direct or consequential relation to social welfare policy formulation. It is true that the Poverty Commission and the Repatriation Commission had been established by the previous Liberal government but it was the existence of all these bodies, with their overlapping and conflicting ambits, that made some rationalisation of their activities and proposals crucial for a Cabinet which was ultimately responsible for the policies adopted. And that was where much of the problem lay. Cabinet had the responsibility but very little in the way of long term analysis that drew together the competing sources of advice on all sides.

One approach to the problem would have been to establish service bodies to perform these tasks for Cabinet while acting under

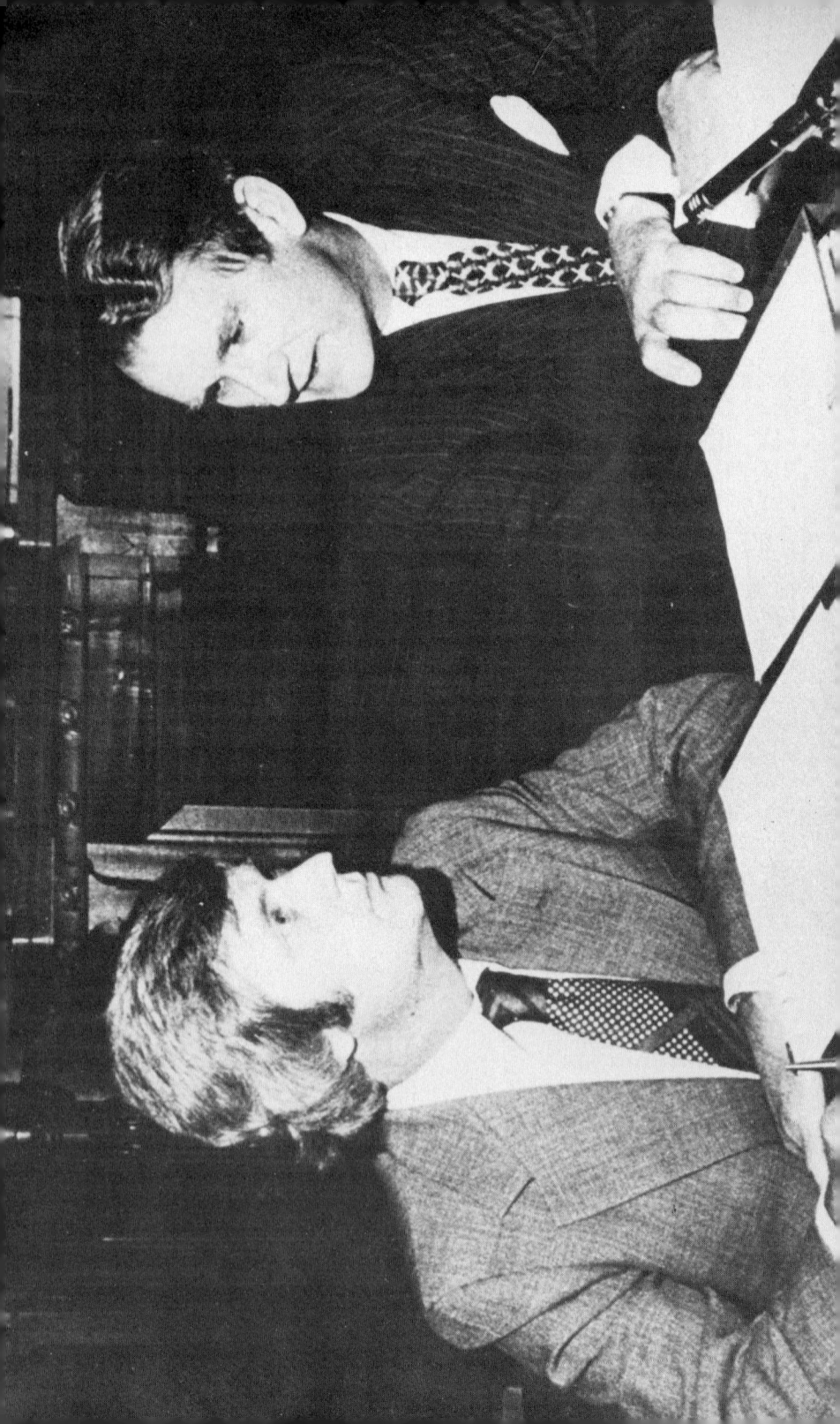

its general direction, but only the PCU approximated this role in any way in its tentative efforts to ensure that the policy proposals of individual departments were related to the government's strategy as a whole. It was nowhere near as high-powered a body as the one on which it was modelled — Harold Wilson's policy unit, created in 1974, which comprised a small group of specialists in various areas of domestic policy who examined all submissions to Cabinet and its committees to inject the government's political values and policy priorities into these proposals for government action. While experienced in administration, the unit's staff were not necessarily civil servants and all were sympathetic to the aims of the government, even if not members of the British Labour Party. Such a requirement in Australia would no doubt draw the usual criticism that it constituted politicisation of the administration — a criticism that of course ignores the fact that any judgment made by any person in the formulation of a policy that will maintain or alter the distribution of power or resources within the community has, by definition, a political connotation.

It would be possible eventually to make this kind of body, functioning in groups that corresponded with Cabinet committees, the central point of co-ordination for policy development — a unit providing Cabinet with a consistent basis for setting priorities and then choosing the best means of achieving the desired end — but only if it were given a much greater and more diverse staff than the PCU and provided that it always retained the total support of the Prime Minister. Even then it would only deal with what went into the Cabinet pipeline, not with how it was later put into operation. What would also be required, therefore, would be a second group along the lines of the first to monitor the carrying out of decisions once made by Cabinet. This second process would logically include a system, also brought into existence by the Wilson administration, under which a small group evaluated government programs in operation through a section in each department set up for the purpose. The findings of this group would be fed into the original policy co-ordination unit to complete the information cycle.

Opposite: John Menadue, permanent head of the Prime Minister's Department 1975-77, advising his second Prime Minister

It is obvious from those aspects of Labor's administration so far discussed that it relied heavily on the traditional structure of the bureaucracy. It is worth emphasising this point if only to contrast the practice of most ministers with their strong contentions before gaining office that they would not rely exclusively on the advice of the public service, as their predecessors had, but would venture much further into the community in search of ideas. There is no doubt that in 1972 the bureaucracy was apprehensive in anticipation of an attempt to dilute the monolithic quality of advice with outside contributions. In the long run their apprehension was unjustified. By 1975 outsiders had chalked up some isolated successes but had not established themselves as a genuine alternative source of advice. They had also gained a new opponent — the most powerful so far — in John Menadue who would discourage non-departmental advisers and neutralise some previously powerful outside influences on ministers.

The rationale for an alternative source of advice had always been that no one group, including the bureaucracy, had a monopoly on ideas and that the formulation of public policy should not be left exclusively to a restricted class. It rapidly became obvious also that departments were confined in the extent to which they would recommend drastic courses for each other, let alone for themselves, by a determination to preserve their own interests and by a consequent reluctance to alienate powerful colleagues unless absolutely necessary. It was for this reason that the hard-fought compromises produced by IDCs were often found to be ineffective for tasks that involved substantial changes to an existing structure of the administration.

The result then, in the first year of the government, was a proliferation of commissions and committees set up to carry out inquiries and make recommendations to the government directly. Many had public servants as members and most relied heavily on the resources of the bureaucracy. They were, however, often able to cut across departmental lines in their inquiries and consider the interests of the administration as a whole. These bodies took a variety of forms. Small task forces were used to report rapidly on a specific question such as the 25 per cent across-the-board tariff cut in 1974. Broader studies were carried out by more elaborate bodies such as the National Compensation Inquiry, or by royal commissions such as the Coombs Commission into Government Administration. In some cases permanent bodies were established to supplement departmental policy proposals as was done with the Social Welfare Commission and the Law Reform Commission. To prevent these bodies representing a continuing threat, departments argued constantly for their assimilation into the bureaucratic structure or 'departmentalisation' as the process became known.

The body that was to epitomise the 'alternative advice' exercise was the Priorities Review Staff (PRS) modelled on the Wilson government's 'think tank' — the Central Policy Review Staff headed by Lord Rothschild. The PRS was set up in early 1974 with a staff of public servants and academics under Austin Holmes, a Reserve Bank economist. Its original concept was one of clarifying long term goals consistent with overall government policy and reviewing existing policies and activities in the light of these goals to see if they were moving closer towards or deviating from them. What the PRS mainly did, however, was to carry out short term reports on specific proposals which were referred to it on an ad hoc basis. Its influence was therefore quite limited and it was further handicapped by being transferred from the Special Minister of State to the Treasurer to the Prime Minister in less than a year. Probably, in a reflection of the preoccupation of its Director, it also had an over-emphasis on economic expertise within its staff. When the government was dismissed, the PRS was disbanded and its staff absorbed into the Prime Minister's Department.

The most flamboyant attempt Labor made to draw on non-departmental advice was the use of advisers on the staff of ministers. Under previous Liberal governments, ministers generally had small staffs drawn chiefly from their department who were not expected to carry out other than routine tasks on the grounds that all matters of substance would be handled by the department. Many Labor ministers opted for larger staffs and some recruited highly-qualified people from universities, journalism, business, and from the bureaucracy itself. Others followed the traditional pattern and were totally dependent on their departments for even the smallest tasks. Yet not all non-bureaucratic ministerial staff advised their ministers on matters of policy — perhaps only about 30 did so at any given time, at various levels and with varying success. Departmental officers, particularly permanent heads, generally resisted this development and attempted to shut out advisers from access to departmental information and also, where possible, from access to

permanent head-to-minister communications. The Chairman of
the Public Service Board, Sir Alan Cooley, no doubt reflected
the feelings of many of his colleagues when he said in April
1974:

> The Permanent Head is supported by the resources of his depart-
> ment, with its extensive knowledge of the implications of policy im-
> plementation at the operational level. While other sources of advice
> may complement or supplement that of the permanent head and his
> department, none can be an effective substitute for it. (Cooley 1974),

The strength of feeling about outsiders can be gauged by the
resistance in some departments even to the notion that the
minister should be able to seek advice directly from officers other
than the permanent head. Sir Arthur Tange, Secretary of
Defence, commented in a submission to the Coombs Commission:

> I do not resist the idea of a minister informing himself better than
> many ministers do and of expressing himself more to his permanent
> head on the kind of organisation which he thinks is needed to achieve
> the government objectives. But my experience leads me to believe
> that there should be no role whatsoever for the minister in:
> (a) the appointment of senior officers (where he should not have the
>   right of veto);
> (b) the minister should not have the right to specify the officers
>   whom he wishes to advise him, or the officers to perform tasks
>   which he directs the department to perform. (Coombs 1976)

Occasionally these tensions emerged into public view. In
January 1973 Clem Lloyd, Press Secretary to Deputy Prime
Minister and Defence Minister Lance Barnard, resigned after he
had been excluded from a meeting with the British Defence
Secretary on the instructions of Sir Arthur Tange. Lloyd had
been one of Labor's most trusted advisers for six years and the
incident attracted considerable publicity. It also provoked bad
feeling against Barnard within the government. Dr Jim Anthony, Private Secretary to Social Security Minister John
Wheeldon, held a press conference in July 1975 to announce that
he was resigning because of obstruction from 'yesterday's men',
as he called the permanent head of the department and his senior
officers. There were also examples of public servants who had
been seconded to work in a minister's office being directed by
the permanent head of the department not to offer advice to the
minister that varied from advice offered to him by the department. Yet most ministerial advisers realised quickly how little

challenge they represented to a department, even when they had the support of the minister in their activities — and this support was by no means always forthcoming. The time and resources available to the department gave it every advantage in such a contest.

It is true that by acting as a filter, advisers could often play a negative role, separating out difficulties in proposals advanced by departments, but positive contributions to policy seldom emerged from the melee of parliamentary business and routine administrative tasks. In many cases a departmental submission to a minister did not allow even the negative 'fail-safe' mechanism in his office to operate on a proposal, as submissions often reached the minister at a stage where his practical options were effectively reduced to blanket acceptance or rejection, modifications being impossible either because of cost factors or because complementary measures had already been initiated through another minister. It became obvious that unless an adviser could gain access to the department at a much earlier stage in the development of a policy or project and inject a contribution there — in other words, down the line, long before the matter reached the minister's office — he could make little real impact on the final result.

One further innovation by way of outside or non-bureaucratic advice was the use by the Labor government of consultants. This allowed an outside expert to work, on a contract basis and either full-time or part-time, on particular projects or as a general adviser in a particular area for one or more ministers. Some consultants enjoyed periods of considerable influence, such as economics professors Brian Brogan and Fred Gruen who had wide access to Whitlam in 1974, and some like Medibank architects Dick Scotton and John Deeble and urban planner Pat Troy who fulfilled the role of Deputy Secretary in the Department of Urban and Regional Development, were able to penetrate the policy infrastructure of departments in a way that ministerial staff could not because of other work pressure. Some advisers produced very little, if anything at all. All were subject to the same objection of principle from the bureaucracy and by late 1975, as part of his overall plan for the institutionalisation of outside advice, Menadue had been pressing the Public Service Board for all consultants to be made temporary public servants and so be responsible to permanent heads rather than to ministers.

It should be re-emphasised at this point that the problem was not, as a rule, that the bureaucracy was deliberately obstructing the programs of a Labor administration because of an ingrained conservative bias. It was rather that, as a large institution comprising 30 departments with certain aims and interests peculiar to individual departments, the bureaucracy could only be directed towards the priorities of the government by clear and considered ministerial directions. It is true that in any government there will probably be some ministers who do not appreciate how their department can be used, in an administrative sense, to advance the policies of the government. Yet the ability of the bureaucracy to adhere to its own interests in the face of the clearest government policy cannot be underestimated.

Nowhere during the Labor government was this better illustrated than by the bureaucracy's determination to keep its own secrets. The issue of freedom of information provided a case study of the problem because it was an area in which the bureaucracy had what it perceived as a clear interest to protect — the confidentiality of its advice to governments — and it was also an area in which the bureaucracy felt that it appreciated the dangers of the subject much better than the politicians.

In his 1972 policy speech Whitlam had said:

> A Labor Government will introduce a Freedom of Information Act along the lines of the United States legislation. This Act will make mandatory the publication of certain kinds of information and establish the general principle that everything must be released unless it falls within certain clearly defined exemptions. (Whitlam 1972b)

On 19 January 1973, a little more than a month after Labor had been elected to government Murphy, as Attorney-General, put up a Cabinet submission which sought approval for the preparation of legislation on public access along the lines of the US Freedom of Information Act. It also proposed that an IDC consider whether any modifications should be made to the US system for Australian purposes. In one of the earliest decisions of the Labor Cabinet, No 30, Murphy obtained approval for both proposals. The IDC was established immediately by the Attorney-General's Department under the chairmanship of Lindsay Curtis, a First Assistant Secretary in the Department. The other departments with representatives on the committee were Prime Minister's, Treasury, Defence, Foreign Affairs, the Public Service Board and what was then Special Minister of

State (SMOS). With the exception of the newly-created SMOS these were the heavyweight departments of the Public Service.

The role of an IDC (of which there were 180 in existence at the last published count in late 1975) can be compared to that of a mincer. It takes proposals of varying shapes and sizes and produces bland consistency. IDCs do not vote on questions, they progress tortuously to consensus. If one member holds out for the most rigid defence of his department's interests he must be accommodated as the IDC grinds towards a report.

The process was well-described by one of the departments represented on the freedom of information IDC, in its submission to the Coombs Commission when it commented on IDCs generally:

> Not only are they often cumbersome and slow, but their recommendations are ultra-cautious, merely reflecting the lowest common-denominator of agreement. In many cases their written reports are too long, complex and imprecisely phrased, being designed to paper over differences in the search for a fragile consensus. Moreover, those Departments which believe their interests are being compromised fight a long, delaying action in the hope that others will eventually give in to their pressures for the sake of producing a 'unanimous' recommendation.

IDCs are normally initiated by departments not by ministers and, even where a minister is involved, the terms of reference are usually drafted by the department providing the chairman, so that the direction of the deliberations is not necessarily that intended by the minister.

Ironically this particular IDC was more likely to produce a natural consensus than many others because of the number of departments that saw a need to preserve the confidentiality of all departmental material. It was not, however, a consensus that would bring freedom of information legislation — the supposed goal of its deliberations — any nearer.

Some departments represented on the IDC had particular interests in secrecy. Defence, and Foreign Affairs considered their own material inviolate for reasons of security; Treasury had always refused to produce its statistics and economic forecasts even to other departments, let alone to the public; and Attorney-General's had no intention of making its legal opinions available.

The IDC met regularly during 1973 and early in 1974. In early 1973 it was assisted, at Murphy's direction, by Tony Mondello who had presided over the implementation of the US Freedom of

Information Act. At an early stage a special sub-committee was established to draft the all-important exemptions to the general rule of disclosure of government documents.

The three-man sub-committee comprised the Defence, Foreign Affairs, and Treasury representatives. After some efforts by this group, even they recognised the absurdity of the three departments with the greatest records of secrecy deliberating as to what government documents should be made available to the public. The sub-committee suggested that other departments might make a better fist of the exercise. The full IDC, however, requested the sub-committee to continue as before.

In December 1974, almost two years after the establishment of the IDC, its report emerged and was tabled in parliament. It contained eighteen pages in its body and seventeen further pages of appendices — somewhat less than a page of text per month of its life time. In the meantime the Labor government had survived an election in May 1974 at which Whitlam had re-affirmed the pledge concerning freedom of information legislation.

In its introductory passages, however, the IDC omitted all mention of the cabinet's instruction to prepare legislation (which had obviously not been done) and referred only to its task of considering modifications to the US legislation. The essentials of the US legislation can be briefly stated:

- All government departments and agencies must give a right of access to documents in their files.
- Any member of the public can exercise this right by specifying the document he wishes to see.
- A department may not refuse to make a document available unless it falls within a class exempted by the legislation from disclosure — chiefly national defence or foreign policy documents, trade secrets, files compiled for law enforcement purposes and the personal or medical files of individuals.
- A refusal to disclose may be appealed to the courts.
- Publication and indexing is required of the internal rules of government agencies.

In the US the exemptions granted had come under heavy fire for being too broadly framed and for allowing the concealment of documents that the legislation had always been intended to cover. For exactly this reason Mondello had advised the IDC that the US exemptions should not be copied. In a cryptic reference to Mondello, the report stated that he had advised that 'the formulation of the [US] exempt classes was unsatisfactory and ought not to be copied in Australian legislation'. This might suggest that Mondello had argued for less disclosure than the US legislation demands whereas he had argued for more but had had no effect on the IDC members.

Not content to adopt the existing US exemptions, the IDC added to these a set of exemptions of their own which would have effectively suppressed almost all material not already available without freedom of information legislation. Naturally, Cabinet documents were added — but also any document considered by a minister to be 'of the same status' as a Cabinet document.

Departmental advice to ministers was always to be exempt — but it was expanded now to include purely factual documents and investigatory reports used in formulating the advice, with the IDC's dark comment that 'the very selection of facts may reveal the deliberative process involved'. Then, to ensure that nothing could escape the net, it added an exemption for 'drafts of documents' and 'documents not brought into the final form for which they were prepared'.

Documents relating to dealings between the Australian and State governments were also proposed for exemption — even though Whitlam had gone on record favouring their tabling in parliament. An appeal to the Administrative Appeals Tribunal from the refusal to disclose was to be provided — but in many cases not if a minister himself certified the document as falling in one of the exempt classes. After this negation of the very purposes of the legislation there was a massive Catch 22 in that the whole scheme was not to apply to any existing material but only to documents created in the future. And finally, to spare ministers the onerous task of claiming exemption from disclosure for documents, the IDC recommended that their discretion to make claims should be delegated to senior public servants.

For the first nine months of 1975 the copies of the IDC report sat quietly in boxes in Attorney-General's, unsung and unread. In the increasingly frenetic survival exercises of 1975 (particularly the loans affair, in which Attorney-General's played a large role) Murphy, and later Enderby, were often distracted from policy questions. The department pushed some of its own projects, like the National Companies Bill, but somehow ignored the freedom of information issue.

In the meantime, Paul Munro, who had been Secretary of the Council of Australian Government Employee Organisations before being appointed to the Coombs Commission, found the interest he had had in the freedom of information question as a union secretary re-kindled by his discovery that approximately one in ten of all submissions to the commission complained of difficulty in gaining access to documents or information from government departments.

Munro was sceptical that any legislation would ever emerge from Attorney-General's (where he had once worked briefly) and enlisted John McMillan, from the University of NSW Law School, to produce a draft bill which he hoped would become a focus for public debate and bureaucratic action. As it was obviously pointless to duplicate whatever work Attorney-General's had already done, however little of it was exhibited in the IDC report, Munro had Coombs write to Enderby in late 1975 requesting their files on the subject. The request was deliberately directed through Enderby to counteract the opportunity for protracted delay that would have been available to the department if it had received the request. In its reply (sent after the dismissal of the Labor government) the department produced, as a result of nearly three years' work, four short papers which basically did no more than discuss the US position and four submissions to the IDC from bodies outside the governmental structure. The main files, which contained minutes of all the IDC's meetings and submissions to it from most departments, had been transferred to the Public Service Board but no reference was made to this fact. Munro's task force ultimately produced draft legislation which was published as an appendix to the Coombs Report and this influenced the Fraser government to reconvene the IDC and to direct it to revise its report. And so, almost three years from their first meeting, they sat down to do just that.

The case study of the freedom of information legislation — or lack of it — demonstrates not only the difficulties any government will encounter with a powerful and permanent institution in the form of the bureaucracy, but also that there must be a genuine determination on the part of ministers to grapple with the problems of administration. But assuming that determination — a large assumption considering past performance — it is only a beginning.

The administrative lessons from the Whitlam government seem clear. At the outset any reform government would face the basic tasks of securing control over the machinery of government and directing the energies of that machinery towards the political and economic priorities of the new administration. It appears difficult, if not impossible, to achieve these aims without a system of policy co-ordination, adequately staffed and adequately financed, to ensure that what is decided is within the government's broad national aims and that when the decision is implemented it actually operates within the context of those aims. If it considers them necessary, a new government should not hesitate to establish alternative sources of advice and information. It should certainly ensure greater internal movement of senior public servants as a means of breaking down the isolation of many departments that has stifled much administrative initiative. More significant still would be the ending — for the Second Division of the public service at least — of the system of lifetime tenure that entrenches bureaucratic interests and prevents genuine exchange with other sectors in society. A system of contract employment, with contracts of increasing length as staff grew older, would protect employees while at the same time allowing a degree of mobility in and out of the public service. None of these measures would alter its basic structure. What they would do is begin to make the bureaucracy as an institution more responsive than it has been in the past to the policies of the government of the day.

In this exercise the ministers of that future government would have their own responsibilities. After leaving his post as permanent head of the British Department of the Treasury, Lord Armstrong when asked the extent of his power gave this answer:

> Obviously I had a great influence. The biggest and most pervasive influence is in setting the framework within which the questions of policy are raised. We, while I was in the Treasury, had a framework of the economy basically neo-Keynesian. We set the questions which we asked ministers to decide arising out of that framework and it would have been enormously difficult for any minister to change the framework, so to that extent we had great power. I don't think it was used maliciously or malignly. *I think we chose that framework because we thought it was the best one going. We were very ready to explain it to anybody who was interested, but most ministers were not interested,* were just prepared to take the questions as we offered them which came out of that framework without going back into the preconceptions of them. (*The Times* 15 Nov 1976, emphasis added)

Lord Armstrong's answer demonstrates that a bureaucracy tends to set its own standard of the public interest against which proposals are evaluated and does not automatically adopt the values of the existing government. But it also demonstrates that very often ministers do little, if anything, to impose their government's priorities on the bureaucracy. That was certainly true the Whitlam government and would constitute as great a danger for any future reform administration.

10   Supply and demand
Blocking the budget

On 16 October 1975 the Opposition in the Senate deferred passage of the Budget until the government agreed to call a general election. It was an action entirely consistent with their approach to the government since its earliest days. They had seldom disguised their intention to remove Labor from office and they had never pretended that they would wait three years for an opportunity to do so, even after the April 1974 attempt failed. And this action, as much as any, reflected the general pattern of resistance to the Labor government — resistance spearheaded by the Opposition in the parliament but reinforced by the governments of the non-Labor States and by powerful forces outside the sphere of party politics, in this case the Chief Justice of Australia and the Governor-General.

The situation of the government on 16 October was parlous. In the preceding six months, inflation and unemployment figures had continued high or increasing and the Deputy Prime Minister and the next most senior minister had been dismissed from the Cabinet for misleading Parliament. In these circumstances it was almost certain that the government could not survive an election held before the end of the year. In fact the Opposition's only reservation was inspired by the realisation that the government probably could not survive an election any time in the next eighteen months, including the end of that period which was the limit of its term. The only possible danger in forcing an election now was that of making the fact of forcing the government to the polls well before the end of its term a major issue in the campaign — as had occurred in May 1974. Yet in October 1975 Labor's stocks were so low that even the most specious and ephemeral issue would have been sufficient to distract attention from *how* the election had been brought about.

For six months before 16 October, both sides engaged in a battle of tactics. It was a battle in which events increasingly favoured Malcolm Fraser. As the overseas loan imbroglio gathered momentum it seemed unlikely that he would find himself on 16 October without a plausible reason for demanding an election — even if no more specific incident emerged before that date. He continued, however, to maintain the Opposition strategy.

Immediately after his election to the Opposition leadership in March 1975 he had said:

> I generally believe [that] if a government is elected to power in the Lower House and has the numbers and can maintain the numbers in the Lower House, it is entitled to expect that it will govern for a three-year term, unless quite extraordinary events intervene.

And on 21 August, in the midst of a wave of media speculation on the possibility of the Senate blocking the Budget, he had stated:

> At this stage, with the knowledge available to us now, it is our intention to allow the Budget passage through the Senate.

On 3 September, Opposition strategy received a significant boost when the LCP-controlled Queensland Parliament nominated Albert Field to fill a casual vacancy in the Senate created by the death of Queensland Labor Senator Bert Milliner. Field, although president of the Furnishing Trades Union and described by Queensland Premier Joh Bjelke-Petersen as a Labor man, had already gone on record as saying the Whitlam government should be removed from office at the first opportunity. Since the present proportional representation method of electing Senators was adopted in 1949, it had been the practice that a deceased Senator was replaced by a person of the same party no matter what the political complexion of the State legislature making the appointment. The convention was observed for 26 years by all parties, until March 1975 when NSW Premier Tom Lewis chose an Independent, Cleaver Bunton to replace Lionel Murphy after Murphy had been appointed to the High Court.

Field's appointment was, however, more important as it materially affected the balance of power in the Senate. Even if Field failed to appear for a vote, as later occurred when his eligibility to sit in the Senate was challenged, the Opposition had deprived the government of a Senate seat and had thereby ensured a minimum of 30 votes for themselves (even without Field) against a maximum of 29 for the government, including both Liberal Movement Leader Steele Hall and Bunton who often voted against the government but who had both declared that they would not vote against the Budget. With a clear majority of one, the Opposition could not only reject legislation (which was the effect of even a tied vote) but could also pass its own amendments and motions to achieve variations on the theme of rejection.

Meanwhile both sides watched the opinion polls. Normally a government can afford to disregard poor ratings in the middle of its term on the grounds that in the last year of its term all its actions, including the Budget, can be directed at the susceptibilities of the electorate. These were not normal times, however, and it was appreciated that the polls were not only a passive reflection of how an election would be decided but also a factor in whether or not an election would take place. A poll was published in the *Age* three days after Field's appointment to the Senate. It gave Labor a 36 per cent level among voters. If the poll was at all close to the mark, it indicated that Labor would be annihilated in any election in the immediate future even allowing for some revival of support during a campaign as had occurred in May 1974.

In the next week, Whitlam went on the attack. Speaking in the sleepy NSW country town of Goulburn to a small and disinterested audience who had come to see him open the College of Advanced Education, he remarked:

> There is no obligation by law, by rule, by precedent or by convention for a Prime Minister in those circumstances which are threatened to advise the Governor-General to dissolve the House of Representatives and have an election for it. Under the traditions of the Westminster system of British Parliamentary government, the Government is composed of that party which has a majority of members in the Lower House. The Prime Minister is the leader of that party, and as long as it has a majority of members in the House of Commons in Britain and the House of Representatives here, then he is entitled to remain Prime Minister.

As members of the press picked up the reference next day and approached Whitlam's office for elaboration, they were all assured that the Prime Minister was deadly serious in his resolve to sit tight if the Budget was blocked. The story that the government intended to tough it out took off in the media. Fraser's uncharacteristically shrill reaction suggested that this was not part of what the Opposition had foreseen; that, in fact, it had not for a moment occurred to them. Dismissing Whitlam's threat as 'arrant nonsense' he replied:

> If the supply of money is cut off to the Government by a House of Parliament which constitutionally and lawfully has been given the power to deny the Government money, then that Government cannot continue. It is absurd to suggest that a power properly and lawfully given to a House of Parliament ought never to be exercised by that House of Parliament. That clear power in the Constitution carries with it greater force than any convention.

Although the exercise was a deliberate counter-attack by the government designed to disrupt Fraser's undeviating course, it was no bluff. To some extent it was a reaction by Whitlam to Labor history. He was always conscious of the example of Scullin — and to a lesser extent Lang — who had been pursued relentlessly by their opponents until they finally succumbed, at the end, without a struggle. Even Lang, who was dismissed by the Governor of NSW, appears on evidence uncovered later to have anticipated, perhaps courted, his dismissal. Whitlam saw himself as reversing this tradition of submission — Labor would not surrender government even if under siege and it would be necessary to wait and see who was blamed by the community for any disruption that occurred. This was definitely *not* part of the Opposition scenario.

The role of the press at this time was important if only because of its impact on the members of Parliament on both sides. A few days of encouraging headlines or editorials had a dramatic effect on morale among those favoured, who seemed convinced that these reports either reflected community feeling or would form it in their own image. In fact the overall approach of the editorials was ambivalent. No newspaper was supporting the proposal that the Budget should be rejected as a means of forcing the government to an election — although this lack of support was not due to any enthusiasm for the Whitlam government.

Some editorialists opposed the Labor government from its earliest days and most of the others had expressed the view after the loans revelations of June and July that it should be removed at the earliest possible date, but none were prepared to say that the date should be advanced by breaking a 75-year convention that the Senate did not reject money bills. Some, like the *Age*, were even asserting that it was irresponsible of Fraser to allow speculation on rejection of the Budget to continue and that he should put it to an end by announcing that the Budget would pass whenever it went to the Senate. These comments intensified when Fraser told a Brisbane rally on 22 September that the Opposition's attitude to the passage of the Budget would not be revealed until the day of the vote in the Senate, or thereabouts.

Fraser was unruffled by the editorials. He took the view that even if the papers held this view right up until the Senate's vote on the Budget (and further loans revelations might well alter their outlook) they would certainly take a different tack the day after the Budget had been rejected. While possibly deploring the breach of convention that had led to the current crisis, they would say that there was now no alternative to the holding of a general election and in those circumstances it should be held as soon as possible. When an election was called, the editorials might still express concern as to the way in which it had come about, but they would support Fraser's argument that the overriding issues were the economy and the competence of the government — two areas in which they had been almost unanimous in their scathing attacks on the Labor administration.

Fraser's strategy required *every* Opposition Senator to vote for the blocking of the Budget. Some were not enthusiastic about the breach of convention involved, others recalled that the same tactic had backfired in May 1974 when it had appeared to have every chance of succeeding at the subsequent election. Accordingly, there was wide speculation as to whether one or more Senators might refuse to be party to the exercise. Those Senators who were most often mentioned were Alan Missen from Victoria, usually categorised as a small-l liberal, Neville Bonner of Queensland who was reported to have told an Aboriginal delegation at Parliament House that he could not and would not see money for Aboriginal advancement cut off by the Senate, and Donald Jessop of South Australia who wrote to the Adelaide *Advertiser* on 17 September to stress that he was opposed to a rejection of the Budget except in the most exceptional circumstances. All these Senators were Liberals — there was no suggestion that any Country Party Senators had any reservations — and they were to come under increasing pressure in the next few weeks.

In South Australia, for example, the former Liberal Premier, Sir Thomas Playford, wrote to one of the State's Liberal Senators, Condor Laucke, drawing attention to the breach of convention in the appointment of Albert Field to the Senate and pointing out that Laucke had himself entered the Senate to fill a casual vacancy created by the death of another Liberal Senator in conformity with the convention the Queensland government had now broken. Playford's letter, widely publicised in South Australia, also argued that chance Senate majorities ought not to reject a Budget. At the same time Steele Hall was working behind the Senate scenes to persuade the suspected waverers against Fraser's course.

Fraser's supporters within the Liberal Party attempted to counter Steele Hall's efforts by approaching any possible waverers individually to discuss their doubts. It was never established that any of them considered the possibility of crossing the floor in the Senate at the Budget vote or of even abstaining. They were under no illusions: to do this would mean the end of their political careers. They may have hoped to make a stand to thwart the Fraser proposal in the party room, but that would have been their only attempt. Even then they apparently felt they needed at least six Senators of the same opinion before they could afford to take that stand, but the problem was that they could not risk approaching other Senators of their own party — or even each other — in case they failed and so isolated themselves.

On 29 September Whitlam tried again to upset the momentum of the Opposition's campaign. While stating categorically that he would not call a House of Representatives election if the Budget were blocked, he said he would consider calling an election for half the Senate if this occurred. A half-Senate election was not required until the middle of 1976 but on past precedents could be held before the end of 1975 if the Prime Minister so decided. This announcement immediately sparked off speculation as to the possibility of a temporary Labor majority in the Senate.

The discussion centred on the fact that the Labor government had enacted legislation providing for the creation of four more Senate seats — two from the ACT and two from the Northern Territory. Those Senators were to be elected for the first time at the proposed half-Senate election and were to take their places immediately. The legislation had been defeated by the Opposition in the Senate but had become law after the Joint Sitting which followed the May 1974 double dissolution. It had subsequently been challenged in the High Court by the non-Labor State governments but the court had not yet handed down its decision. If the court upheld the legislation, the four territorial Senators would, under its provisions, take their places immediately after an election, whenever held. So would the two candidates who filled the casual vacancies arising from the resignation of Lionel Murphy and the death of Bert Milliner, which were filled only temporarily by Cleaver Bunton and Albert Field. All other Senators elected from the States, however, would not take their places until 1 July 1976.

It was theoretically possible for Labor to win the two casual vacancies and one seat in each of the ACT and the Northern Territory. In addition, former Liberal Prime Minister John Gorton had announced his intention to stand for the Senate in the ACT as an Independent. If Gorton were to poll well enough to snatch the second ACT seat from the Liberal candidate, the numbers in the Senate from December 1975 until June 1976 could be Labor 31, LCP 31, with Steele Hall and Gorton holding the balance of power. While there were many measures on which these two would not vote with Labor, the blocking of the Budget was not one of them. Nor was Labor's electoral legislation, which was a source of constant concern to the Opposition, being designed to remove some of the inequalities between electorates which had resulted in the substantial over-representation of the Country Party in the House of Representatives.

Whitlam's tactic of introducing the prospect of a half-Senate election misfired. Far from halting the Opposition's rush towards 16 October, it appeared to give it added momentum, particularly when the High Court on 10 October upheld the validity of the territorial Senators' legislation and made a half-Senate election a genuine option for the government.

Yet both sides appear to have been deluded. Although called by the federal government, no election for Senators in any State can be held unless writs for the election are issued by the State Governor — which means, in effect, by the State government. In the past this process had been automatic and writs had been issued in all States whenever a Senate election had been called. On this occasion, however, Queensland Premier Joh Bjelke-Petersen and NSW Premier Tom Lewis made it clear that they would ensure that no writs were issued in their States. As it was in those States that the two casual vacancies were to be filled, Labor's chance of a temporary majority, however slight, evaporated at once.

Even if the issue of writs could have been guaranteed, that chance was extremely slight. Had Labor polled well, it was not guaranteed the complex fall-out of votes needed in each State and territory to obtain 31 Senators plus Gorton and Steele Hall. How it would in fact have polled is best suggested by the report of ANOP Director Rod Cameron at the time immediately after 16 October when there was a strong public reaction against the blocking of the Budget:

> I believe there is some confusion in the minds of many Labor party people I have spoken to recently that is operating to equate the new found apparent reaction against the Opposition's stance with an increase in the likely vote for Labor in an early election. The two are by no means any more than marginally related. I would suggest that voting for Labor is by no means the same thing as supporting an emotional bandwaggon movement which is for the preservation of the democratic system as we know it. It would appear as if Labor and general media communications efforts are doing very well to help the success of the latter. However, I would urge you strongly not to assume that such support automatically transfers to a vote for Labor in a 1975 election . . .
>
> Moreover, the major issue, as I have suggested previously is 'competent government'. In a strictly election oriented campaign, rather than the pre-season effort we have at the moment with both sides playing under different rules, Labor may hope to divert some attention away from competent government as an issue. It is unlikely, however, to be able completely to defuse it. We cannot hope no matter how impressive Gough will be on the campaign trail, no matter how skilful we can make the communications effort to defuse in a short period a year's worth of constant, repetitious reinforcement of the incompetent government theme. Other things being equal, we have a show of doing it in six months — not in six weeks.

Into October, with approximately two weeks before the Budget introduced in the Senate, government and Opposition both tried to shift the debate to their own ground. Labor spokesmen, somewhat ironically from an historical viewpoint, emphasised questions of constitutional propriety and stability in government. In an effort to narrow the issue to these principles, they tried to draw into the controversy persons not normally associated with Labor but concerned at the precedent that would be set by a Senate cut-off of supply. One of the most effective was a well-publicised statement on 11 October by four of the country's leading professors of constitutional law who argued:

> The rejection of the budget by the senate in the present circumstances would be a constitutional impropriety of the first order. It would be likely to do irreparable damage to the parliamentary system as we have known it. It would be an act which

future generations will have cause to regret . . .

Governments have to put up major money bills at least twice a year. If they have to run the gauntlet of an election threat every time they do so, orderly government and rational long-term decision-making will become impossible . . . The reduction of an ultimate constitutional sanction — if indeed it should ever be used at all — to the level of a routine political tactic is a debasing of our constitutional system and the democratic values it is supposed to protect. (*Australian* 11 October 1975)

This statement did much to offset the effect of the Melbourne *Herald*'s 'Khemlani Tells' series published during the preceding week and the presence of Khemlani himself in Sydney. For it was for this kind of question — really one of competence and credibility underneath the exotic facts and fictions — that Fraser stressed at every opportunity over this period. What the Opposition basically had to do was to concentrate on the performance of *this* government and to play down its constitutional significance as *a* government elected for three years.

No sooner had the government regained the public initiative with the professors' statement, however, than it received the knock-out blow of Connor's 23 May telex in the *Herald* of 13 October. That night everyone on the government side realised that Connor would resign; that the Budget would be blocked in the Senate within days; that they had lost this battle and might as well start thinking about the next.

Fraser's decision was made known to the morning papers that evening. The *Age*'s editorial on the Tuesday was representative when it said:

We will say it straight and clear, and at once. The Whitlam government has run its course; it must go now, and preferably by the honourable course of resignation — a course which would dispel all arguments about constitutional proprieties, historic conventions and 'grabs' for power. It must go because it no longer has the degree of public support and acceptance that permits governments to govern effectively. (*Age* 14 October 1975)

The Opposition met on Wednesday morning and resolved that the Budget should be blocked. The decision was unanimous, although Alan Missen voiced open reservations. His was the only dissenting voice and he agreed to abide by the decision of the majority. At 2.45 pm that Wednesday afternoon, Fraser announced to a packed press conference that the Appropriation Bills would be delayed, rather than rejected, until a general

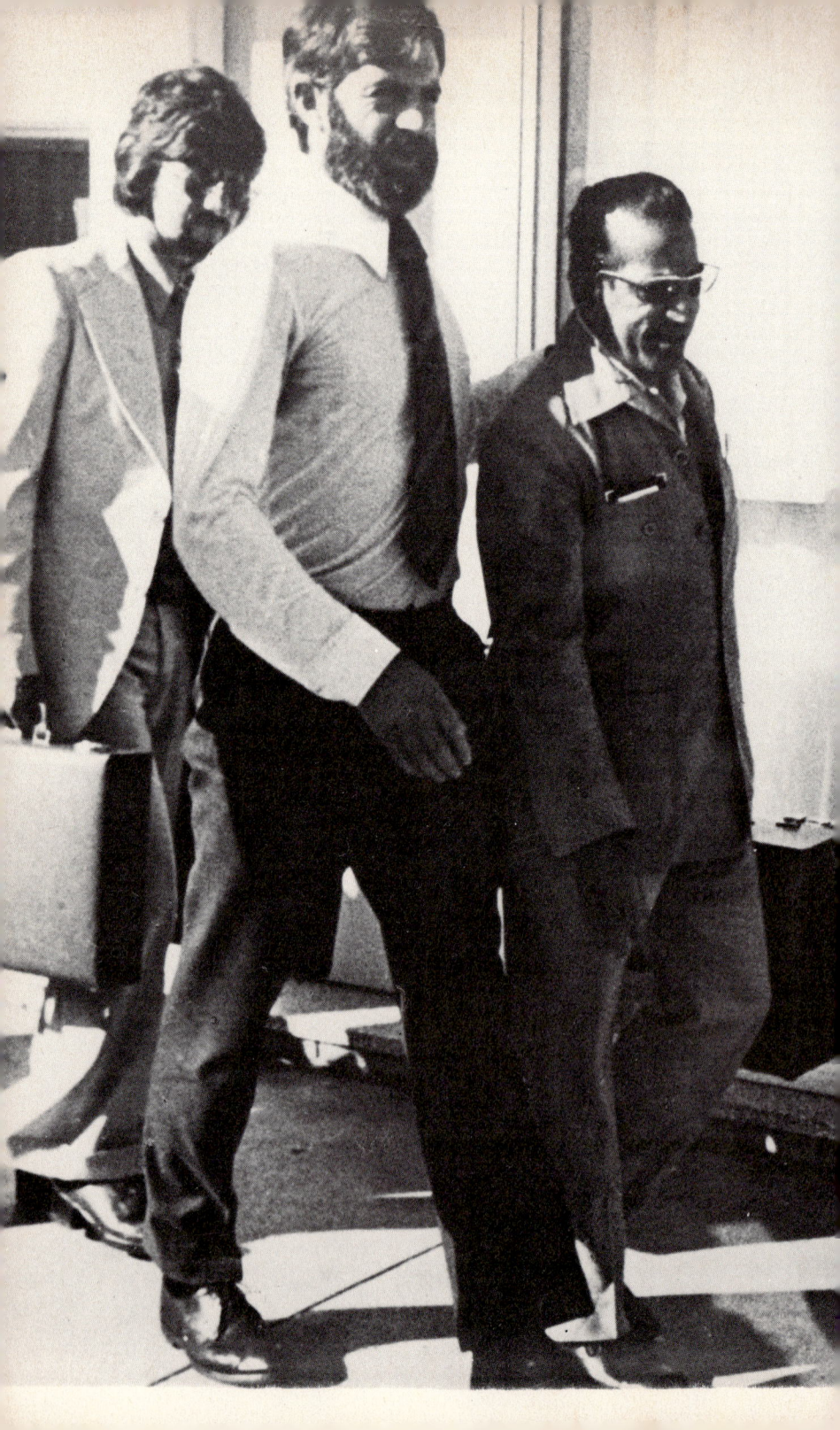

election was called. At 4.45 pm, Withers moved in the Senate for
the deferment of the Loan Bill 1975 and indicated that the
Appropriation Bills would be subjected to the same treatment
the next day. When the Senate divided, Withers' motion was
carried by 29 votes to 28.

Yet, after weeks of tension and suspense, the feeling in the
government was now almost one of relief — and an angry and
resolute unity. Any camaraderie there may have been in the
corridors of Parliament between members and staff on differing
sides ceased on that day and was replaced by a silence that would
continue until the election and beyond. Internal differences
within the government were put aside in the face of a common
enemy and some remarkable, if temporary, reconciliations were
effected. The spirit of unity was reflected at the Labor Caucus
meeting held that afternoon. Only Senate Leader Ken Wriedt
and Social Security Minister John Wheeldon raised the question
of seeking a double dissolution then and there. Most members
responded enthusiastically, some quite emotionally, to
Whitlam's call to stand firm. And in an address to the nation that
evening, Whitlam declared flatly:

> We will not yield to blackmail. We will not be panicked. We will not
> turn over the Government of this country to vested interests,
> pressure groups and newspaper proprietors whose tactics would
> destroy the standards and traditions of parliamentary government.

Whitlam took his stand in the arena he knew best — the
Parliament. Even as the Senate voted to defer the Appropriation
Bills the next day, the House debated a motion expressing
confidence in the government, condemning the tactics of the
Opposition, and calling on the Senate to pass the Budget Bills
forthwith. Whitlam led the debate with a ringing speech that
demonstrated that he was still without equal on the floor of the
House. Glaring at Fraser across the bar table, his measured
phrases edged with genuine indignation, he put his
government's case:

> The House of Representatives — the people's House — alone
> determines who shall govern Australia. Only 17 months ago, the

Brian Buckley, Press Secretary to Opposition Deputy Leader
Philip Lynch, escorts Tirath Khemlani from his motel room
to a waiting car in October 1975, the month the Opposition
decided to block the budget

people, for the second time in less than 18 months, elected the Australian Labor Party to govern for a further 3 years. I state again the basic rule of our parliamentary system: governments are made and unmade in the House of Representatives — in the people's House. The Senate cannot, does not, and must never determine who the government shall be.

For Fraser himself, slouched casually in his chair and affecting a politician's disinterest in his opponent's words, he kept his strongest jibes:

The Leader of the Opposition is refusing to pass the Appropriation Bills in the Senate which provide for the ordinary annual services of the Government. He will be responsible for bills not being paid, for salaries not being paid, for utter financial chaos, and this will continue as long as the Leader of the Opposition refuses to allow the Senate to pass the Supply already authorised by this House, the people's House. And now, like a pyromaniac he dances around the fire. He will get burnt.

He quoted to Fraser his own words in the House about John Gorton when he resigned as Minister for Defence in March 1971:

This man is unfit to be Prime Minister of Australia.

and added with overwhelming assurance:

His own reproach will be his own epitaph. And it will be my exquisite duty soon to ram this message home to the people of Australia, in terms that neither they nor the Leader of the Opposition will ever forget.

It was a breathtaking parliamentary performance. But Malcolm Fraser was no Billy Snedden who could be destroyed on the floor of the House. In his reply, delivered in a flat monotone without any of Whitlam's alliterations or symmetry, Fraser seemed to sense this when he said of Whitlam:

His world has shrunk to this Parliament. He does not realise that performance here does not meet Australia's needs.

Then, ignoring the constitutional issue, he returned to his constant theme of incompetence and misconduct:

The impropriety of this Government's actions date in particular from 13 December of last year, a date which will live in infamy in the records of this Government, this Caesar's Ides of March.

He was simply not intimidated by Whitlam's dominance of the parliamentary stage. Parliament was not where the issue would be resolved. His concern was with the media and with the other groups outside the Parliament whose support was vital for dislodging the government.

Whitlam had, however, electrified his own supporters, even Clyde Cameron, one of his greatest detractors within the government since his removal by Whitlam from the labour portfolio. Cameron spoke later in the debate and amazed those listening when he said:

> Why is it that the Federal Parliamentary Labor Party is now being seen at its magnificent best? Why is it that the Labor movement outside the Parliament is now more solidly united than ever before? It is because of the inspiration given by the Prime Minister in this present crisis, the man who in this Parliament stands out like a giant against the intellectual and moral pygmies who sit opposite him. It is because the Prime Minister has thrown down the gauntlet in defence of parliamentary government that I stand proudly beside him. That is why I and my ministerial colleagues stand solidly behind the Prime Minister in this, the most important fight of his life, the most important fight that the Australian people have ever fought in their lives.

Over the next month, the government's morale was to be held together largely by the brilliance of Whitlam's performances in the House, and it was a forum Whitlam had no intention of abandoning as long as the Senate continued to delay the Budget. He announced that Parliament would not adjourn for normal recess but would sit every week until the Senate either passed or rejected the Budget.

Meanwhile, in the public arena, the Opposition planned a series of large-scale rallies and also began a series of full-page newspaper advertisements in every State based on the theme: 'We must do it'. It was an extraordinary case of political role-reversal. Labor had taken its stand on the traditions of the Westminster system and was using the Parliament as its chief forum. Its opponents, who had for decades offered themselves to the electorate as the defenders of these institutions against Labor, now conducted their campaign in the streets and through the media. Labor continued to rely on the established forms of government. The conservatives abandoned them. The political issue was simple — would the government be forced to an election or would the Opposition in the Senate back down and pass the Budget. In this situation, whether or not the framers of the Constitution had intended the Senate to have the power to block a money bill was not really relevant. What was clear was

NSW Premier Tom Lewis and Opposition Leader Malcolm
Fraser acknowledge the cheers of supporters at a Sydney rally
during the supply crisis, October 1975

that on its face the Constitution provided no means of resolving
such a deadlock.

Faced with this constitutional vacuum, Fraser had turned for
advice to Robert Ellicott QC, Liberal front-bencher, former
Solicitor-General, and cousin of Chief Justice Sir Garfield
Barwick. Ellicott had built up an extensive and lucrative practice
at the Sydney Bar in the 1950s and 1960s, specialising in
commercial and patent law. Unlike his cousin, he was normally
reserved, quietly spoken, almost colourless but his skill in
analysing complex legal problems and reducing them to lucid
options for his corporate clients was considered formidable. He
had been appointed Solicitor-General in 1969 by the Gorton
government on the recommendation of Attorney-General Nigel
Bowen, one of his closest colleagues at the Bar. Beneath the
placid exterior, Ellicott was a determined man. He first moved to
enter Parliament in 1972 but was defeated for Liberal

preselection for the blue-ribbon seat of Berowra on Sydney's North Shore.

The loss was embarrassing for Ellicott — not only because Prime Minister William McMahon had encouraged him to nominate but also because it meant returning to his non-political post as Solicitor-General after publicly declaring his ambitions, and it was even more embarrassing for him when a Labor government took over at the end of 1972. Ellicott stayed on but continued to look for preselection. The seat he chose was Wentworth, this time in the eastern suburbs of Sydney but also a blue-ribbon seat, held by the former Treasurer, and Minister for Labour and National Service, Les Bury, who had indicated he would not seek re-election.

Having won preselection shortly before the May 1974 election, he entered Parliament at that poll and was quickly promoted to the front bench by Snedden, although as shadow Minister for Aboriginal Affairs rather than as shadow Attorney-General because of the presence of the former Attorney-General and Deputy Liberal Leader in the Senate, Ivor Greenwood. When Fraser took over from Snedden as Leader, Ellicott survived on the front-bench but only after a public argument with Fraser over the principle of whether as a shadow minister he should conduct a private legal practice.

It was to Ellicott, however, that Fraser turned for legal advice on the unprecedented deadlock situation following the blocking of the Budget. In a five page statement released to the press the day after the Budget was blocked, Ellicott argued that, if the government could not obtain supply, and would not advise an election, it was within the Governor-General's powers to dismiss the government and appoint ministers who would advise an election. For Fraser it was to provide a basic strategy — to defer the Budget until the Governor-General was persuaded that it was necessary to act as Ellicott was convinced he ultimately would. His conviction must have been re-inforced by a special request from Yarralumla for a copy of his press statement on the powers of the Governor-General.

Within the government the overriding problem had suddenly become a shortage of money. This was not the balance-of-payments-type problem where all shortages were book entries but rather a literal drying-up of funds as if it were an employee whose salary had been cut off. An ad hoc Cabinet Committee comprising Whitlam, Crean, Hayden and Enderby was established to oversee the spending of what monies remained and the arranging of further funds when existing supplies were exhausted. On 16 October, all public service departments were asked if their current reserves would last until 30 November and what the shortfall or surplus would be. A week later Treasury had received estimates from departments and collated the figures. Their estimate was that there was a shortfall of approximately $93 million for salaries and essential administrative costs. Since there was approximately $193 million available in the Treasurer's Advance for just such purposes, there was no prospect of not being able to meet departmental expenses before 30 November.

During the same week, a task force of officials from Treasury, Prime Minister's, and Attorney-General's began to consider methods by which the government might carry on after 30 November. The scheme which was first considered involved the CTB borrowing funds from the Reserve Bank and then lending members of the armed services and public servants sums equivalent to their net salaries in return for an assignment to the CTB of future payments of their salary arrears. When the arrears were eventually paid, the public servants would discharge their loan except for the interest due, which would be met by the government. A similar scheme could also be established to enable the suppliers of goods and services to the government to be paid. The possibility of a moratorium on debts at some stage was raised tentatively for discussion.

When Parliament resumed the week after the blocking of the Budget, both sides took up their positions like Napoleonic armies for a set-piece battle. Whitlam played the role, rich in historical precedent, of the Leader of the Lower House locked in confrontation with an upper chamber. Referring to 'my distinguished predecessor Asquith' he took up this theme on the first sitting day:

> The present crisis caused by the action of the Leader of the Opposition and those in the Senate who have been prepared to follow him is in the grand line of the great constitutional struggles of the past — of 1640, 1688, 1832 and 1910. At stake is the same great issue — the people's control of the Executive and the moneys raised and spent by the Executive through the people's control of the Lower House, the people's House. The taxpayers' control over their money through their elected representatives in the people's House is in the foundation of parliamentary democracy. Under our Westminster system of control this is firmly lodged in the Lower

House — the people's House — this House. It is precisely for this reason that in Australia whichever Party has the majority in the House of Representatives forms the Government of Australia.

It was a role that Whitlam had been born for. He dominated Question Time and the major debates over these weeks with a mercurial performance seldom seen in any Parliament. Fraser's responses were, however, undeviating. To Whitlam's tales of 1640 he asked:

What about the Connor documents?

and took up *his* theme of

that infamous and evil December 13 Executive Council minute.

Towards the end of the second week Fraser was nevertheless on the defensive. Polls published at the time indicated increased support for Labor, and a further swing to the already large majority opposed to an election. Media speculation on a resolution of the deadlock referred only to the prospect of the Opposition cracking, possibly by means of some 'arranged' defections in the Senate so that Fraser would not be completely humiliated. The Melbourne *Herald*'s editorial of October was typical of the second thoughts in the press:

Malcolm Fraser and our opposition parties should reconsider their present strategies. We believe our national system is in serious danger. However beneficial a change of government now would be, we must consider the long-term effects of the way in which such change comes about.

Yet some people in the government were still concerned. They could not see how Fraser could back down without permanently damaging his standing in the Liberal Party. Therefore, he would not back down. And it was unlikely that any Liberal Senator would cross the floor to save Fraser from a situation entirely of his own making. Withers had told Wriedt that there was no possibility of an Opposition Senator buckling as they had all been told in the clearest terms that any who did so would end his political career on the spot. Wriedt did not think Withers was bluffing. So the deadlock would continue and, when the money finally ran out and chaos ensued, one side would be the object of the electorate's wrath. But it could not be said with confidence which side. There was, therefore, no reason for heady optimism on the Labor side.

Indeed had they been aware of a legal opinion completed on 23

October they would have had cause for much concern. The opinion was prepared by Keith Aickin QC, long the leader of the tax and commercial sector of the Melbourne Bar, and to be appointed a Justice of the High Court by the Fraser government in 1976; Murray Gleeson QC, a leading Sydney barrister; and Pat Lane, Professor of Constitutional Law at the University of Sydney Law School and a vociferous opponent of what he considered Labor's centralism. The opinion was written for John Rothery, a partner in the Sydney law firm of Freehill Hollingdale and Page which acts as solicitors for the NSW Liberal Party.

It is worth setting out at length if only because very nearly all its legal and political propositions would be followed to the letter by John Kerr nineteen days later. It will be observed that it does contain certain political, as well as legal, propositions including the need for a Governor-General to consider the likely result of a half-Senate poll and to assess the voting intention of the electorate for a general election. In view of the other opinions sent to Kerr during this period from Opposition sources, it seems unlikely that Kerr would not have had this one on, or soon after, 23 October and that, because of its authors, he would not have attached great weight to its contents. In fact the specific nature of the advice requested suggests that he was always intended as the real recipient of the opinion. It began:

> We have been asked to advise in relation to the following matters:
> 1. Is the Senate entitled and empowered under the Constitution of Australia to reject the budget?
> 2. If the budget is rejected by the Senate, in the event of the Federal Executive Council advising the Governor-General that a course of action should be taken other than a double dissolution of both Houses of Parliament or the House of Representatives:
>   (i) Is the Governor-General bound to act in accordance with the advice of the Federal Executive Council?
>   (ii) If the Governor-General is not bound to so act:
>   (a) What powers and discretions may be exercised by the Governor-General;
>   (b) What considerations should determine the exercise of the powers and discretions by the Governor-General;
>   (c) Particularly, should the Governor-General have regard to the events of great national importance outlined by the Treasurer, in forming his decision as Governor-General in the exercise of his powers and discretions?

After answering yes to the first question — the Senate was able to block the Budget — the opinion continued:

Bearing those matters of principle in mind we answer to specific questions asked as follows:

(i)   The answer to this question depends upon precisely what action is contemplated.

If the action in question is either dissolving or not dissolving the House of Representatives then, as we have said, the Governor-General's powers are discretionary. He would not be bound to take positive action to dissolve the House because he was advised by his Minister so to do. He would not, however, be entitled to dissolve the House without being supported by the advice of responsible Ministers.

If the Governor-General were advised to call a half-Senate election, it would be a matter in which he would have the discretion to refuse to do so, although the Constitution does permit such an election at this stage. However, the situation is quite novel in that no more than six of those elected will take their seats immediately whereas up to 30 newly elected Senators not until July 1976. It would be a matter for careful consideration that such an election might produce a temporary effect contrary to the overall result of that election and equally it might not resolve the problem of obtaining a grant of supply with the serious consequences which delay in restoring supply may then entail for effective government.

(ii)   The possibility which faces the Governor-General at the moment is that the Government will be unable for a substantial and possibly indefinite period to obtain supply from Parliament.

The mere statement of that possibility reveals the magnitude of the problem.

We are not qualified to measure the likelihood of the occurrence of the various practical consequences that could flow from the present impasse, and this involves political and other considerations upon which the Governor-General would be entitled to seek advice and information from appropriate sources. In particular, we are aware that it is said that the holding of a half-Senate election could bring about a practical resolution of the problem by giving the Government sufficient voting strength in the Senate to procure supply. This is a matter that would presumably be of considerable significance to those advising the Governor-General. No doubt any discussion of this possibility would require close consideration of the precise facts concerning the availability of funds to carry on the business of Government pending the outcome of a half-Senate election. Moreover, an important consideration relevant to an exercise of the ultimate discretion under consideration would be the question of the extent to which the immediate results of a half-Senate election could be said to constitute an effective expression of the will of the people. The evident purpose of a half-Senate election under the Constitution is to fill the places of the Senators whose seats become vacant at the expiration of their three year term; it is not to produce a temporary change in voting power in the interim for the purpose of attempting to pass supply bills, where such change in voting power does not reflect the will of the people as expressed in that election.

Procedures of consultation are available. The Governor-General is entitled to seek advice on his powers from sources outside the Ministry. There is, for example, precedent for the seeking of advice from the Chief Justice of Australia. The Senate itself would be entitled to explain its position in the form of an address to the Governor-General. But the Senate could not advise the Governor-General on how he should exercise his discretion.

We understand, however, that we have been asked to consider the legal position that would exist in the event that after all remaining possibilities had been explored there was still a situation where there was a refusal of supply by Parliament.

The Governor-General is, in our opinion, vested with sufficient discretionary authority to overcome that position by an exercise of his personal discretion.

It would be open to the Governor-General, having regard to the necessity to maintain the law and the constitution, and to the welfare of the nation, to exercise his power to dissolve the House of Representatives and, consequently, to seek an expression of the will of the people at an election.

We have said above, however, that this power is exercised on the advice of responsible Ministers.

What is the position of a Governor-General whose Ministers are unable to procure supply from Parliament, who are supported by a majority in the House of Representatives, and who are not prepared to advise the Governor-General to dissolve the House and to call an election?

There is precedent to support the view that in such a case it would be within the power of the Governor-General to dismiss his Ministers and to seek the advice of other Ministers if it is available. By the time such a state of affairs had been reached the political situation could be so fluid that it is difficult to predict the source of such alternative advice. If, however, the Governor-General were advised by new Ministers to dissolve Parliament he could act on that advice.

There is one particular problem involved in what we have said above that requires special emphasis.

For a Governor-General to dismiss Ministers who commanded the support of a majority in the House of Representatives has such serious implications that one would normally say that it would only be likely to occur in a case where the Governor-General was satisfied that the majority in the House of Representatives did not also represent a majority in the electorate; (and the consequences upon the authority of the Crown of a mis-judgment of the mood of the electorate in such a case would be far-reaching).

Nevertheless, the power is there and it would be available to be exercised in a case where the Governor-General considered that the maintenance of the law and the Constitution, and the welfare of the nation required its exercise, and that the manner and possible consequences of its exercise would not impair the authority of the Crown.

With regard to the last-mentioned consideration it is possible to envisage a situation where the basis of the dissolution was not the opinion of the Governor-General that the electorate would not support the majority in the lower house but rather that the parliamentary situation had become such that it ought to be resolved by the electorate.

In addition to setting out the exact steps which would later be followed by the Governor-General the opinion concluded with the tempting proposition that 'the power is there' awaiting a situation where 'the Governor-General considered that the maintenance of the law and the Constitution and the welfare of the nation required its exercise'.

Although parliament had been due to adjourn for two weeks on 23 October, it continued to sit the next week, rising at 6.00 pm each day instead of 11.00 pm (to save overtime payments for staff) in accordance with Whitlam's insistence that the Budget would be presented again and again to the Senate until passed, or rejected outright. The House of Representatives passed the Appropriation Bills for a third time. The Opposition in the Senate refused to allow them to be listed for debate on the Notice Paper. So confrontation continued. Yet, in an incongruous spectacle, Parliament continued to function as usual when it was not actually debating the rights and wrongs of the blocking of the Budget. On 30 October, for example, the House of Representatives solemnly debated such legislation as the Wool Marketing (Loan) Bill 1975, the Roads Acts Amendment Bill 1975 and the Queensland Grant (Proserpine Flood Mitigation) Bill 1975.

In the third week, public opinion polls were running even more strongly in favour of the government. An *Age* poll had 70 per cent of people interviewed in favour of the passage of the Budget, 41 per cent of these being LCP voters, and a majority of the opinion that the Opposition was to blame for the crisis. It also surveyed voting intention and put the government and Opposition level at 47.3 per cent in the capital cities where the poll was taken. Although this was still below the Labor Party's 1974 city vote and omitted the rural areas which traditionally favoured the Opposition, it represented a dramatic rise for Labor since the beginning of the crisis.

The danger for Fraser was that the longer an election was delayed, the greater was the possibility of the polls reaching a point of balance where an election victory could no longer be predicted with confidence. At that stage, even if the polls did not really reflect voting intentions, he came under increasing pressure from within his own Party to allow passage of the Budget. Ellicott continued to maintain that Kerr would have to step in if the money actually ran out but according to all reports (and to Treasury's assessments) that would not happen for at least a month. These misgivings were considerably increased by Whitlam's comment in a television interview on 31 October that the government was investigating ways of carrying on for some time after the existing funds ran out. Fraser's angry reaction, and his insistence that the High Court would declare any such scheme invalid, indicated that this possibility had not been taken into account by the Opposition.

Over these last two weeks the task force of officials considering alternative sources of funds had continued to work on its original proposal after enlarging its membership to include representatives of the Reserve Bank and the CTB, and they put forward a more detailed submission to the ad hoc Cabinet Committee on 31 October. Not every aspect of government expenditure was involved, since many programs were financed by specific legislation which had already passed through the Senate earlier in the year. Pensions, child endowment, sickness and unemployment benefits and most funds for educational institutions fell into this category. At risk were those items of expenditure contained in the Budget Bills — in particular the salaries and administrative costs needed to keep public service departments running from day to day.

The submission of the task force began confidently:

> The scheme is considered by officers of Attorney-General's Department to have every prospect of withstanding legal and Constitutional challenge; it is regarded as a technically feasible scheme.

It then set out the basic elements of the arrangements:

> In essence the scheme involves:
> (a) The Government issuing certificates of indebtedness to those to whom payments were due for wages and salaries, under commercial contracts, and under existing legislation.

(b) The banks accepting from employees, and to the extent practicable from other non-suppliers, assignments, by way of mortgage, of the debts referred to in the certificates as the basis for a loan.

(c) Suppliers using certificates to make individual arrangements with banks for finance; banks could take an assignment if they wished.

(d) Banks funding the loans from their own resources.

(e) The Government announcing its intention to pay banks an agreed interest rate on loans they made to employees and non-suppliers, and to pay suppliers interest at the same rate on the Government's outstanding indebtedness to them.

(f) Enactment of legislation to authorise the payment of such interest.

An example of the form public servants would have to sign for their banks was then set out:

I, A.B. of . . . . Public Servant hereby request an advance from the . . . . Bank (hereinafter called 'the Bank') in an amount of $, and I undertake to repay the said sum upon demand being made by the Bank. I acknowledge that interest on the amount advanced will be payable at the rate of   % per annum on the daily balance outstanding.

In consideration of the Bank making the loan to me of the amount of $ this day (the receipt whereof I hereby acknowledge), I hereby assign to the Bank by way of mortgage the debt or sum of $ due and owing to me from the Commonwealth of Australia, being the gross amount referred to in certificate of indebtedness No   dated   1975.

Provided that the amount recoverable by the Bank shall not at any time exceed the net salary shown in the Certificate of Indebtedness.

Dated this   day of   1975

(signed) . . . .

A.B.

The rate of interest to be paid was estimated at 9-10 per cent. As the actual payment of interest could only be authorised by an Act of Parliament, it was proposed that, after the Budget passed, the government would pass legislation to pay out both loans and interest to the banks and to suppliers, thereby discharging all obligations of employees and enabling suppliers to settle with their banks.

Immediately after outlining the scheme, however, the report gave the following warning:

There are a number of qualifications to the practicability of the scheme:—

(a) The participation of banks would be an essential element of the scheme and they would need to be consulted before detailed planning was commenced. The scheme would require the co-operation and participation of most of the banks if it were to be workable.

(b) The Government administration machinery would be subject to very heavy additional work loads. A minimum period of 3 weeks would apparently be needed for relevant Government printing and distribution requirements; such work would need to follow discussions with banks, which would have their own significant banking distribution and administrative problems.

(c) Unforeseen legal complications, which would need to be solved, could arise in the administration of the scheme.

(d) Parliamentary approval of legislation to authorise the payment of interest would be required; this could raise questions of Parliamentary proprieties and tactics.

(e) The co-operation of the States would be desirable, particularly in the area of handling stamp duty problems.

These considerations point up the very large administrative complexities and burdens. They suggest that, legal and constitutional considerations apart, too wide a coverage of the scheme could lead to its complete breakdown. Also, the longer the scheme was in operation, the greater would be the administrative burdens and the chances of breakdown.

It is emphasised that the overall practicability of the scheme, and the practicable extent of its coverage, could only be finally determined after discussions with the banks and after the working out of detailed administrative procedures.

The need for the co-operation of the private banks, and possibly the States, rang alarm bells. In addition the administrative exercise was daunting. The report calculated that if each individual loan transaction took five minutes on average for a bank to process, a total of 27,000 working hours would be entailed in each fortnightly pay cycle.

Treasury had of course assisted in the preparation of the report but viewed the entire exercise with mounting distaste. Wheeler also made the point that there were now legal difficulties for departments in ordering future supplies of goods and services as they could not guarantee, as they were required to do under the Treasury Regulations, that they would eventually be able to pay for them. The Department of Prime Minister and Cabinet had made the running on the alternate arrangements and continued to press on with them. It was almost certainly a misconceived strategy as it exposed the government to the charge of trying to govern without Parliament at a time when it was winning the public relations battle handsomely, and it tended to relieve the pressure on the Opposition Senators who were uncertain as to what would happen if the money was to run out. It also aroused the interest of Sir John Kerr who at this stage asked for details of the scheme.

Whitlam, however, still gave every appearance of being in complete control of the situation. At Question Time on 4 November he gave one of his most dazzling displays, visibly affecting the Opposition's morale. He rejected out of hand Fraser's proposed compromise — that an election for the House of Representatives be held with an election for half the Senate in May 1976. Taunting them with the reversal in the opinion polls and in the editorials, he speculated with mock solemnity on whether he should take advantage of the High Court's decision concerning territorial Senators and hold a half-Senate election before Christmas, at the same time dangling an offer to postpone it until May:

> My ordinary view is that elections should take place closer to the expiry time of the shorter term senators. Nevertheless, I am influenced by the advice of the editorials in the *Age* and the *Australian Financial Review* to consider an earlier Senate election — on a date such as Sir Robert Menzies and most of my predecessors would have advised. But I want to assure honourable gentlemen and right honourable gentlemen that I am still thinking over the matter. I am not over-euphoric because of the overwhelming results of the opinion polls. I am not unduly swayed by the editorials in the *Age* and the *Australian Financial Review*. I still want to look at the matter.

It was swaggering bravado and the government benches reacted with laughter and applause. The Opposition was silent.

The next day, however, the debate was back to normal. Ministers continued to emphasise the effects on the various community services of the drying up of funds — and it had become clear that they *were* drying up. Whitlam led the assault as usual.

> The Budget must pass, and it will pass. While it is not my intention, or desire, to provide needless fear of alarm, we must be quite clear about the consequences of the continual refusal to pass the Budget. This refusal is already damaging the business community, threatening the normal life of the nation and endangering the delicate process of economic recovery. As I have said before, there can be no surrender to the Senate on this issue. The fundamental

principle of democracy is too important. I call on all honourable
members to condemn the actions of the Opposition in the Senate. I
call on that Opposition to pass the Budget without further
procrastination, without further delay.

But Fraser was back in stride, however, ready to juxtapose
again the twin charges of incompetence and impropriety:

> This is a government of economic mismanagement, of.massive un-
> employment, of massive inflation, of greater industrial unrest than
> the country had previously seen and of higher interest rates than
> Australia has previously seen. We know quite well what occurred in
> the conspiracy of 13 December last year to which the Prime Minister
> was a direct party.

On Thursday 6 November, Kerr received some of the
information he had been asking for. Hayden briefed him on the
alternative arrangements and Enderby gave him two legal
opinions, both in the names of Enderby and Maurice Byers. The
first dealt with the alternative arrangements and concluded that
they were 'clearly constitutional'. The second was essentially a
rebuttal of Ellicott's published views on the role of the
Governor-General which Kerr had requested from Whitlam. It
rejected Ellicott's views flatly:

> No [British] Government has been dismissed by the Sovereign since
> 1783. . . .
> Nor do we agree with the suggestion that were the Prime Minister
> unable to suggest means which solve the disagreement between the
> Houses, and left the Government without funds to carry on, it would
> be His Excellency's duty to dismiss his Ministers.

The same afternoon, Treasury, Attorney-General's, and Prime
Minister's officials were meeting with the Reserve Bank, the
CTB the State banks and the private banks to discuss the alternate
arrangements proposed in the task force's report. After being
welcomed by Menadue, the bank officers, who were chiefly at
the Assistant General Manager level, listened to an explanation
of the arrangements. While blanching at the idea of having to
administer the scheme, most did not reject it as impossible. They
did, however, raise other difficulties, most particularly:

- their obligation to their regular customers who would also be
  experiencing financial difficulties if government funds ran out
  but whose salaries would not be guaranteed like those of public
  servants;
- their need to be indemnified by the government against losses due
  to forgeries and frauds that occurred in the confusion of the first
  weeks;

- their concern that agreement by all banks on a standard rate of interest for these transactions would violate the price-fixing provisions of the Trade Practices Act.

The meeting concluded with the bank representatives leaving Canberra to report to their chief executives in the State capitals and to obtain legal opinions on the validity of the scheme. Their feeling was that they would have an answer for the government within a week.

In fact the banks had already had the documents relating to the scheme for one or two days and most had already passed copies to their legal advisers. Two significant opinions were obtained in Sydney, one by the Bank of New South Wales, and the other by the Commercial Banking Company (CBC) of Sydney. The Bank of New South Wales obtained advice from William Deane QC, who had advised the Liberals on the merits of Murphy's opinion that the $4000 million loan was for temporary purposes, and who would be appointed a federal judge by the Fraser government in 1977. Working with William Gummow, a member of Allen, Allen and Hemsley, the Bank's solicitors, he produced an opinion that expressed serious doubts about the legality of the arrangements. The CBC sought advice through its solicitors, Dibbs, Crowther and Osborne, from John Lockhart QC, who would also be appointed to the federal bench in 1978 by the Fraser government. Lockhart's opinion was highly critical of the scheme and its legal basis. At least one of these opinions was in the hands of the Governor-General before it reached the bank for whom it was prepared, which meant that Kerr probably now had a number of opinions provided through his old Sydney legal world, all counselling the end of the existing government. Further copies of the opinions on the arrangements were sent to Kerr in the following week — one arriving on 11 November and one a few days later — possibly by board members of the banks who had received copies for themselves and were not aware that Kerr had already been supplied with at least some of the material.

This last exercise illustrates the difficult position that the general manager of a private trading bank was in at this time. Being ultimately responsible to a board of directors which would almost certainly contain a number of the most prominent Liberals in the State, he would be under great pressure to reject the government's proposals. But, as the person who actually carried on the day-to-day business of the bank, he would be

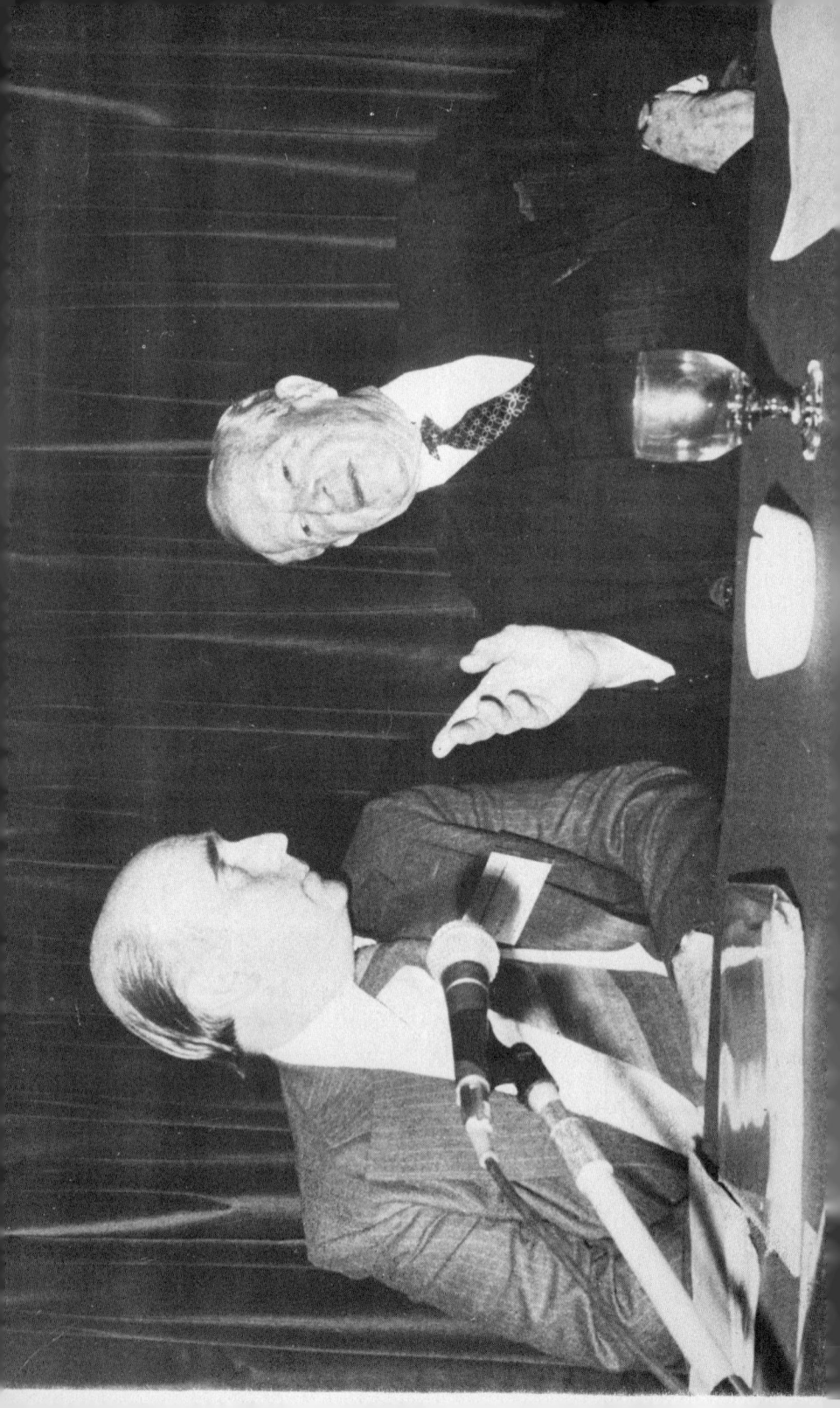

conscious of how difficult any federal government could make life for a bank because of the complete control it exercised over the whole area through the Banking Act — if that government survived, of course.

There was also the problem of pressure from customers, many of whom, particularly among the largest depositors, would be opposed to the present government. All these difficulties are apparent in the telex sent to Hayden on the morning of 10 November by George Bowen, Managing Director of the CBC which had, as its most prominent Liberal board member, Sir Robert Crichton-Browne, the federal Treasurer of the Liberal Party, who became chairman of the board in 1977. The telex read:

Hon Bill Hayden
Treasurer
Parliament House CANBERRA

In view of the note of urgency contained in your second communication to me despatched 6.30 pm 7th instant I feel constrained to let you have this interim advice on the subject matter STOP You refer in your urgent telegram to proposals but it is important to note that in banking parlance we do not in fact have any proposal from you before us STOP I must also add I am surprised that the scheme outlined to us should have been placed before us officially for decision while still incorporating assumptions of quite doubtful legality and apparently ignoring community reactions STOP Clearly a considerable amount of time and research will be required of banks if we as it appears are looked to to develop the scheme into an acceptable proposition STOP In the unlikely event (as it now appears) that it might be possible to overcome all legal barriers we would still be faced with commercial realities attaching to funding concerning which depositors are already expressing opposition to our participation in no uncertain terms STOP Being a bank dependent on customer support we share their basic views and would look for a very specific cover from the Government to ensure that our depositors funds would not be appropriated for the purposes of the scheme either directly or indirectly STOP

I would hope you appreciate we are restricted under the trade practices legislation from conferring with competitors on the scheme and that for us to offer any suggestions which could assist in making the scheme into a proposition worthy of consideration we would want to be sure beyond all doubt that our directors officers and the

Opposite: Chief Justice Sir Garfield Barwick making a point to his cousin Robert Ellicott QC

bank itself would not be implicated in any way under the Crimes Act or any more obscure legislation STOP

However we will continue to examine the many facets of the scheme and will let you know our considered reaction as soon as we are in a position to do so STOP Meanwhile if you require an answer inside our own time requirement it would have to be that we are unable to participate for fear of the reasons outlined STOP

I think you are fully aware of our announced intentions which I again confirm to consider sympathetically any requests from existing customers affected by the foreshadowed disruption to Supply STOP This you will appreciate is strictly on the basis of a banker/customer relationship STOP I understand you are also aware that even this limited operation will need special funding if banks are exposed to it for anything more than a short time.

G. F. Bowen
Managing Director
The Commercial Banking Company of Sydney Limited.

The very act of sending the telex indicated Bowen's concern not to alienate the government, and in the previous week he had strongly protested to a board member who had attempted to put pressure on the CBC's representatives at the 7 November meeting in Canberra. Yet the thrust of his message was clearly that the Bank would not be able to go along with the scheme as it had been proposed at that meeting.

Meanwhile, Fraser had asked Whitlam for a meeting to discuss the proposition — already rejected by Whitlam — of passing the Budget if a House of Representatives election was held in May 1976 at the same time as a half-Senate election. The meeting was set for 9 am on Tuesday morning in Whitlam's office. And on Monday afternoon Sir John Kerr lunched at his Sydney residence, Admiralty House, with the Chief Justice of Australia Sir Garfield Barwick.

11   Death in the afternoon
11 November 1975

Tuesday 11 November 1975 was hot and clear in Canberra —
even by 8.45 am when a large group of reporters and
photographers were already clustered at the side entrance to
Parliament House waiting for Whitlam and Fraser to arrive for
their 9.00 am meeting. Few of those waiting expected the
meeting to resolve the political crisis which had been with them
for almost a month. Much of the early tension had evaporated,
for even crises develop a routine of their own if they go on long
enough and it was generally accepted that the likely crunch point
— the end of the government's funds — was still some weeks
away. Within that curious routine, Tuesday was scheduled as a
full-day with Parliament House for the government and the Opposition. Both had arranged party meetings for the morning —
the government for 10.00 am and the Opposition for 10.30 am.
Parliament was to begin later than usual — at 11.45 am, instead
of 10.00 am — because of the ceremony at the War Memorial at
11.00 am. It was the 47th anniversary of Remembrance Day,
when the guns stopped firing in the first World War. At the
eleventh hour of the eleventh day of the eleventh month, wreaths
would be laid as usual at the War Memorial by various
dignitaries — including the Governor-General.

That day's program for the House of Representatives indicates
just how unprepared the government was for what was to happen. The business schedule was mundane, except for an Opposition motion of censure which was of course intrinsically a
criticism of the government's actions as a *government*. The
program read:

Prayers
Mr Daly (Leader of the House) to announce that he accepts the

notice of motion given by the Leader of the Opposition as a censure
motion for the purposes of standing order 110.

General Business
NOTICE NO 1 — Censure of the Government — Mr Fraser (Leader of
the Opposition) to move motion appearing on the Notice Paper in
his name.
(Time limits: Mover 30 minutes
                  Prime Minister or one Minister
                     deputed by him — 30 minutes
                  Any other Member — 20 minutes)

If motion of censure is defeated—
Petitions — The Clerk to announce petitions lodged for presen-
tation.
Mr Speaker to call on—
    Notices
    Questions without notice
    Presentation of Papers — Ministers
    Ministerial statements, by leave
Mr Speaker to report a message from the Governor-General
notifying assent to Bills.

Report from Committee
PUBLICATIONS COMMITTEE — Mr McKenzie (Chairman —
Diamond Valley) to bring up Eleventh Report (copies circulated to
Members in Chamber).
    Mr McKenzie to move, by leave — that the report be agreed to.
DISCUSSION OF MATTER OF PUBLIC IMPORTANCE — Mr Peacock
(Kooyong) —
The Australian Government's inept handling of the Timor crisis
which has resulted in prolonging the tragedy, alienating all parties
and diminishing Australia's responsible role in our region.
Requires support of 8 Members; Time limits: Discussion 2 hours;
Proposer and Member next speaking 15 minutes; other Members 10
minutes.

Government Business
NOTICES No 1 — Authors Fund Bill — Mr Whitlam (Prime
Minister) to present Bill. First reading. Second reading to be moved.
Debate adjourned.
No 2 — Australia-Japan Foundation Bill — Mr Whitlam (Prime
Minister) to present Bill. First reading. Second reading to be moved.
Debate adjourned.

At this point the Budget Bills were to be debated again. In the
Senate the two notices of motion standing on the Notice Paper
related to the Postal Services Regulations and the ACT Liquor
Ordinance. Ministers had additional commitments beyond
parliamentary business. Some would be attending a meeting of

the Legislation Committee of Cabinet at 2.30 pm; Fred Daly and Kep Enderby were to attend an Executive Council meeting with the Governor-General at Yarralumla at 6.30 pm; the full Cabinet was scheduled to convene in the Cabinet room at 7.30 pm for its usual weekly meeting during parliamentary sittings. This agenda also indicated a relatively routine collection of matters for consideration:

CABINET
7.30 pm to 9.30 pm Tuesday 11 November 1975

BUSINESS LIST

	Minister Responsible
Long Service Leave ACT Ordinance (Submission to be circulated)	Senator J. McClelland
Location of Curriculum Development Centre (Submission No 2055)	Mr Whitlam
National Aboriginal Consultative Committee (Submission No 2006)	Mr Johnson
Proposed New Chancery and Official Residence — Brasilia (Submission No. 2035 Decision No 4155 [ERC])	Senator Willesee
Acquisition of Freehold Land in the ACT (Submission No 1996 and Addendum Decision No 4157 [ERC])	Mr Bryant
Amendment to Health Insurance Act 1973-1975 Part II — Medical Benefits (Submission No 2046)	Senator Wheeldon
Review of Australia's Customs Valuation Legislation and the Brussels Definition of Value — Amendment of Customs Act 1901-1975 (Submission No 1983)	Senator Cavanagh
Review of Grants-in-Aid Administered by Australian Government Departments (Submission No 1951)	Senator D. McClelland
Aboriginal Land Rights Commission — Second Report Financial Implications (Submission No 2028)	Senator D. McClelland
Maritime Industry Commission of Inquiry — Second Report Navigational Aid Systems (Submission No 2027)	Senator D. McClelland

Australian Extension Services Grant and Special Research Grant (Submission No 2031 Decision No 4098 [ERC])	Dr Patterson
Australian Industry Development Corporation: National Interest Committee (Submission No 2014)	Mr Bowen
Industrial Research and Development Grants Act 1967-73: Review and Proposed Amendment (Submission No 1882)	Mr Bowen
Reference to Industries Assistance Commission on Assistance to Innovation in Manufacturing, Mining and Tertiary Industries (Submission No 2047)	Senator D. McClelland

The arrangements for the Fraser-Whitlam meeting at 9.00 am had been well-publicised. It had been agreed that Fraser would be accompanied by Country Party Leader Doug Anthony, and Deputy Liberal Leader Philip Lynch. Whitlam was to be accompanied by Deputy Prime Minister Frank Crean, and the Leader of the House, Fred Daly. Fraser had wanted officials from Treasury and the Prime Minister's Department to attend so that the question of the alternative arrangements could be discussed but Whitlam had refused. The Opposition trio appeared at Whitlam's office right on 9.00 am but retreated to their own rooms two corridors away when they found that Whitlam had not yet arrived. They returned five minutes later when informed by telephone that the Prime Minister was now in his office.

During the meeting, which lasted about 40 minutes, Whitlam stated that, unless the Budget Bills were passed by the Senate later that day, he would advise the Governor-General to call a half-Senate election before the end of the year. Fraser demanded a House of Representatives poll. After this perfectly predictable confrontation, the Opposition leaders returned to their own rooms to report to their parties. At 10.00 am, Fraser called Whitlam to say that the Opposition would continue to defer the Budget Bills in the Senate. Whitlam immediately put a call through to Kerr and explained that he wished to see him as soon as possible in order to make arrangements for a half-Senate poll before Christmas. Kerr replied that he would be attending the ceremony at the War Memorial at 11.00 am and would be tied up after that until almost 1.00 pm, to which Whitlam answered that he would be out at Yarralumla at 1.00 p.m.

The Labor Caucus had begun its meeting at 10.00 am and was discussing the question of Australian government assistance to the Old Sydney Town project when Whitlam arrived to report on his meeting with Fraser and to announce his intention to call a half-Senate election. Bouyed by the break in the month-long impasse, the prospect of taking the refusal of supply question to the people, and the confidence and aggression Whitlam displayed, Caucus gave him a standing ovation and voted unanimously to support his plan. Within minutes news of the decision spread through government offices in Parliament House and discussions began on such detailed questions as itineraries for the coming campaign. Those who had opposed the idea of a half-Senate poll realised that they had been unsuccessful and took out their airline timetables as well.

At 11.00 am precisely, the official ceremony to mark Remembrance Day commenced at the War Memorial when Sir John Kerr laid the first wreath on the tomb of the Unknown Soldier. When the ceremony concluded minutes later, the Governor-General set off for Yarralumla and the politicians present rushed back to Parliament House for the 11.45 am start. When the House of Representatives assembled, Fred Daly, as Leader of the House, duly announced that the motion of censure standing in Fraser's name would be debated immediately. Fraser spoke to the motion, dealing chiefly with the loans affair and Whitlam's intention to make alternative arrangements to supply. Whitlam replied with a forceful attack on Fraser and on the Senate, moving an amendment to the censure motion that would make it a censure of Fraser for his breach of constitutional precedent. There was nothing either party could add to what they had been saying inside and outside parliament for the last month but both sides sat through the speeches as a demonstration of support for their leaders.

Whitlam was followed by Anthony who spoke until 12.55 pm when the House rose for lunch — to resume at 2.00 pm. The Senate had begun its proceedings at 12 noon and, after the usual opening period of questions without notice and presentation of papers, had risen until 2.00 pm.

Whitlam, however, had already set off for Yarralumla at 12.50 pm, carrying a formal letter advising Kerr to call a half-Senate election. What he did not know was that Fraser was already on

his way to the same destination. A message had been left in Fraser's office soon after noon by Kerr's Official Secretary, David Smith, to say that Kerr would see Fraser at about 1.00 pm. Fraser was told to arrive shortly after Whitlam but only after Fraser had left Parliament House did some of his colleagues realise that because Whitlam had been late getting away, Fraser would arrive first. Their efforts to contact his driver failed and Fraser arrived shortly before 1.00 pm. He was met by Smith and taken to a sitting room where they waited together. When Whitlam was driven up to the official Prime Minister's entrance five minutes later, Fraser's car was no longer visible and a military aide was waiting to escort Whitlam to the study which was used as a meeting room.

As soon as Whitlam was shown in, Kerr asked, without preliminaries, if Whitlam had come to advise a general election. When Whitlam answered, taken by surprise, that he had not, Kerr handed him a letter terminating his appointment as Prime Minister and the appointments of all his ministers. Even at that numbing stage, Whitlam's mind still functioned quickly and focused on the Queen in London. 'It's too late — your commission is withdrawn' Kerr answered, with the finality of the lawyer who had closed off all loopholes and knows there is no way out. As Whitlam sped from Yarralumla to the Lodge, Fraser was being sworn in as Prime Minister by Kerr in the same study. It was agreed that he would lead a caretaker government until an election was held, and that his first act as Prime Minister would be to advise the Governor-General to dissolve both Houses of Parliament and call a general election.

Although Parliament House is only ten minutes drive from Yarralumla, Whitlam went to the Lodge — a few minutes closer — and had calls put through to his own Parliament House office and to the offices of the men he wanted — Crean, Daly, James McClelland, Enderby, Menadue, the Speaker of the House Gordon Scholes, the Party's National Secretary David Combe, Whitlam's chief Private Secretary John Mant, and his longtime speechwriter Graham Freudenberg. Some were in their offices having a working lunch, some were in nearby restaurants where their own staff contacted them. Without knowing the reason for

Opposite: Governor-General Sir John Kerr and Labor's second Attorney-General Kep Enderby at the Remembrance Day ceremony

the summons they all dropped what they were doing, as they had no doubt done before in response to Whitlam's calls — and no doubt expected to do again. Most of them were gathered, glazed by Whitlam's news, in the summer room of the Lodge a little after 1.15 pm.

It was Whitlam who made the only proposal for action — a demonstration in the House of Representatives that Labor still retained a clear majority there and that Fraser was unable to have even the smallest procedural motion passed, let alone conduct the business of government. As the day's events were to demonstrate, however, the House of Representatives was not where the business of government was conducted. Whitlam had a view, rooted in British history and nurtured by two decades as a member of Parliament, of the Lower House as the place where governments were made or broken.

What John Kerr, never a parliamentarian, and Malcolm Fraser, two decades an MP but seeing the House chiefly as a means to an end, realised was that no motion of the House of Representatives could affect the change of government that had already taken place — and that, if supply could be forced through the Senate, the House of Representatives, complete with its Labor majority, could be simply terminated. What was at issue was power, not precedent, and it would become clear that Parliament was not the focus of power. As if to emphasise how power was draining out of the Labor administration even while it was still physically present, the news spread quickly through Canberra's offices, and public servants scheduled to brief Labor ministers that afternoon in Parliament House remained in their departments or tried to find out who their new Liberal minister would be. And at the Lodge a little after 1.30 pm, the first of those public servants, John Menadue, left abruptly to find his new minister, Malcolm Fraser.

While Whitlam and Enderby worked on draft motions, Crean started back for Parliament House with instructions to talk out the censure debate that would resume in the House of Representatives at 2.00 pm. The plan was that Crean would speak for half an hour to allow the Labor tactics to be formulated and then finish so that Whitlam could move a motion of no-confidence in the new government.

Punctually at 2.00 pm, when the Speaker re-convened the House of Representatives, Crean rose and walked slowly to the bar table. For 20 minutes he engaged in a bizarre defence of a government which no longer existed. The only hint of reality came when, speaking of the blocking of the Budget, he remarked:

> To condone that sort of conduct, of course, is to turn the Senate into a monster. The Senate would be exceeding the powers that properly are provided for it. As the Prime Minister has asserted, governments are made and unmade only in the House of Representatives. What should happen, for argument's sake, if someone else were to come here in a few minutes and say he was now the Prime Minister of this country. He would be voted out immediately in this House. This is the test of constitutionality.

Even as he spoke the galleries were filling with staff and press who had heard garbled versions of what had happened. In the offices of Labor ministers, the staff listened to Crean over the closed circuit broadcast which goes into every office in Parliament House. As they listened they packed books and papers into the large cardboard boxes used to store or shift material when ministers changed offices for normal administrative reasons. Already boxes had been taken to the side entrances of the building and placed in private cars or in removal vans that had been urgently ordered, to be taken from there to the airport or to various parts of Canberra. What inspired these wild scenes was the fear that the ministerial offices, together with their contents, might be taken over at any time by the new government. Everything was packed indiscriminately — personal papers, political material that would be needed in the campaign, departmental documents — to be sorted out later at a more secure location.

Meanwhile in the Senate there had been business as usual at 2.00 pm with a discussion of the Postal Regulations followed by the Tertiary Education Commission Bill 1975. The Budget Bills were, however, listed as the first Order of the Day, which meant that they would be called on for debate automatically when these items were finished. Until 2.15 pm, Labor's Leader in the Senate, Ken Wriedt, still did not know that he was no longer Leader of the government and that he was about to move the passage of a Budget that could now benefit only his LCP opponents. In the last hour no one from Whitlam's office had contacted him. At 2.15 pm, he was told in the Senate Chamber by a member of his own staff.

At 2.20 pm, the Budget Bills were called on by the President of the Senate, Labor's Justin O'Byrne. Even with the support of

Independent Senators Steele Hall and Cleaver Bunton, Labor could not have directly prevented this as they would have lost any vote 29-30 (Albert Field was absent in Brisbane). But they could have moved various procedural motions, such as a motion that the business of the Senate be re-arranged, or simply that it adjourn for that day. And once a Labor Senator had the call to speak from O'Byrne, he would have been entitled under the Senate Standing Orders to speak for an hour, even on a procedural motion. Labor could, therefore, almost certainly have delayed the bringing on of the Budget Bills until the Senate adjourned at 6.00 pm, leaving the caretaker government without supply overnight and the Governor-General unable to dissolve Parliament — a situation that would have graphically heightened the events of the day. But it was scarcely feasible for Wriedt to devise this kind of strategy in the five minutes' notice he had of the government's dismissal before the Bills came on. That kind of exercise would have required some time before 2.00 pm when the Senate resumed sitting.

It should be noted, however, that O'Byrne could not have suspended or adjourned the sitting of the Senate without the concurrence of the Opposition — clearly, this would not have been granted. Nor could he have prevented the Senate meeting by not appearing at the scheduled time of 2.00 pm. The Standing Orders of the Senate provide that in the absence of the President another Senator may be elected by those Senators present to preside over the Senate and so the Opposition could simply have chosen one of their own number to take the Chair.

The result was that when the Budget Bills automatically came before the Senate for consideration at 2.20 pm, Wriedt simply moved the motion he had prepared — a motion for passage similar to other motions he had been moving for the last month. On this occasion his motion was carried on the voices. Both Labor and Liberal Senators had voted for it and no division was taken. At 2.24 pm, the sitting of the Senate was suspended until the ringing of the bells, a reference to the shrill bells that summoned Senators to sittings. The bells would not ring again that day and that Senate would never sit again.

The Budget Bills were taken straight to Gordon Scholes in his Speaker's chair in the House of Representatives. Scholes signed the usual certificate which stated that the Bills had passed both Houses and were ready for the Governor-General's assent. The Bills were then despatched to Yarralumla. While the Speaker's

Malcolm Fraser surveying the scene outside Parliament
House in his first hour as Prime Minister

certificate is usual, it is not strictly necessary. A refusal by
Scholes to sign would not have stopped the transmission of the
Bills to Kerr where they immediately received his assent and
became law. At the same time a proclamation announcing the
dissolution of Parliament was being typed up in the Prime
Minister's Department.

In the House of Representatives, Crean finished his speech a
little before 2.25 pm and a vote was taken in which the censure
of the no longer existing government was defeated. At 2.34 pm
Fraser rose to make the following statement:

> Mr Speaker, this afternoon the Governor-General commissioned me
> to form a government until elections can be held . . .

At that point he was drowned out by shouts of angry abuse from
the Labor benches. When the shouting died down he went on to
read portions of Kerr's statement of reasons and to announce
that Parliament would be dissolved as soon as possible. He could
not of course control the House and, when he finally moved that

it adjourn, Labor defeated this motion 64-55 and then forced the suspension of Standing Orders to allow Whitlam to move the following motion:

That this House expresses its want of confidence in the Prime Minister and requests Mr. Speaker forthwith to advise His Excellency the Governor-General to call the honourable member for Werriwa to form a government.

Whitlam's motion was an impeccable study in the niceties of parliamentary process, referring to Kerr as 'His Excellency', to Fraser as 'the Prime Minister' and to himself now simply as 'the honourable member for Werriwa'. It was an attempt to overturn on the floor of the House, a forum which he had mastered and then dominated over 20 years, a decision carefully designed to exclude the House from any influence. Kerr and Fraser both realised that Labor retained a majority in the House of Representatives. It followed that they could only intend to disregard any expressions of its opinion and have it dissolved as soon as possible. How well Whitlam was playing the parliamentary game really did not matter — they were playing a different game.

Whitlam's motion was passed and Speaker Scholes, intending to take it to Kerr, suspended the House at 3.15 pm until 5.30 pm. By 5.30 pm, however, a copy of Kerr's dissolution proclamation would be attached with adhesive tape to the polished doors of the chamber and that House of Representatives would, like that Senate, never sit again.

Scholes had telephoned Yarralumla, as soon as the House rose, to request an appointment but was told that he could not meet Kerr until 4.45 pm. The proclamation dissolving both Houses of Parliament was signed into law at Yarralumla by Kerr and Fraser before 4.00 pm.

Inside Parliament House, Labor ministers and their staff sat in their almost empty offices only fully realising what had happened now that they had stopped moving. Some were already thinking coolly of the coming election and Defence Minister Bill Morrison, sitting behind an empty desk with a drink, speculated bleakly on the harm that Kerr's action would do Labor in the eyes of the elderly ladies in his suburban Sydney electorate of St.

Opposite: Outside Parliament House on the afternoon of
11 November 1975

George. Outside, a crowd of about 2000 from nearby government offices had gathered in the afternoon sun and kept up the chant of 'We Want Gough' that became an ovation if any of the Labor members emerged from the main doors.

4.45 pm was the end. At Yarralumla Kerr was receiving Scholes, thanking him politely for bringing the House of Representatives motion which had no significance whatsoever in the absence of the House itself. On the steps leading to the main doors of Parliament House, Kerr's Official Secretary David Smith, wearing a formal black jacket and standing before a lectern, was reading the proclamation that dissolved both Houses of Parliament

What he was reading, unheard over the jeers of the crowd, was the following:

PROCLAMATION

Australia   By His Excellency the
JOHN R. KERR   Governor-General of
Governor-General.   Australia

WHEREAS by section 57 of the Constitution it is provided that if the House of Representatives passes any proposed law, and the Senate rejects or fails to pass it, or passes it with amendments to which the House of Representatives will not agree, and if after an interval of three months the House of Representatives, in the same or the next session, again passes the proposed law with or without any amendments which have been made, suggested, or agreed to by the Senate and the Senate rejects or fails to pass it, or passes it with amendments to which the House of Representatives will not agree, the Governor-General may dissolve the Senate and the House of Representatives simultaneously:

AND WHEREAS the conditions upon which the Governor-General is empowered by that section of the Constitution to dissolve the Senate and the House of Representatives simultaneously have been fulfilled in respect of the several proposed laws intituled—

Health Insurance Levy Act 1974
Health Insurance Levy Assessment Act 1974
Income Tax (International Agreements) Act 1974
Minerals (Submerged Lands) Act 1974
Minerals (Submerged Lands) (Royalty) Act 1974
National Health Act 1974
Conciliation and Arbitration Act 1974
Conciliation and Arbitration Act (No. 2) 1974
National Investment Fund Act 1974

> *Electoral Laws Amendment Act* 1974
> *Electoral Act* 1975
> *Privy Council Appeals Abolition Act* 1975
> *Superior Court of Australia Act* 1974
> *Electoral Re-distribution (New South Wales) Act* 1975
> *Electoral Re-distribution (Queensland) Act* 1975
> *Electoral Re-distribution (South Australia) Act* 1975
> *Electoral Re-distribution (Tasmania) Act* 1975
> *Electoral Re-distribution (Victoria) Act* 1975
> *Broadcasting and Television Act (No.* 2) 1974
> *Television Stations Licence Fees Act* 1974
> *Broadcasting Stations Licence Fees Act* 1974

NOW THEREFORE, I Sir John Robert Kerr, the Governor-General of Australia, do by this my Proclamation dissolve the Senate and the House of Representatives.

Given under my Hand and the Great Seal of Australia on 11 November 1975.

By His Excellency's Command,

MALCOLM FRASER
Prime Minister

GOD SAVE THE QUEEN!

Directly behind and towering over Smith's diminutive figure was Whitlam, eyes fixed grimly on the one-page document which marked the end of his three years as Prime Minister. When Smith finished with the traditional 'God Save the Queen' Whitlam finally exploded:

> Well may we say 'God Save the Queen' because nothing will save the Governor-General.

He had undoubtedly caught the anger and frustration felt by most of those watching. Yet to see Kerr's action as the substance rather than the symbol of Labor's defeat is to misunderstand his role. It was the culmination of a three-year struggle between opposing political forces and was only significant for the time and style of its occurrence. The important decision was the Opposition's decision to block the Budget. It was this that demonstrated graphically the irreconcilable divisions between the Labor and non-Labor forces. Whatever John Kerr had once been, he was by this time a representative of those non-Labor forces in the sense that a commitment to the labour movement formed no element in his reasons for any action and on his record

Labor had no ground for thinking otherwise. As pressure built up on the Whitlam government throughout 1975 and its opponents closed in for the kill, the only question became whether it was strong enough to survive these assaults — by itself, for it could expect no help from outsiders, including an outsider it had appointed as Governor-General. The answer was that it was not strong enough to survive although its resistance carried it closer than most of its opponents ever foresaw.

Ironically, none of the participants in the impending struggle had thought more about these historical patterns than Kerr — and none would have better appreciated the strength of the forces concentrated against Labor. Labor's opponents, also assessing the nature of the conflict, knew they could not necessarily rely on the Governor-General but, more importantly, they knew that Labor could not rely on him either. Their strategy was always more consistently directed because its basic premise was correct, and throughout the crises they demonstrated that they knew their man by emphasising to him his role in its resolution.

In his 17 October statement that was forwarded to Yarralumla, Ellicott had stressed that:

> The Prime Minister is treating the Governor-General as a mere automaton with no public will of his own, sitting at Yarralumla waiting to do his bidding.
> Nothing could be further from the truth. It is contrary to principle, precedent and common sense.

In the statement released in his name on 21 October supporting Fraser's blocking of the Budget, the patriarch of the Liberal Party, Sir Robert Menzies, had observed flatteringly:

> Finally, and I would say this with unfeigned respect for the vice-regal office, I think that it would be a singular piece of impertinence on the part of the Prime Minister to go to the Governor-General, whose reputation is high, and who understands these things very well, and to ask him for a premature 'half-senate' election, calculated and designed, hopefully, because of the recent legislation about senators from the Capital Territory and the Northern Territory, to give the Government control of the Senate for a month or two, in which time, of course, all their legislation which now has been attacked in the Senate, could be carried with permanent (and I think damaging) effects on Australian political structure. To offer advice to the Governor-General on the lines that have been hinted at would, I think, be both improper and insulting.

Two days later Fraser assured questioners:

But if any decision is made by the Governor-General as part of the Constitution of course we will abide by it. If he gives us any advice in relation to the course of action we ought to take within his part of the constitutional process, of course we will give very great weight to it.

On 7 November Fraser was still pressing the point. In a television interview he refused to be drawn on his discussions with Kerr but added:

Sir John Kerr is perfectly capable of talking for himself — and he will.

Labor's strategy was based, on the other hand, on the answer Whitlam gave on 17 October to the question whether the Governor-General was required to accept his advice:

Unquestionably. The governor-general must act on the advice of his prime minister.

He need not and he did not. Once that is assumed, it becomes clear that the government could almost certainly not survive the blocking of the Budget. It was that action that brought it down. It is not really important, therefore, to ask which of the various motivations which have been attributed to Kerr is correct. The answer may be one of them, some of them, all of them, or none of them. It is unlikely that anyone will ever know.

He may simply have concluded that Labor could not last in office and in those circumstances he ought to distance himself from those who had appointed him and ensure his acceptability to the administration which would replace them.

He may have been influenced by the near unanimous advice of his friends and acquaintances. Certainly, few of those who came regularly to Yarralumla or to Government House in Melbourne where he spent most of the week before 11 November, would have counselled anything except a speedy end to the Whitlam government. Most would have maintained that Labor was running down the nation's economy to a point where it could not recover for some years.

He may have been unable to overcome his distaste for Whitlam and his chagrin at having to work constantly with someone who treated him as a cipher in spite of his constitutional position as Head of State.

He may have formed the opinion that the alternative arrangements to supply, proposed by Whitlam, were illegal, or simply administratively impossible, or at least demonstrated that

Whitlam was capable of stepping outside the normal processes of government in his battle to survive — and of taking the Governor-General with him in the same way as he had persuaded him to approve the loan authorisation of 13 December 1974.

He may have believed, as he explained to Bill Hayden in late October, that both Whitlam and Fraser were endangering the system of government by their unyielding confrontation. Or even, as he suggested to Hayden in early November, that Whitlam was resilient enough to be defeated in an election now but to return to power in a short time when the Liberals found the economy as unmanageable as Labor had.

He may have believed when he proposed to James McClelland on 29 October that if any half-Senate election was put off until mid 1976 Fraser might agree to pass the Budget, that the possibility of Labor controlling the Senate for even a short period was the greatest fear of the Liberals, and that he could initiate a compromise between the two leaders — even though Fraser rejected the proposal out of hand when it was floated by Whitlam a few days later.

He may have taken the view that the risk of supply running out could not be taken or that, as 11 November had been suggested as the last practicable date on which to call an election before Christmas, if the Budget had not been passed by that date there was a danger of the money running out before an election could be held — although Fraser had essentially guaranteed that supply would be given for the election period by agreeing to abide by a decision of the Governor-General. He may have considered that, even if a half-Senate election were called by that date, it would not avert the danger since the three State Liberal governments would instruct their Governors not to issue the necessary writs to allow the elections to take place in those States — although it is possible that merely granting Whitlam's request for a half-Senate election would have effectively compelled the Opposition in the Senate to pass the Budget Bills.

He may have regarded the confrontation as a 'constitutional crisis', as he described it in his statement of reasons, requiring a detached judicial approach to its settlement, an application of some of his theories in this area of law. On this approach its causes were irrelevant. It did not matter how the Senate had gained the numbers to block the Budget or why State governments would nullify any half-Senate election by refusing to issue the writs. These political antecedents did not make it a 'political crisis'. Yet his own actions indicate that he approached the crisis from the outset as a *political* exercise in which he was a *participant* — not as a judge removed from the conflict between parties. He realised that he had as much to gain — or to lose — as they did, and acted accordingly.

For, whatever his reasons when deciding upon Whitlam's dismissal, he took every precaution to ensure that it occurred so that it could not be undone — and, in what would be a confrontation between himself and Whitlam, that he was the survivor. This obviously involved the initial judgment of what the result of an election would be. As Sir Philip Game emphasised in 1932, while debating the dismissal of NSW Premier Lang, the real question is whether in such a situation the Governor can be sure of the Opposition winning the consequent election. If he cannot, he must hold back, as he himself faces instant dismissal should the government be returned. It is a situation therefore where a Governor, or Governor-General, is required to ask in essence whether he can defeat the government at the polls — without being able to campaign himself, but of course being able to rely on the Opposition to plead his case. There could be few decisions more intensely political.

By November 1975 Kerr was able to conclude, like Game in 1932, that the government's chances of surviving an election were remote. If for no other reason, this judgment made a double dissolution the goal so far as Kerr was concerned — not an election for the House of Representatives alone or for the House of Representatives and half the Senate only. Either of the last two left the danger of the Senate being as closely divided in future as it presently was and, in those unstable circumstances, another election in the near future at which Labor might be returned, was a possibility. Even a *possibility* of that was out of the question for someone in Kerr's position.

So, while confident of how the electorate would react, he had also to ensure that the issue went directly to them and was not side-tracked into the courts. However little prospect of success a legal challenge to his actions ultimately had, its very existence would be dangerous. It was therefore necessary to determine whether the High Court would stay out of the fracas that would follow the dismissal of a Prime Minister — hence the meeting with Chief Justice Sir Garfield Barwick on 10 November. It is unlikely that he felt the need of Barwick's opinion to confirm that the Governor-General had the power to dismiss a Prime

Minister, although it was a useful debating point later. What he did need was Barwick's assurance that this was an exercise of power that was out of the court's jurisdiction, and that the challenge to the existing electoral boundaries which had been heard by the court in the first week of November and was still awaiting judgment, would not render an election held before Christmas on the existing boundaries in any way invalid.

In this context any prior notice to Whitlam was out of the question. It will always be a matter of conjecture as to what Whitlam would have done had he discovered the plans that were being made. But anyone who witnessed his fierce determination to triumph over his opponents at that time must have concluded that it was almost certain that he would have had Kerr dismissed. Kerr had witnessed Whitlam at close quarters and would hardly lay himself open to such a real and present danger when he was being so meticulous about mere possibilities. For the same reason, it would have done Whitlam no good to ask for time when presented with his letter of dismissal so that he could meet Kerr's objections to his existing course and, if necessary, accept Fraser's compromise offer of a June 1976 election or even recommend a general election now at which he would at least be able to campaign as Prime Minister. The attention to detail was maintained to the last minute.

The logistics of 11 November were fraught with real danger for Kerr. It was necessary to dismiss a Prime Minister, commission his successor, have supply passed through the parliament, and finally dissolve both Houses, without any major period of delay that could raise doubts about the legitimacy of the new government or enable the old government to regain the initiative. That all these took place according to the timetable worked out beforehand was due, even then, as much to Labor's lack of counter measures as to the detailed forward planning. What contingency plans had been made to deal with a situation where Labor refused to accept the decision have not been revealed. It is unthinkable that some were not formulated.

Kerr misjudged the future. He did not envisage the possibility that he, not Malcolm Fraser, would be chief target for Labor and its supporters; that he would receive no real support from those he had bought to power once they had made good use of him; and that within two years he would be forced into permanent and wounded exile, condemned to joylessly wander the world's pleasure spots like some modern version of Wagner's Flying

Dutchman.

The significance of Kerr's decision was not its substance but, to use his own expression, its style. In substance it constituted one element, if a vital and penultimate one, in the three year campaign by Labor's opponents to remove it from government — a campaign in which John Kerr was no more than an agent at the very end. In style, it reflected three years of refusal to accept the legitimacy of the Labor government. In the same way that Opposition Senators and State Premiers acted in a way that no conservative government had ever experienced, Kerr, as Governor-General, broke with all precedents by consulting with the Leader of the Opposition, confiding in him to a greater extent than in the Prime Minister, and finally commissioning him as Prime Minister without a majority in the House of Representatives. Whitlam, who had of course never seen an Opposition Leader consulted by a Governor-General in his two decades in the Parliament under conservative governments, must have flinched to realise that on its last day in office his government was still being treated as an aberration, as never entitled to the power and privileges its opponents had long enjoyed as of right.

As he stood behind Smith and listened to the proclamation of dissolution, these realisations, many of them still only half-appreciated in the rush of events, began to form into the well of bitterness that would first spill over as soon as Smith finished speaking and would still be close to the surface years later. After his opening attack on Kerr and Fraser he appealed to the crowd to maintain their rage throughout the coming weeks. Obviously it would be no problem for Whitlam himself.

Then he went back into the building to call an immediate meeting of Caucus. With an election certain, most members wanted only to return to their electorates that night or first thing next morning. So it was decided that the meeting be held at once in the Caucus Room. Again Whitlam spoke briefly and bitterly to the emotionally charged gathering, simply appealing for a total effort over the next month during the campaign up to the election that was expected to be on 13 December. He led the 92 members of Caucus in single file down the corridor past Fraser's office, through Kings Hall, out the main doors and down the steps into the crowd, all to the tune of the old union song, *Solidarity Forever*, sung badly, but with feeling.

Back inside, Fraser and Menadue discussed some of the administrative details related to the transfer of power. Already the

Ex-Prime Minister Gough Whitlam addressing the crowd from the steps of Parliament House soon after his dismissal

corridor outside Fraser's office, still the suite normally allocated to the Leader of the Opposition, was filled with public servants laden with files and papers, who had business with the new Prime Minister. Only 100 feet further down the same corridor were the Prime Minister's rooms where Whitlam still remained in occupation. That morning some of the very officials waiting outside Fraser's office had been attending on Whitlam. Now they kept their 100-foot distance from the ex-Prime Minister's quarters, dramatising the swiftness of the change-over as no proclamation could ever do.

It was simply too late for Labor to do anything about what had happened. There was talk of a general strike but ACTU President Bob Hawke made a strong plea to the trade union movement that evening to focus their efforts on the election campaign. It seemed startling — an appeal to the union movement for observance of the processes of the parliamentary system — a system under which the House of Representatives, where Labor had established a government, now stood empty with the dissolution proclamation taped to its doors. Hawke was also speaking, however, in his capacity as National President of the Labor Party. He had flown to Canberra that afternoon and after talks with Whitlam and others had shared their judgment that widespread industrial action would alienate a large section of the electorate even before the campaign began. It did not occur to him that Labor's vote might be so low at the election in a month's time that it is unlikely that anything could have worsened the result for the Party. Probably it did not occur to anyone else on the Labor side. That night they took over a Canberra restaurant and kept it open until five o'clock next morning. It was the Labor government's wake.

There was probably only one point at which Labor might have made a significant attempt to retain power. That was when Kerr handed Whitlam his letter of dismissal in his study at Yarralumla. If Whitlam had, at that moment, refused to accept the letter of dismissal and had returned to Parliament House, if he had installed himself in his office, insisting on the status of Prime Minister and attempted to have Kerr's commission revoked in London, it is likely that the formal changeover of power would have been slowed, or even halted, as many public servants would have continued to deal with the existing government until the issue was finally resolved. Paradoxically this would have involved keeping out of the House of Representatives, in order to prevent Fraser having a credible forum to announce Kerr's decision, yet occupying the Senate to attempt to prevent the Supply Bills passing through it. The government could have used its majority to adjourn the House of Representatives and, with sufficient notice, have brought proceedings in the Senate to a virtual standstill by procedural obstruction.

Whether it would then have been possible for Whitlam to convince Harold Wilson's British Labour government to advise the termination of Kerr's commission to the Queen must be doubtful. The initial British reaction would have been to avoid involvement at almost any cost and, if some decision was necessary, it would probably have been to do nothing to alter the status quo which would have left Kerr still as Governor-General, on the ground that removing Kerr would appear more like intervention than allowing Whitlam to be dismissed. Harold Wilson's writings all suggest that he would not have been influenced in any way by the fact that it was an Australian *Labor*

Melbourne police try to halt crowds marching on Victorian
Liberal Party headquarters, 11 November 1975

government which appealed for assistance.

Yet there may have been a chance of saving the situation.
Whitlam was entitled to have Kerr's commission revoked if he
was still Prime Minister and there was at least an argument that
Kerr had exceeded his constitutional powers — and in this kind
of confusion Whitlam would have had the advantage of having
every appearance of being the Prime Minister. Any chance
disappeared, however, when he took the letter of dismissal from
Kerr and left Yarralumla to seek a reversal of the decision in
Parliament. Kerr would have realised this at the time although it
has already been suggested that he must have considered the
possibility of Whitlam refusing to accept the dismissal and to
have formulated a swift point of contact to key bureaucrats. This
was never needed.

When the long file of Labor Senators and Members, all
singing, with Whitlam at their head, emerged from Parliament
House into the still bright sunlight of late afternoon, the crowd

responded wildly to a gesture that appealed to them by its sheer sense of defiance. But nothing could disguise the fact that as they descended those steps they were marching out of office, out of government — and into the streets which would be their only forum for the coming campaign.

12 Dead men running
The election

Yesterdays' ministers woke up on the morning of 12 November to contemplate the bleak vista of the campaign trail stretching for 32 days before them. And they now faced it not only without the status and prestige of government but also without its immense logistic support — not just the VIP aircraft, cars, staff and communications equipment that made campaigning more efficient and more convenient, but also their departments, those storehouses of information and speeches that can be fed into the media day after day up to an election.

At 9.00 am in Whitlam's office in Parliament House there were numerous signs of the new order. In rooms strangely empty of bureaucrats and parliamentary personnel, Whitlam's Private Secretary John Mant was trying, and failing, to get an assurance from the office of the new Defence Minister Jim Killen that the Leader of the Opposition would be provided with one of the RAAF VIP planes for the duration of the campaign. Whitlam himself interrupted Mant:

> Don't press them — I'll fly commercial if necessary. We did it for years in Opposition.

Looking out the window he could see another sign of the times. Walking across the lawns which separated the Attorney-General's Department from Parliament House were Secretary Clarrie Harders and Pat Brazil, head of the Constitutional Law Section of the department. They were not, as they would have been the day before, walking towards Whitlam's office or Enderby's office on the House of Representatives side of Parliament House. They were walking towards the Senate side, to the office of the new Attorney-General, Ivor Greenwood, and carrying with them files of material that Greenwood would want to use over the next four weeks. It was a depressing sight to everyone in Whitlam's office, except seemingly to Whitlam who continued to arrange papers industriously in preparation for doing once more what he had spent a large part of the last 25 years doing — criss-crossing the country for fifteen or sixteen hours every day in an election campaign, giving the same speech and somehow giving it with enthusiasm.

Enthusiasm was something Labor would need. An election campaign has an internal life of its own, often divorced from reality. Surrounded more or less continually by devoted aides and eager supporters, the campaigners tend inevitably to overrate their electoral chances. That was certainly true of the Labor campaign in 1975. When the polls published figures predicting a massive defeat, many Labor campaigners, witnessing the largest and most demonstrative crowds for a generation, felt that the polls could not be correct — at least about the margin of victory and defeat. There was also to some extent a protective suspension of belief. With large numbers of people required over the next month to work long hours and to contribute funds, it was apparent that the campaign would collapse if it was once conceded that the exercise was futile. And it was not necessarily completely futile, despite the poll which had the government's level of electoral support at 33 per cent with the Opposition at 60 per cent, during the first week of July when the Cairns and Connor loan stories dominated the front pages.

On these kinds of figures Labor faced not just defeat but near extinction if the electorate returned during the campaign to its pre-supply crisis mood.

The basic strategies of the campaign emerged almost at once. Labor's invidious situation was best suggested by the comment of ANOP Director Rod Cameron made three weeks earlier and already referred to:

> Moreover, the major issue, as I have suggested previously is 'competent government'. We cannot hope, no matter how impressive Gough will be on the campaign trail, no matter how skilful we can make the communications effort, to defuse in a short period a year's worth of constant, repetitious reinforcement of the incompetent government theme.

It would face for the next month the twin charges of incompetence and impropriety which Fraser had emphasised so effectively throughout the year and which were now firmly lodged

Your choice on

dark or

MURPHY Lionel, Senator: As Attorney-General, led A.S.I.O. Headquarters raid. Involved in initial moves for $4 billion "temporary loan". Left ministry on appointment by Mr. Whitlam as Justice of High Court of Australia.

CREAN Frank: Former Treasurer during period of record inflation, record taxes and growing unemployment. Demoted from Treasury, December, 1974.

CAIRNS Jim: Labor's second Treasurer. Also Acting Prime Minister. His involvement in loan negotiations saw his dismissal by Mr. Whitlam for misleading Parliament.

CONNOR Rex: Was Minister for Minerals and Energy. Acting Prime Minister. Dismissed for misleading Parliament after pursuing overseas loan negotiations beyond authorised period.

CAMERON Clyde: Former Minister for Labour. Demoted June, 1975. His period in Ministry saw record industrial strife, record wage demands.

HAYDEN William: On own admission disclosed Budget details to Mr. Robert Hawke 7 hours before Budget made public. Labor's 3rd Treasurer. Budget deficit heading towards $4 billion against his estimated $2.8 billion.

WHITLAM E. G.: Was Prime Minister for 3 years. Promised Australian people full employment. Presided over record inflation, unemployment, industrial strife, overseas junkets, Ministerial dismissals and demotions.

DALY Fred: Popular leader of the House and Minister for Services and Property. Retired November, 1975. Into the vacancy . . . Tony Whitlam.

WHITLAM Tony: Son of E. G. Whitlam. Named A.L.P. candidate for Mr. Daly's blue ribbon seat of Grayndler, without usual ballot for endorsement.

Labor turned out the lights.

The personal touch. Liberal Party campaign advertising,
November 1975

in the minds of the electorate. Moreover the concepts were sufficiently general to enable individual voters to identify their own particular grievances — often local or regional — with the deficiencies of the national government.

Although aware that the damaging events of 1975 could not possibly be neutralised, the initial response of Labor strategists to this situation was to focus on what they saw as the positive aspects of its administration — the new programs in areas like education, social welfare, urban and regional development. This approach, however, contained its own dilemma. Fraser had also consistently stressed the theme of extravagant spending by a government anxious to centralise programs in Canberra and to substantially expand the bureaucracy to implement them. It was a theme which struck a number of electoral chords — dislike of taxation which was the source of the funds so prodigally dispensed; distrust of government in general and Canberra in particular; distaste for public servants as an overpaid, underworked group. The result was that what seemed like the natural basis of Labor's campaign tended in many ways to reinforce Fraser's charges.

To a large extent this was possible because Labor had never succeeded in demonstrating to the electorate that expenditure on education, for example, resulted in a specific benefit to the great majority in the community who made use of schools even though it was not a benefit that could be readily quantified in individual terms. Out of Labor's multitude of government-funded programs of services over three years, only two had registered a significant electoral impact in ANOP polls carried out by Cameron earlier in 1975 — Medibank, which produced a wide positive reaction, and the ALAO which had a substantial but much weaker degree of penetration. These findings coincided with Liberal surveys with the result that, from the outset, Fraser specifically exempted Medibank from his announced intention of cutting government spending although he was careful not to guarantee that it would continue in its existing form.

Labor's efforts to make capital out of Fraser's promises of spending cuts therefore encountered the threshold difficulty of dramatising for the electorate, in a period of weeks, what a reduction in expenditure on education would entail when it had been unable to do this over a period of years. The extent of Labor's failure to communicate these notions to the electorate during its period of government can be gauged from the extraordinary spectacle of Fraser able to promise, in a reversal of the usual approach of an Opposition party, not increased expenditure on a wide variety of groups, but spending cuts in almost every area — to be able to offer not more, but *less*, to the electorate.

It followed logically from this strategy that there was little reason for the Liberals to put forward a set of detailed policies and programs — indeed such an approach would have been inconsistent with the idea of cutting back government activities — and in the absence of a need to do so it was obviously preferable not to have to set out the kinds of positive proposals for action in government that attract analysis and debate. In the 1974 campaign Snedden had been drawn into questions of policy implementation and suffered some damage as a result.

Only one issue did not fit into this campaign scenario — perfect as it was for the Liberals, and positively nightmarish for Labor — and that was the means by which the election had been brought on half-way through the government's term. The polls had indicated strong public support for the government on the issue of the blocking of the Budget and, while Rod Cameron had warned that much of this support would almost certainly not be translated into Labor votes if an election eventuated, an analysis of the other issues indicated no room to manoeuvre.

So Labor's National Secretary and Campaign Director David Combe informed the Party's advertising agency that it would run on the issue of deprivation of government by the decisions of Fraser to block the Budget and Kerr to dismiss the government, emphasising the former because of possible electoral reaction against continued attacks on the ostensibly non-political figure of the Governor-General. He was aware, like most of his colleagues, that the issue would be a difficult one to sustain over a month — but that there was effectively no alternative.

In fact the issue retained much of its emotional force during the first week of the campaign, aided by the release of the Enderby-Byers opinion by Enderby, the release of Barwick's advice by Kerr in response, and attempts by Byers to extricate himself from the political fracas over his legal views.

Fraser, however, adhered to his own line with a television address to the nation on 16 November in which, his staff promised the press in advance of the broadcast, he would reveal that the country's economic condition was far worse than the government had disclosed to the public. It was the familiar juxtaposition of incompetence in economic management and impropriety in concealing the results from the nation. Although the broadcast did not substantiate these changes with details, 70 Treasury officials protested to Kerr that in this, and in other matters, Fraser was going beyond the role of a caretaker administration by using the bureaucracy as an arm of his election strategy. Their protest highlighted the problem of the very concept of a caretaker government for, despite the use of the term by both Barwick and Kerr, it had no basis or recognition in British or Australian parliamentary history. There was government or opposition but no twilight zone in between and Fraser, being in government, was under no constitutional obligation to observe any diminution of a government's normal powers.

In addition to the logistic advantages of government, the Liberals had at their disposal on 12 November a campaign organisation that had already been activated on a full-time basis for a month since the blocking of the Budget. It had been operating during that time under the supervision of Tony Eggleton from the Liberal Party National Secretariat. In response to dissatisfaction with the 1972 and 1974 campaigns, Eggleton had instituted a fund-raising drive which had enabled the Secretariat to be expanded to provide constant inputs on questions of policy and tactics between elections. For the actual campaign period, a headquarters was established in Queens Road in Melbourne where masses of telephones, telexes and vocadexes were installed to link ministers, candidates, Party officials and the media. In keeping with the emphasis of both sides on media exposure, there were not only sufficient television and radio receivers for several persons to monitor reports simultaneously but also equipment to record the items of coverage on tape or video-disc.

Labor had a similar but less extensive assemblage of electronic aids at its Canberra base, John Curtin House, where Assistant National Secretary Ken Bennett presided over the mechanics of the campaign, using John Curtin House as the co-ordinating point for the information and personnel located in the various State headquarters. Merely to rationalise the availability of former ministers so that all regions were covered during the campaign required the work of three persons full-time throughout the campaign. Manpower was no problem. Although Labor lacked the Liberal Party's large number of paid year-round staff, it was deluged with offers of voluntary assistance in the emotional aftermath of dismissal, many of them from persons who had never previously taken any active role in politics.

Those who were put to work in Canberra could quickly appreciate how dominating the dismissal issue was to Labor within its own shattered world. In John Curtin House they worked beside mountains of boxes containing files and papers from ministerial offices. In Parliament House they worked in ministerial offices from which the Labor members could not yet be ejected only because this was the decision of the Speaker, and there could not be a new Speaker until a new Parliament convened in February. A large proportion of Labor's ministerial staff had initially been seconded from the bureaucracy and most of these took annual leave or leave without pay for a month to work on the campaign. Some of these set up a research unit in Ken Wriedt's office in Parliament House and supplied Labor candidates around the country with information on government programs.

In melodramatic 'secret' meetings on suburban street corners, public servants handed over, usually at their own instigation, some of this material that had not been in Parliament House on 11 November. After one voluminous collection of material on the government's record had been obtained from the Prime Minister's Department and copied, the original was to be fed into the incinerators at the Canberra Hospital — the only fires large enough — in order to protect its source. When even that seemed unlikely to work, all the documents were buried in the garden of a suburban residence.

On both sides, those at the top of the campaign organisations had their minds fixed on two related matters — television advertising, and money. Again the Liberals had a flying start by booking timespots during the blocking of the Budget in the possibility of an election and by setting their corporate fundraising network in operation at the same time. So successful was this last exercise that by 15 November a $1.3 million Liberal campaign budget had been underwritten.

For Labor, the suddenness of the election meant that television time had to be booked before funds had even been solicited, let alone received. One consequence of this precarious financial position was that in addition to the tapping of normal sources — unions and corporations (70 per cent of the funds for the 1974 campaign had been provided by corporations and only 30 per cent by unions) — Whitlam and Combe became involved in their damaging attempt to obtain $500,000 from the Iraqi government. Even the very booking of time presented problems, as November/December had been closed out by the Liberals and pre-Christmas retailers. Only the intervention of the Broadcasting Control Board forced the commercial networks to increase the advertising time available each hour by two minutes. When it all emerged on the evening television screens, the advertising followed largely the pattern of debate already set: the Liberals 'Three dark years' with frame after frame clicking through Labor's misdeeds and mismanagement; Labor's earnest community stalwarts explaining why Fraser's actions in forcing an election were shameful and un-Australian.

Initially Combe had hoped to arrange a series of television debates — Whitlam *v* Fraser, Hayden *v* Lynch, James McClelland *v* Street, with David Frost as moderator. He was unable to sell the idea to the commercial television stations but still pushed the importance of Labor's three 'trump cards' being thrown into debates with their Liberal counterparts on current affairs radio and television. The Liberals were unenthusiastic, recognising the Labor trio as effective debaters but, more importantly, convinced that they were well ahead in the polls and could only lose rather than gain by giving their opponents an opportunity to regain the initiative.

For just this reason the campaign overall was flat and uninspiring after the flurries of the first week. As the issue of the dismissal waned, the Liberals, realising that they had nothing to gain from discussing policies or engaging their opponents, retreated into a bland low-key campaign designed to preserve the existing mood of the electorate. Labor was never really able to penetrate this shell and what had begun in uniquely dramatic circumstances became for most of the electorate a monotonous series of media performances, whether paid advertisements or current affairs treatment, in comparison with the campaigns of 1972 and 1974.

There has been a great deal written about the anti-Labor bias of the media, particularly the print media, during the campaign. Without knowing what effect newspaper coverage over a short period has on voting intention, it seems unlikely that the problem lay in editorials. With the exception of one group of papers in 1961 and another in 1972, no editorials have ever urged the election of a Labor government and it would have been unrealistic for Labor to expect a change in 1975. What was alleged in 1975 as being unprecedented was that all three

Three dark years. Liberal Party campaign advertising,
November 1975

newspaper groups cut back on comment by political correspondents, and that the Murdoch group injected political bias into the reporting of news, as distinct from editorials, on a wide scale. The cutback of political correspondents was clearly designed to restrict their analysis of Fraser's policies and presumably arose out of the assurances of support Fraser sought and received from proprietors during the supply crisis. The attitude of the Murdoch papers was the cause of a strike in Sydney by journalists working for the *Daily Telegraph*, the *Daily Mirror* and the *Australian*.

Before the strike, 75 members of the staff of the *Australian* had presented Murdoch with a letter in which they said:

> We are loyal to the best traditions of journalism and must remain so to retain our sanity.
> We cannot be loyal to those traditions, or to ourselves, if we accept the deliberate or careless slanting of headlines, seemingly-blatant imbalance in news presentation, political censorship and on occasion, distortion of copy from senior, specialist journalists, the political management of news and features, the stifling of dissident and even unpalatably impartial opinion in the paper's columns. All these things have happened to greater or lesser degree in recent months, and the tragedy is that because of this more are mistakenly imputed, by people both inside and outside the paper.

The coverage can be best illustrated by three examples from the campaign period. On the evening of 4 December, the latest unemployment figures were released. The *Australian*'s headline for 5 December read:

UNEMPLOYMENT UP 18,368 TO 4.5 PER CENT.

The *Age*'s headline for the same day read:

20,000 FALL IN JOBLESS.

The difference was that the *Age* was using the seasonally adjusted figures normally used in discussing unemployment.

On 26 November, the first edition of the *Daily Mirror*, one of Sydney's two afternoon papers, carried on the front page a story that Whitlam had proposed a scheme of low cost rental accommodation for persons under a certain income level. Its headline read:

GOUGH'S PROMISE: CHEAP RENTS

In the second edition, however, the headline read:

GOUGH PANICS: CHEAP RENTS

On 1 December both the *Daily Mirror* billboards on Sydney's street corners and its headline were the same:

GOUGH GUILTY! LOANS SCANDAL ERUPTS

It was a reference to a statement made by Fraser that day in which he had accused Whitlam of being a party to illegal loan negotiations while Prime Minister.

The last example, however misleading, indicates Labor's vulnerability to hostile media treatment during the 1975 campaign. What Whitlam was guilty of, or who had been his judge, did not need elaboration. After the events of 1975 and Fraser's emphasis on them, these were things that could be filled in by the imagination of those returning home that evening as their eyes caught the billboard through bus or train windows. Vulnerability in politics invites attack and, however unfair some sections of the media may have been during the campaign, it would have been naive for Labor to expect otherwise given the fact it is normally opposed by all sections of the media during campaigns.

In the area of television and radio news coverage, the Liberals ensured that there was no repetition of the 1974 campaign when Snedden had been shown in filmed and recorded press conferences floundering under the aggressive questioning of newspaper correspondents. Each day Fraser held a press conference for newspaper reporters without any video cameras or recorders. Then each television and radio station was given a separate interview. The result was that in all his speaking media performances, Fraser was fully in control of the situation and appeared so to anyone watching or listening.

In addition to their media efforts, both sides maintained throughout the campaign the daily procession of public meetings where political leaders preach fiercely to the converted. These meetings may well be useful for intra-Party morale but their only chance of reaching uncommitted members of the electorate depends upon attaining media coverage, either because of the stature of the speaker, the news value of his announcements, or the sheer size and frenzy of the meeting. Of these the first could be guaranteed, in one city at least, on a daily basis by use of the Party leader.

Two meetings guaranteed to attract coverage were the formal campaign openings. In many ways the openings reflected the approach of each side to the election. Labor decided upon an

opening in Sydney and Melbourne on the same day — 24
November. In Sydney it was held in the Domain at 1.00 pm
before 40,000 people. On the platform, under a black and white
'Shame Fraser, Shame' backdrop, were former ministers
Hayden, Enderby, Bowen, Jones and Crean, together with NSW
Opposition Leader Wran. They listened to NSW ALP President
John Ducker, then to Hawke and finally to Whitlam. Although
the crowd responded fiercely to his emotional plea for a reversal
of 11 November, it proved impossible to sustain the tension in
the vast area of the Domain and there was a general feeling that it
had been anti-climactic.

By contrast the ALP meeting in Festival Hall in Melbourne at
8.00 pm that evening had only 7000 people present but they
jammed every inch of floorspace and gave deafening applause to
Hawke, Dunstan and Whitlam who spoke before a massive backdrop that said:

> Stability not Chaos
> Democracy not Piracy
> Honour not Shame
> Whitlam not Fraser

Whitlam's speech had been televised live and Labor's hope was
that something of the electrifying atmosphere at Festival Hall
had been transmitted into the living rooms.

Three days later in the Dallas Brooks Hall in East Melbourne,
Fraser gave his policy speech before 2000 eager members of the
Liberal Party and a national television audience. His theme was
undeviating:

> This election results from the dishonesty and incompetence of the
> Whitlam Labor Government.

If the cheers for Whitlam at Festival Hall were part of the
passion that often attends a lost cause, the disciplined applause
that punctuated Fraser's address expressed the relief of those
who were supremely confident, after three years in exile, of
returning to what they saw as their rightful role of government.

Although some of Labor's advertising in the latter part of the
campaign attempted to focus on positive concepts like Medibank
or the ALAO, it continued its basic strategy with an endorsement
by Gorton who stressed that the dismissal issue should be
paramount and a film clip of Fraser stating earlier in the year
that a government should normally be allowed to complete its
term. The Fraser television advertisement was taken off in NSW

when the Liberal Party obtained an order in the NSW Supreme
Court restraining its playing on the grounds that it could be
defamatory of Fraser. Although a similar order was refused in
the Victorian Supreme Court, the Federation of Australian Commercial Television Stations (FACTS) ruled that it could not be
shown in Victoria either. Labor had a number of its advertisements rejected by FACTS, who appeared to take the func-
tional view that there was no great danger in offending a party
that was certainly going to lose the election.

And still during the campaign the long tentacles of that
Executive Council meeting of 13 December 1974 intruded to
dramatise Labor's difficulties. Conspiracy charges against the
participants were set down for hearing on 9 December and so
raised the issue anew in the media even though they could not be
heard until after the election. Premier Bjelke-Petersen recalled
the Queensland Parliament for a special sitting on 9 December to
announce to the press under parliamentary privilege that two
Labor ministers were to receive 'staggering sums' in kickbacks
out of the loans affair. Ten days before the poll, Alan Reid reported in the *Bulletin* that Frank Stewart, Minister for Tourism and
Recreation in the Whitlam government, had told Kerr that
Whitlam had approved Connor's loan-raising efforts up to the
very end. The story became headlines in all other papers and
focussed attention on the issue once again in case anyone had lost
sight of it in the course of the campaign.

The result of the 13 December poll can be stated briefly.
Labor gained 42.8 per cent of the national vote — a drop of 6.5
per cent on May 1974 — and the LCP 52.9 per cent. Because of
the existing House of Representatives electoral boundaries, the
result in terms of Labor members elected was much worse — 36
members out of 127 or only 28 per cent of the total, 30 members
less than in the last Parliament. In the Senate the numbers would
be LCP 36, Labor 27 and Independent one — a breakdown that
meant that Labor would be unlikely to achieve a majority of
Senators for at least five years if the normal pattern of half-
Senate elections was maintained, no matter how well it polled.

Labor retained only one House of Representatives seat in
Queensland, one in Western Australia, and none in Tasmania.
As the swing against Labor was weakest in the rural and safe LCP
electorates where in May 1974 Labor's vote had been lowest,
this result really reflected a drop closer to 7-8 per cent in the
outer suburban electorates which had fallen to Labor in 1972

and 1974, and in the metropolitan electorates that were traditionally Labor strongholds.

In some ways the last of these figures was the most depressing for Labor. It indicated that a significant proportion of its 'thick-and-thin' supporters had voted against the Party for the first time in many years, even though the only effect in those seats was to reduce Labor's majority. Naturally, members from these electorates predominated among Labor's 36 survivors and that also made the result more damaging as they tended to be the older and less imaginative members who had gained their seats years, in some cases decades, before. The new faces of 1969 and 1972 had been swept away and six members of the Cabinet with them. What remained was indeed a shadow of what had been.

13 Limits of power
The future of reform

The Whitlam government and its aftermath has left three basic questions.

Can a government committed to genuine reform be elected to office in the immediate future?

Can that government hold office for the length of its three year term?

Can that government, if it does gain and hold office, exercise real power — by harnessing the resources of government and exerting the public interest over private interests in the community?

The first question — can a reform program receive sufficient electoral support to form a government in the immediate future — must be asked, since the result in December 1977 almost exactly mirrored that of December 1975, to leave the Fraser government with the largest effective majority ever enjoyed by *any* party in the House of Representatives.

The electoral system itself presents a threshold problem. On the existing electoral boundaries, Labor would need 51.5 per cent of votes cast, either won directly or gained after a distribution of the preferences of minor parties, to achieve office. In a close result, 1.5 per cent of the vote could represent the handful of seats that means the difference between winning and losing. In 1954 and 1961, Labor polled just over 50 per cent of the vote after distribution of preferences but narrowly failed to gain office — in 1954 by 7 seats and in 1961 by 2 seats.

In terms of electoral appeal, Labor's greatest short term problem is the memory of the Whitlam government. Not for nothing did the Liberals run a television advertisement in the 1977 campaign on the 1972-5 period entitled simply 'Memories'. There can be no doubt that in the aftermath of that period, Labor has to re-establish an image of competence and reliability in the eyes of much of the electorate — no easy task in Opposition where there are few opportunities to demonstrate these virtues.

The substantial long term problem, however, is to isolate why Labor has been consistently unable in the post-war years to cut into Liberal votes the way the Liberals have on a number of occasions such as 1955, 1966, 1975 and 1977, cut deeply into the normal Labor vote. Even in 1972 when Labor appeared to have everything going for it, the margin of victory was only nine seats.

Today Labor begins with an enormous initial handicap because of its almost total exclusion from rural seats in all States. At present it holds only two of 32 rural seats and even in its victories of 1972 and 1974 held only twelve out of 33 and eight of 33 rural electorates. Obviously this places greater pressure on the Party in its efforts in the metropolitan areas where it needs to gain much more than 50 per cent of the available seats.

A serious discussion of Labor's electoral difficulties would require a book of its own — although most contemporary surveys demonstrate how little is still known of voter motivation. Factors such as the competency rating of a party in voters' eyes and their own assessment of their class position appear to be important but neither equally nor consistently. What does seem fairly clear is that Labor's own image of what is most appealing in its presentation is inaccurate in many respects. In contrast to Labor's emphasis on the egalitarian thrust of its programs, many Australians appear uninterested in equality as an end in itself, suggesting something of the puritan ethic with its acceptance of unequal material rewards for earthly effort — although their enthusiasm seldom extends to the effort demanded by the ethic in its native America.

Early in the 1977 campaign, Labor made an attempt to portray Malcolm Fraser as an extremely wealthy member of Victoria's western district squattocracy — which he is — and thus remote from the everyday world of mortgage repayments and supermarket prices. The strategy met with little success, not least because most Australians simply appeared not to resent Fraser's wealth and position. It is possible that they envy him these advantages but even the fact that, in Malcolm Fraser's case, it is essentially inherited wealth does not appear to inspire ill-will. Perhaps it is a classic example of traditional social Australian egalitarianism — not to hold a man's money against him!

The erosion of some of Labor's strongest bases is illustrated by the evidence that in 1975 and 1977 more than 50 per cent of persons in some lower-income groups voted for non-Labor parties. This phenomenon is even more disturbing for Labor in the long term than the significant proportion of trade union members who have voted Liberal in recent years, as trade union membership for many Australians represents a licence to work rather than a commitment to the industrial wing of the Labor Party. It is possible that these developments are manifestations of increased flexibility in the electorate, of a loosening of the traditional party loyalties. Nevertheleess Labor does not appear to have made parallel inroads into traditional Liberal areas of strength.

On the second question — Labor's ability to hold office — it is almost certain that if Labor were able to break through the electoral barriers by gaining a majority of seats in the House of Representatives, it would face a non-Labor majority in the Senate, half of which will have been elected two or three years earlier when Labor was unable to poll enough votes to win government.

If the events of November 1975 serve no other purpose, they dramatise the fact that some of the most powerful sections of Australian society are not prepared to tolerate a reform government in any circumstances. This ought to make it impossible, for at least a generation, for the supporters of reform to be again lulled into a sense of false security as they were in the early days of the Whitlam government. If so, it may be that the action of Malcolm Fraser and his colleagues radically altered what would otherwise have been the historical role of the Whitlam government. Their action certainly changed its immediate aura from an administration that was heading towards internal disintegration and electoral annihilation in 1976 to a martyred government forced prematurely out of office by its opponents.

There is no reason to believe, however, that the pressures that were brought to bear on the Whitlam government — by the Liberals in Parliament, by State governments, by private interest groups — would not recur in the case of any reform administration. And although a future government might be better able to withstand those pressures than the internally unstable Whitlam government, there is no watertight defence to a blocking of supply by the Senate. Even if the Governor-

General of the day could be relied upon to follow the advice of the Prime Minister, this would not necessarily prevent the fall of the government in the chaos that would result if the money began to run out.

The Senate's power to block supply appears to be recognised as consistent with the Constitution by a majority of present High Court judges. Like any other aspect of the Constitution, this situation can only be changed if a reform measure is approved by over 50 per cent of votes in four of the six states — the rock on which so many past referenda have foundered. Finally, the circle is closed by the requirement that any proposal for altering the method of amendment — by making the approval of only three States necessary, for example — has to pass the present system first. By accident or design, those who framed the Australian Constitution in the 1890s have ensured that its essentially anti-democratic structure cannot be significantly altered without the approval of those who would never consent to such an alteration.

Malcolm Fraser may have discovered, consciously or unconsciously, the fact that Labor has no practical choice but to seek office under the existing constitutional system yet finds in office that the system contains an expulsion mechanism that its opponents can employ as soon as unpopular decisions have to be made (as ultimately they have to be by any government). It is important to remember, however, that changes to the role of the Governor-General and the Senate are simply means to an end, not ends in themselves.

The third and most demanding task for any reform government, once it has gained office and can stay there for one full term at least, is that of exercising the powers of government, although paradoxically this presents on its face less institutionalised barriers than those in the electoral and constitutional areas. The view, prevalent for some years after Chifley's attempt to nationalise the private trading banks was struck down by the courts, that the Constitution poses almost insuperable problems for the implementation of reform policies, has been slowly replaced by the realisation that most reform programs can be brought within the often cryptic terms of this 1901 document. A national government could not abolish the existing State boundaries or monopolise particular industries but by means of financial grants to State governments, by taxation measures and by setting up its own commercial enterprises, it could establish a legislative and administrative structure for basic programs within the Constitution.

But that is not by any means the same thing as *implementing* those programs. That requires, as a first step, the identification of the centres of power in Australia with which a national government must be concerned and an appreciation of the degree to which each of them can be controlled. Some of those power centres — such as State governments and the federal bureaucracy — are essential to the implementation of policies.

Some of the private sources of power in the community — such as the media — are not immediately necessary to a government. But, particularly in the case of the media, they do exercise a strong negative influence for any government. This influence can be minimised only by a concentration on programs within the government. Labor's media problems in the period 1972-5 were in the main caused by matters unrelated to the policies of the government. This is not to say that those policies were not also unacceptable to sections of the media and would not have been the subject of attack in the absence of more lurid events. The media is on the whole a deeply conservative factor in Australian society — perhaps quite naturally in view of the family structure of the industry — but its capacity for damage is certainly decreased if it is forced to concentrate on issues rather than personalities.

The important area which the Whitlam government found itself virtually powerless to influence was the collection of private investment decisions, particularly those in the manufacturing, mining and finance sectors, that inevitably set economic priorities and determined the allocation of the nation's resources. Ironically, a government has more control over foreign investors than over domestic business concerns. In its last days the McMahon government introduced measures to regulate takeovers of Australian businesses by foreign corporations or the establishment of foreign businesses in Australia although, once the takeovers or establishments had been approved, there was to be no further government impact on the firms' activities. Yet the investment decisions of the major Australian corporations and those transnational corporations which operate in Australia can inhibit, and ultimately destabilise, any government's long-range programs for employment maintenance, monetary management, overseas trade or income distribution. Thus by using the threat of large-scale lay-offs, the automobile industry — almost 100 per cent foreign-owned — can directly contribute to the maintenance of protective tariffs at a time when these barriers are an increasing source of friction between Australia and other nations. In early 1975, it will be recalled, the industry persuaded the government to increase these barriers by making that threat.

It is pointless to complain about this kind of conduct to corporations as they are currently constituted. Corporations, whether foreign or domestic, are premised upon the goal of profit-maximisation and if they manufacture automobiles in Australia, they will naturally be more concerned with capturing the Australian market than with the economic implications for the country's trading partners. A government, however, must be concerned — and so it must have some means of influencing the policies of these corporate decision-makers. What became clear during the time of the Whitlam government was that simply being the government did not carry this capacity with it. It was quite possible to take economic decisions, as was done with tariffs, and then be unable to adhere to them in the face of opposition. How is real power to be grounded in a future reform administration?

It is possible that its economic decision-making power could be increased by nationalisation of key industries. The ALP's objective still stands as the 'democratic socialisation of industry, production, distribution and exchange' but only 'to the extent necessary to eliminate exploitation and other anti-social features in those fields'. This could obviously cover anything, or nothing — and to date has covered nothing. There are two problems about nationalisation. One is legal. It is likely that a majority of the present High Court would view nationalisation of any industry as unconstitutional, as the court did in 1947 when it invalidated Chifley's banking legislation. It is possible, however, that the same result could be achieved by less direct provisions that would satisfy the technical requirements of the court.

The second problem is economic. To acquire the assets of entire industries, or even the shares of existing firms in particular industries, may well strain a government's current resources to the point where it is unable to carry out other programs. There has been considerable debate on whether ownership of a majority of shares in corporations would in fact enable a government to exercise a more substantial influence on investment decisions. The nub of the dispute concerns the extent to which any shareholders can impose their will on corporate management. It is quite correct to point out that the numerous small shareholders in many public companies are unlikely to be able to unite in order to affect the decisions of an entrenched management. The influence of one or more large shareholders, individual or corporate, is less easily discounted and it cannot be said that the 'management thesis' has been generally established. One thing that is clear is that, by acquiring only failing and unreconstructed firms as the British Labour government has done, it is impossible to make a serious impact on the national economy.

The serious and more feasible alternative is the establishment of government corporations in key sectors to carry on business either alone or in association with private corporations in a way that will, over the long term, give the government a substantial impact on the operation of that sector. While regulatory legislation such as the Trade Practices Act is obviously necessary to deal with the various sectors of the economy as they now exist, it cannot as a rule alter the basic structure of those sectors. That can be done only by direct government participation which influences the direction in which they develop. This point is at the centre of any reformist program. It will only be possible to change the existing pattern of the *distribution* of resources in Australia if changes are made to the system of *production* of those resources. Without actual government involvement in the system of production, there can be no more than cosmetic changes brought about to that system and so to the system of distribution also.

Australian Government corporations exist now in some areas — banking, airlines, shipping — but they have never functioned on this basis. Most, like TAA or the Commonwealth Trading Bank, have been dedicated followers of the uncompetitive practices of their private counterparts. Rex Connor's Petroleum and Minerals Authority was, however, intended to take a major role in the financing and development of natural resource projects until it was stifled by the Senate. The AGIC was very modestly empowered although it would have quickly become a source of capital funds as it began to collect premiums.

Any program of public enterprise will need to overcome the strong feeling in the electorate — and assiduously fostered in the post-war period by the conservative parties — that the public sector is by definition unproductive and inefficient in comparison with private commercial activity.

Even in the public sector itself, this long campaign has achieved its ends. As Hugh Stretton describes it,

> Day after day I sat around coffee tables and conference tables with public servants and private consultants who banked Commonwealth, flew Qantas and British Airways and TAA, enjoyed high-speed trains and geometrically designed superhighways, trusted the radio beams in the sky and the admiralty charts at sea and the ordnance maps in the bush, used government loans to buy government houses framed and lined with government softwood, preferred public to private superannuation, shot their children with Salk and Sabin, smoked Gauloises and fuelled their Leylands and Renaults with BP — but still knew in their bones as a fact of life, beyond any rational dispute whatever, that the private sector is the only productive sector, and that public ownership and management are always, everywhere, incurably inefficient. (Stretton 1978)

This lack of enthusiasm for governmental activities was probably heightened by the tenure of the Whitlam government. Because an increased role for government was a feature of its administration, that feature has been identified in retrospect with its decisive rejection by the electorate in December 1975 although it was clearly submerged at that time in more personal aspects of Labor's administration. Only practical demonstrations of productive public enterprise possibly combined with a demonstration of the extent to which some areas of private 'enterprise' are supported by public funds, will answer these objections.

In general it would not be necessary to fund public enterprises out of taxation, except possibly for establishment cost. This would obviously be an advantage electorally although it might be noted that Australia ranks in the bottom 25 per cent of OECD nations in terms of total tax revenue (direct and indirect, including social security levies) as a percentage of Gross National Product. In other words Australia is at present one of the most lightly taxed of the western industrialised nations. Quite apart from taxation, however, it will clearly be necessary for a future government committed to public enterprises to channel some of the nation's limited capital into public — and, it must be insisted, more productive — use.

Sources of capital do exist in Australia. The Australian Mutual Provident Society (AMP) had available for *investment* in 1978 approximately $500 million and expressed its difficulty in finding sufficient investment projects. This is despite the provisions of Australian tax legislation that effectively force the placing of 30 per cent of the Society's funds in government or semi-government loans, and its ongoing commitments to its massive real estate projects — in particular the Collins Place development in Melbourne. In early 1978, as a result, the AMP had \$50 million on the short term money market for want of any other repositories for its overflowing resources. Of the \$500 million available for investment in 1978, almost \$350 million had come from individual policy holders who held whole-of-life or endowment policies with the AMP. The remaining \$150 million was provided by corporate superannuation plans. This last figure is a reminder of the reservoir of capital held by private and government superannuation schemes across Australia. The NSW State government scheme, for example, holds assets of over \$1 billion. If a greater proportion of these funds could be directed to public investment projects, it would significantly lessen the total dependence of public sector policies on private investment decisions.

For a reform government it would be crucial therefore, from the viewpoint of economic management, to gain a greater influence over corporate investment decisions. It is not only their decision-making power in this area that makes large corporations the real alternative source of power to modern governments. Their activities reach into every corner of the community and have finally led to proposals that those most directly affected should have some say in the decision-making process, most particularly the consumers of their products and services and the employees of the organisations.

Representation of consumers and employees in corporate management will obviously be an issue for a reform government. Both concepts are designed to provide a greater degree of public accountability from these sources of private power. European experience suggests, however, that the results may not be dramatic in the short term and that much more work needs to be done on how to genuinely democratise the work place. It must be recalled that in Australia, in contrast with industrial organisations in Germany and Scandinavia, the majority of trade unions are among the most institutionally conservative bodies in the community. Instead of building up research capacity and political expertise, they have dissipated much of their resources in intra-union disputes between factions competing for the rewards of office and inter-union disputes between competing organisations for jurisdiction over groups of employees. On occasions they have also been the employers' strongest allies in promoting sectional policies, as in the case of the Vehicle Builders Union which has consistently supported the pressure exerted by the automobile companies on governments, including their successful efforts to impose tariff policies on the Whitlam government in January 1975.

This raises the question of the relationship between the trade union movement and the supporters of reform, as there is little doubt that over the years the close identification between the ALP and the union movement has been effectively used by its opponents. It is somewhat paradoxical that, in an electorate containing one of the highest proportions of individual union membership in the world, there is such hostility to the collective notion of unions. If Labor retains its present links with the union movement, it faces a long and difficult exercise to transform unions in the public mind into specific organisations that must be assessed separately, rather than as a monolithic and threatening abstraction. It is, however, an exercise that would only be worthwhile if there were to be a simultaneous effort to broaden the activities of unions and to involve them to a much greater degree in productive activities.

While the sum of decisions of all corporations theoretically represents corporate decision-making power, it is true that in most western nations — and in none more so than in Australia — this power is essentially exercised by a relatively small group of very large corporations. The following figures summarise this phenomenon:

- Manufacturing Industry: 200 corporations produce 51 per cent of goods and 30,000 small and medium-sized companies produce the remainder.
- Mining Industry: 79 concerns account for 72 per cent of turnover and over 1,300 for the remaining 28 per cent.
- Retail Sales: 6 firms are responsible for 22 per cent of sales out of approximately 127,000 establishments.
- Life Insurance: 4 corporations possess 81 per cent of the industry's total assets.
- Finance: 13 finance companies account for 80 per cent of all advances.
- Banking: 7 banks are responsible for 87 per cent of all loans.
- Media: 3 groups effectively control 94 per cent of all metropolitan daily newspapers and 4 groups 47 per cent of all metropolitan television stations.

It will be obvious that while there is considerable overlap in some of these sectors, for example between banking and finance where banks have taken substantial interests in finance companies, there are areas of conflict as well. On the issue of tariffs, to take one case, there is a clear division between the manufacturing sector which benefits from increased protection against imported goods, and the mining sector which has to purchase those goods at higher prices. Nevertheless, the degree of concentration of economic power is striking.

It is this factor that also explains much of the continuing debate in Australia (and in other countries) on the role of foreign investment and on the multinational corporations that are its chief sources. While multinational corporations do possess characteristics which make them less amenable to regulation than domestic corporations — it is, for example, more difficult to ascertain their profits for tax purposes — the main reason for assessing their role is their sheer size in comparison with domestic firms, and their consequent impact on the national economy. The most recent figures of the Australian Bureau of Statistics reveal that:

- Over the period 1971-72 to 1974-75 foreign ownership of the mining industry increased from 49 per cent to 52 per cent and foreign control from 54 per cent to 60 per cent.
- Over the period 1966-67 to 1972-73 foreign ownership of manufacturing industry increased from 25 per cent to 31 per cent and foreign control from 29 per cent to 34 per cent. Of the 200 largest enterprises 87, amounting to 45 per cent of production, were classified as foreign-controlled. Particular industries may have a much higher figure for both ownership and control. The figure for foreign control in the pharmaceutical industry is 78 per cent, in cosmetics 91 per cent, in non-ferrous metals 79 per cent, and in automobiles 99.8 per cent.
- On 1973 figures foreign ownership of finance companies was 48 per cent and foreign control 42 per cent.
- On 1973 figures foreign ownership of life insurance companies was 37 per cent and foreign control 19 per cent.

Finally, the following table gives some idea of the assets of the subsidiaries of major foreign corporations operating in Australia and demonstrates their preference for as near as possible total ownership and control by the parent corporation:

Company	Assets Aust. $ Million	% Owned by Parent
Alcoa	471	51 (U.S.)
Amoco	72	100 (U.S.)
Australian Oil Refining	70	100 (U.S.)
Borg-Warner	77	77 (U.S.)
Cadbury Schweppes	109	61 (U.K.)
Caltex	152	100 (U.S.)
Caterpillar	37	100 (U.S.)
Chrysler	167	97 (U.S.)
Cottee's	31	100 (U.S.)
Esso	179	100 (U.S.)
Ford	280	100 (U.S.)
General Electric	45	100 (U.K.)
General Motors	387	100 (U.S.)
Heinz	28	100 (U.S.)
ICI	405	62 (U.K.)
IBM	67	100 (U.S.)
International Harvester	132	100 (U.S.)
Kodak	71	100 (U.S.)
Kraft Foods	50	100 (U.S.)
Mobil Oil	313	100 (U.S.)
Nestle	95	100 (Switzerland)
Philip Morris	144	72 (U.S.)
Philip Industries	139	78 (Netherlands)
Reckitt & Coleman	71	70 (U.K.)
Shell	531	100 (U.K.)
Sperry Rand	55	100 (U.S.)
Standard Telephone & Cables	49	100 (U.S.)
Sunbeam	35	100 (U.S.)

(Department of Industry and Commerce 1976)

These figures make clear that the argument for regulation by government of foreign and domestic corporate action is about the accountability of private power to public power, about who ultimately makes the influential decisions for society. There are two reasons why these decisions should be made by government and not by other groups in the community. One is rooted in traditional democratic political theory — that a society's directions should be charted by those elected to public office for that purpose and answerable to the community at regular intervals. The other is based on the narrow horizons of the multinational and domestic corporations who provide the alternative source of directions.

These organisations are concerned with selling automobiles — not with transporting people efficiently and cheaply in the still-

growing urban areas, with advertising cigarettes — not with
building hospitals to house the victims of lung cancer, with
dominating the entertainment media — not with providing
educational services for the school age population. If these social
functions are to be carried out and carried out in a way that
moves Australian society closer to an equitable and productive
distribution of its resources, it will only be done by an exercise of
public power, power that has its authority in government and its
source in the people. The debate over the use of the term
'socialism' is not really relevant to these goals. Some would
describe them as socialism but the term has never had an agreed
meaning and it is unlikely to acquire one at a time when
economic and social problems, and so their solutions, are
becoming increasingly complex. It is the goals that are
important, not how they are described.

Ironically, few of the Whitlam government's proposals were
directed to the sort of major structural changes necessary to
move significantly towards these goals. Most were attempts to
make some improvement to the existing system while essentially
preserving it intact, of which Medibank is a good example. Yet
Labor's opponents were unwilling to wait even the three years
between elections to prevent the implementation of its measures.
So it is unlikely that they would tolerate substantial change
without the most desperate action.

The removal of the Whitlam government by its opponents is,
therefore, all the more striking in view of the fact that they had
effectively prevented the implementation of many of its major
programs and that they must have appreciated how difficult the
government was finding the employment of its administrative
machinery. Such a reaction to the shadow of power presages a
truly violent response to its substance. In this situation there is
little room for gradualism. Fifty years later, Tawney's remark
remains apposite:

> Onions can be eaten leaf by leaf, but you cannot skin a live tiger paw
> by paw. Vivisection is its trade and it does the skinning first.

The difficulties for a reform government in gaining office at
the national level — and of achieving that goal in circumstances
that give it an opportunity seriously to exercise governmental
power — have been emphasised. Yet the instability that has
infected the international economic system since the early 1970s,
and the inherent weaknesses of the Australian economy, makes

even the most entrenched governments and constitutional impasses vulnerable in comparison with the 1950s and 1960s. In this kind of situation the economic and social measures already discussed would become not simply more feasible but also necessary for national survival.

What is clear, however, is that if such an opportunity becomes available to any national government, it will again encounter ferocious opposition in its attempts to govern. It must therefore come to office with a coherent program already devised. This will provide the only chance of resisting the obstruction of its opponents, the pressure of interest groups, the conservatism of the bureaucracy and the personal conflicts within its own ranks. In the context of implementing such a program it is apparent that Parliament is only a tool — although a vital one — in the process of implementation. It is, therefore, important to be able to use the parliamentary machinery but not to become immersed in its intricate procedures for their own sake. This simply constitutes a distraction from real priorities.

It is possible for conservative parties to live from day to day, from hand to mouth, because they are chiefly concerned with government on a day to day basis, reacting to issues but not anticipating them. It is not possible, however, for a Labor government to function effectively in this fashion. To allocate this society's resources, both tangible and intangible, over the coming decades with vision and justice while at the same time restraining inflation by any but the most draconic methods, will require the clearest of aims and the most precise of programs. And they are required not just when a government comes to office but years before to achieve acceptance by its own supporters and the community.

If these goals are the government's lodestar, they will inevitably influence relations between ministers, appointments made to public positions, and the government's approach to the bureaucracy — as they must if the government is to exercise real power. Without such goals a government will inevitably oscillate uncertainly between piecemeal reforms and placating its opponents when they react against those reforms, until its opponents once again assume power — probably with the concurrence of the electorate who can recognise that the government's opponents at least know what they want to do, or not to do. No collection of *ad hoc* responses to particular problems, however attractive some may seem in isolation, can substitute for a long-term strategy based on a directing ideology.

No amount of plans and policies can of course be sufficient without the will to achieve and keep power. The Whitlam government failed because of the assaults mounted on it by its opponents and because of its own internal weaknesses. The external pressures will always be present. The surest means of surviving its internal pressures — and perhaps the attacks of its opponents as well — is to have a clear appreciation of what is necessary to achieve not just office, but power, and how power duly achieved can be used to shape the Australia of the 1980s.

Note on sources

In addition to the particular sources referred to below (almost all of them published or accessible) it will be obvious that throughout the book there has been constant drawing on public material — *Hansard*, the *Australian Parliamentary Handbook*, the Australian Statutes — law reports, and the various Australian editions of *Who's Who*. Where documentary material not published or readily accessible is drawn upon, the text usually incorporates the document in whole or part, thereby identifying the source. Interviews with persons involved in the events discussed in the book (almost all of whom would insist on confidentiality) did produce some information but usually this could be checked against documentary material, public or otherwise. Each of the three books published within the first six months after the dismissal of the Labor government provides a reliable chronology and record of events of the periods within the years 1972-1975 on which they focus. Those books are:

Kelly P. (1976) *The Unmaking of Gough* Angus & Robertson, Sydney

Lloyd C. J. and Clarke A. (1976) *Kerr's King Hit!* Cassell, Australia

Oakes L. (1976) *Crash Through or Crash: The Unmaking of a Prime Minister* Drummond, Melbourne

Chapter 1

The formal details of the Executive Council Meeting of 13 December 1974 are contained in the Executive Council Minute Paper read by Senator James McClelland in the Senate on 12 June 1975 (See *CPD* (Sen) 12 June 1975 at 2611).

Chapter 2

Freudenberg G. (1977) *A Certain Grandeur* Macmillan, Melbourne

Whitlam E. G. (1957) *The Constitution versus Labor:* Chifley Memorial

Lecture, Melbourne University ALP Club
— (1960) *An Urban Nation* Victorian Fabian Society
— and Grant B. (1972a) *Labor in Power — What is the Difference?* Victorian Fabian Society
— (1972b) Policy Speech: Opening of the 1972 election campaign, 13 November
— (1974) Policy Speech: Opening of the 1974 election campaign, 29 April
— (1975a) Chifley Memorial Lecture, University of Melbourne, 14 August
— (1975b) *The New Federalism: A Review of Labor's Programs and Policies*: Address to Conference of the Centre for Research on Federal Financial Relations, ANU, 27 August
— (1975c) Curtin Memorial Lecture, ANU, 29 October
— (1975d) Policy Speech: Opening of the 1975 election campaign, 24 November
— (1979) *The Truth of the Matter* Penguin, Melbourne
Woodhouse A. O. (1974) *Compensation and Rehabilitation in Australia: Report of the National Committee of Inquiry (Vols. 1-3)* AGPS, Canberra
The Australian Labor Government: Some Highlights — By Portfolio; Record of Government Achievements — Notes (Both unpublished documents prepared by the Department of Prime Minister and Cabinet in October 1975)

Chapter 3

Cairns J. F. (1963) *Socialism and the ALP* Victorian Fabian Society
— (1971) *Tariffs or Planning?* Lansdowne Press, Melbourne
— (1972) *The Quiet Revolution* Widescope, Melbourne
— (1974) *The Impossible Attainment*, Chifley Memorial Lecture 1974, Melbourne University ALP Club
— (1975) Monday Conference Transcript for 24 February 1975, ABC Television
— (1976) *Oil In Troubled Waters* Widescope, Melbourne
Documents tabled by Mr Whitlam in the House of Representatives on 9 July 1975 (See *CPD* (HR) 9 July 1975 at 3557-3595)
Harris S. (1975) *The Processes of Economic Policy Making in Australia* (Report to the Royal Commission on Australian Government Administration by the Task Force on Economic Policy) AGPS, Canberra
Industries Assistance Commission, *Annual Report 1974-75*
Sheehan N. (1971) *The Pentagon Papers as published by The New York Times* Bantam, New York

Chapter 4

Edwards J. (1976) 'The Adelaide Spy Caper' *National Times* 29 May
    1976
Hope R. M. (1977) Royal Commission on Intelligence and Security
    (*Reports* I-IV) AGPS, Canberra
Senate Select Committee on Civil Rights of Migrant Australians. This
    Committee, which was established by the Senate on 17 May 1973,
    never brought down a final report but heard evidence concerning,
    inter alia, the ASIO raid of 14 March 1973

Chapter 5

The figures relating to foreign investment in Australia can be found in
Sexton (1977) 'Transnational Corporations: Is Regulation Feasible?' 54
Current Affairs Bulletin 16 (No. 6)

Chapter 6

Basic Wage, Margins and Total Wage Cases (1966) 115 *Commonwealth
    Arbitration Reports* 93
Hall R. (1978) *The Real John Kerr* Angus & Robertson, Sydney
Kerr J. R. and Wootten J. H. (1958) 'Re-opening The Orr Case' 4 *The
    Free Spirit* 3 (No. 10)
— (1960) 'The Struggle Against Communism in the Trade Unions' 4
    Quadrant 27 (No. 4)
— (1964) 'Higher Education in New Guinea' 18 *Australian Outlook* 266
— (1969) 'Wanted — a Constitution before it is too late' 4 *New Guinea*
    19 (September/October)
— (1971) 'A Constitutional Suggestion: Mixing the Systems' 5 *New
    Guinea* 51 (January)
— (1978) *Matters for Judgment* Macmillan, Melbourne
Lloyd C. J. and Clarke A. (1976) *Kerr's King Hit!* Cassell, Australia
Sugerman B. (1963) *Alfred Conlon: A Memorial by Some of His Friends*,
    Benevolent Society of NSW

Chapter 7

MEDIBANK: Unpublished Department of Health working papers

AGIC
 Edwards J. (1975) 'How the big guns of the insurance industry sank the
    AGIC' *National Times* 15-20 September
Power F. R. *The Fight for "Life"* 1975, F. R. Power, Melbourne

Rivers L. and Hyde J. (1975) 'The Dominance of Finance Capital' 39
Arena 5

ALAO
*Re Bannister and Legal Practitioners Ordinance 1970-1975; Ex parte
Harstein* (1975) 5 ACTR 100
Material circulated to members by the Victorian Law Institute in con-
nection with a general meeting of the Institute on 20.2.75

Chapter 8

Documents tabled by Mr Connor in the House of Representatives on 9
July 1975 (See *CPD* (HR) 9 July 1975 at 3612-3625)
Transcript of evidence in *Sankey* v. *Whitlam & Others* before Quean-
beyan Court of Petty Sessions between 30 January - 16 February,
1979
See also: Whitlam v. *Sankey & Others* [1976] 2 *NSWLR* 570; *Sankey* v.
Whitlam & Others [1977] 1 *NSWLR* 333; *Sankey* v. *Whitlam &
Others* 53 *ALJR* 11
Statutory Declaration of Tirath Khemlani (Publication authorised by the
Senate 4 November 1975)

Chapter 9

GENERAL
Coombs H. C. (1976) *Royal Commission on Australian Government
Administration* (Report and Appendices Vols. 1-4) AGPS, Canberra,
(together with many of the [unpublished] submissions made to the
Commission)

DEPARTMENT OF PRIME MINISTER AND CABINET
Mediansky F. A. and Nockles J. A. (1975) 'The Prime Minister's
Bureaucracy' 34 *Public Administration* 202

CABINET AND ITS COMMITTEES
Lloyd C. J. and Reid G. S. (1974) *Out of the Wilderness* Cassell,
Australia

FREEDOM OF INFORMATION
Attorney-General's Department (1974) *Proposed Freedom of Information
Legislation: Report on Inter-departmental Committee* AGPS, Canberra

Chapter 10

Opinion: *Ex Parte J. M. Rothery,* by K. A. Aickin QC, A. M. Gleeson
QC and P. H. P. Lane, dated 23 October 1975

Opinion: *The Governor-General's Powers*, by R. J. Ellicot QC dated 16 October 1975

Opinion (unsigned): *The Governor-General's Powers* by K. E. Enderby QC (Attorney-General) and M. H. Byers QC (Solicitor-General) dated 4 November 1975

Opinion (unsigned): *Possible Assistance to Employers and Some Others to Obtain Finance in the Absence of Appropriations* by K. E. Enderby QC (Attorney-General) and M. H. Byers QC (Solicitor-General) dated 3 November 1975

Chapter 11

On the events at the actual moment of dismissal both participants have written their own, slightly differing, accounts. *See:*

Kerr J. R. (1978) *Matters for Judgment* Macmillan, Melbourne

Whitlam E. G. (1979) *The Truth of the Matter* Penguin, Melbourne

A great deal has been written about the legal and constitutional aspects of the dismissal. This chapter concentrates rather on the political aspects. But for those who wish to pursue the legal questions the best overall coverage (as it is on all of the legal and constitutional issues that arose over the period 1972-75) is Sawer G. (1977) *Federation Under Strain* MUP Melbourne

Chapter 12

Much of the material on the coverage of the campaign by News Ltd. newspapers and the subsequent protests by some of those papers' journalists is collected in (1976) *New Journalist* (No. 21)

Chapter 13

The figures used come from the Australian Bureau of Statistics and the Department of Industry and Commerce.

The debate about the role of government in general and Labor governments in particular is illustrated in Australia by, on one side, Carr R. (1978) *Social Democracy and Australian Labor* (NSW Labor Day Committee), and, on the other, by the press release *There is an alternative* signed by 29 federal Labor parliamentarians in 1978.

In Britain the most recent contributions of substance to the debate have been:

Holland S. (1975) *The Socialist Challenge* Quartet, London

Coates D. (1975) *The Labour Party and the Struggle for Socialism* Cambridge University Press, Cambridge

Select Bibliography

Aitkin D. (1977) *Stability and Change in Australian Politics* Australian National University Press, Canberra

Albinski H. S. (1977) *Australian External Policy Under Labor* University of Queensland Press, Brisbane

Altman D., Santamaria B. A. and Butler G. (1973) 'The First Six Months' 50 *Current Affairs Bulletin* (No. 2)

Archer J. and Madox G. (1976) 'The Concept of "Politics" in Australia' 11 *Politics* 7

Arndt H. W. (1975) 'The Economics of the Loans Affair' 19 *Quadrant* 11 (No. 6)

Atiyah P. S. (1975) 'Compensation and Rehabilitation' 51 *Current Affairs Bulletin* 24 (No. 8)

Basic Wage, Margins and Total Wage Cases (1966) 115 *Commonwealth Arbitration Reports* 93

Blazey P. and Campbell A. (1974) *The Political Dice Men* Outback Press, Melbourne

Briot G. T. (1975) 'The Ermolenko Affair' 19 *Quadrant* 29 (No. 1)

Brogan B. (1975) 'The Hayden Budget' 52 *Current Affairs Bulletin* 9 (No. 5)

Buckley K. (1974) 'The Human Rights Bill' 50 *Current Affairs Bulletin* 25 (No. 11)

Butler D. (1976) 'An Election Reflection' 20 *Quadrant* 6

— '20 Questions Left by Remembrance Day' 50 *Current Affairs Bulletin* 4 (No. 10)

Caiden G. E. (1977) 'Tackling bureaucratic inertia: some personal reflections on the Royal Commission on Australian Government Administration' 49 *Australian Quarterly* (No. 1)

Cairns J. F. (1963) *Socialism and the ALP* Victorian Fabian Society

— (1971) *The Eagle and the Lotus* Lansdowne Press, Melbourne

— (1971a) *Tariffs or Planning?* Lansdowne Press, Melbourne

— (1972) *The Quiet Revolution* Widescope, Melbourne

— (1974) *The Impossible Attainment* Chifley Memorial Lecture 1974, Melbourne University ALP Club

— (1975) Monday Conference Transcript for 24 February 1975 ABC Television

— (1976) *Oil in Troubled Waters* Widescope, Melbourne

Carr R. *Social Democracy and Australian Labor* NSW Labor Day Committee

Castles A. (1975) 'Constitutional Conventions and the Senate' *Australian Current Law Digest* 286

Catley R. and McFarlane B. (1974) *From Tweedledum To Tweedledee: The New Labor Government in Australia* ANZ, Sydney

Coates D. (1975) *The Labour Party and the Struggle for Socialism* Cambridge University Press, Cambridge

Colston M. (1976) 'The Stacked Senate of 1975', 11 *Politics* 57

Connell R. W. (1977) *Ruling Class Ruling Culture* Cambridge University Press, Cambridge

Cooley A. S. (1974) 'The Permanent Head' 33 *Public Administration* 193

Coombs H. C. (1976) Royal Commission on Australian Government Administration (*Report and Appendices* Vols. 1-4) AGPS, Canberra

Coper M. (1976) 'The Constitutional Crisis' *Australian Current Law Digest* 281

Coxsedge J. and Harant G. (1975) 'A Question of Intelligence: Australia's Secret Agencies' 10 *Politics* 158

Craig J. (1976) 'Senatorial Prime Ministers and Presidential Governors-General' 11 *Politics* 62

Crossman R. (1975) *The Diaries of a Cabinet Minister* (Vols. 1-3) Hamish Hamilton & Jonathan Cape, London

Daly F. (1977) *From Curtin to Kerr* Sun Books, Melbourne

Department of Industry and Commerce (1976) *Directory of Overseas Investment in Australian Manufacturing Industry* AGPS, Canberra

Edwards C. (1974) *Labor Pains* Hill of Content, Melbourne

Edwards J. (1975) 'The economy game: Treasury and its rivals' 51 *Current Affairs Bulletin* 4 (No. 12)

— (1975a) 'How the big guns of the insurance industry sank the AGIC' *National Times* 15-20 September

Encel S., Horne D. and Thompson E. (1977) *Change the Rules: Towards a Democratic Constitution* Penguin, Melbourne

Enderby K. (1976) 'Difficulties facing federal Labor governments' 48 *Australian Quarterly* 33 (No. 4)

Epstein L. (1976) 'Australian bicameralism: a comparative perspective' 11 *Politics* 27

Evans G. (1976) 'Labor and the Constitution' 35 *Meanjin Quarterly* 3 (No. 1)

— (ed.) (1977) *Labor and the Constitution 1972-1975* Heinemann, Melbourne

Foot M. (1975) *Aneurin Bevan 1897-1945* Paladin, London

Forward R. (1977) 'Editorial Opinion and the Whitlam Government'

12 *Politics* 136 (No. 1)

Freudenberg G. (1977) *A Certain Grandeur* Macmillan, Melbourne

Goldring J. (1975) 'The royal prerogative and the dissolution of the Commonwealth Parliament' 49 *Australian Law Journal* 521

Griffin D. 'The will of the people: a comment on 11 November 1975' 48 *Australian Quarterly* 103 (No. 3)

Groenewegen P. (1975) 'What are the causes of the current Australian inflation rate?' 52 *Current Affairs Bulletin* 4 (No. 5)

Gruen F. H. (1976) 'What Went Wrong? Some Personal Reflections on Economic Policies Under Labor' 48 *Australian Quarterly* 15 (No. 4)

Hall R. and Iremonger J. (1976) *The Makers and the Breakers: The Governor-General and the Senate vs the Constitution* Wellington Lane Press, Sydney

Hall R. (1978) *The Secret State* Cassell, Australia

— (1978a) *The Real John Kerr* Angus & Robertson, Sydney

Hanks P. (1975) 'Vice-regal Initiative and Discretion' *Australian Current Law Digest* 294

Harries O. (1975) 'The Self-criticism of E. G. Whitlam' 12 *Quadrant* 42 (No. 5)

Hartnett L. (1975) 'Crisis in the Motor Industry' 52 *Current Affairs Bulletin* 4 (No. 6)

Haster G. (1977) 'The Press and Labor 1972-1974' 12 *Politics* 130 (No. 1)

Hawker G. (1975) 'The bureaucracy under the Whitlam government and vice versa' 10 *Politics* 15

— (1977) 'The Implementation of RCAGA: What Happened to the Coombs Report' 49 *Australian Quarterly* 17 (No. 1)

— (1977a) 'Problems of administrative change: unlearned lessons' 53 *Current Affairs Bulletin* 13 (No. 2)

Holland S. (1975) *The Socialist Challenge* Quartet, London

Holmes J. (1976) 'Swingers and Stayers, 1974-75' 11 *Politics* 47

Hope R. M. (1977) Royal Commission on Intelligence and Security (*Reports* I-IV) AGPS, Canberra

Horne D. (1976) *Death of the Lucky Country* Penguin, Melbourne

Howard C. (1975) 'Constitutional Conventions and Gentlemen's Agreements' *Summons* 18

— (1976) 'Constitutional Conventions and Gentlemen's Agreements' *Summons* 18

— (1976) 'Constitutional Amendment and the Office of Governor-General' 48 *Australian Quarterly* 55 (No. 4)

— (1976a) The Constitutional Crisis of 1975 48 *Australian Quarterly* 5 (No. 1)

Industries Assistance Commission (1975) *Annual Report* AGPS, Canberra

Jackson R. G. (1975) *Policies for Development of Manufacturing Industries*: Report of Committee to Advise on Policies for

Manufacturing Industry, AGPS, Canberra

James F. (1975) 'A letter to a great "Chinese" friend' *Nation Review* November

Katz L. (1975) 'The simultaneous dissolution of both Houses of the Australian Parliament' 54 *Canadian Bar Review* 392

Kelly P. (1976) *The Unmaking of Gough* Angus & Robertson, Sydney

Kemp D. A. (1978) *Society and Electoral Behaviour in Australia* University of Queensland Press, Brisbane

Kerin J. (1976) 'Labor: dilemmas of reformism' *Politics* 39

Kerr J. R. and Wootten J. H. (1958) 'Re-opening The Orr Case' 4 *The Free Spirit* 3 (No. 10)

Kerr J. R. (1960) 'The Struggle Against Communism in the Trade Unions' 4 *Quadrant* 27 (No. 4)

— (1964) 'Higher Education in New Guinea' 18 *Australian Outlook* 266

— (1969) 'Wanted — a Constitution before it is too late' 4 *New Guinea* 19 (September/October)

— (1971) 'A Constitutional Suggestion: Mixing the Systems' 5 *New Guinea* 51 (January)

— (1978) *Matters for Judgment* Macmillan, Melbourne

Lane P. H. (1973) 'Double Dissolution of Federal Parliament' 47 *Australian Law Journal* 290

— (1974) 'Double Dissolution of Federal Parliament — the Third Double Dissolution' 48 *Australian Law Journal* 515

Litvin J. (1976) 'The rhetoric of crisis' 11 *Politics* 20

Lloyd C. J. and Reid G. S. (1974) *Out of the Wilderness* Cassell, Sydney

— and Clarke A. (1976) *Kerr's King Hit!* Cassell, Sydney

McAuley J. (1976) 'Commentary: John Kerr's judgment' 20 *Quadrant* 25 (No. 1)

McCawley P. (1976) 'Labor: destined to fall' 11 *Politics* 30

McClaren J. (ed.) (1972) *Towards a New Australia* Cheshire, Melbourne

McNair I. (1977) 'Three Years of Labor — Some reasons why Labor was elected and defeated' 49 *Australian Quarterly* 94 (No. 3)

McQueen H. (1976) 'None dare call it conspiracy' 11 *Politics* 23

Mackerras M. (1974) 'City vs country: Analysis of 1974 election results' 9 *Politics* 195

— 'Uniform Swing: analysis of the 1975 election' 11 *Politics* 41

Martin J. V. (1976) 'Australia and Japan Under Labor' 19 *Quadrant* 37 (No. 8)

Mediansky F. A. and Nockles J. A. (1975) 'The Prime Minister's Bureaucracy' 34 *Public Administration* 202

Millar T. B. (1975) 'Defence under Labor' 52 *Current Affairs Bulletin* 4 (No. 7)

Minogue D. (1975) 'The Departments of Bumpf' 19 *Quadrant* 41 (No. 4)

Murray R. (1970) *The Split: Australian Labor in the fifties* Cheshire, Melbourne

— (1976) 'Labor: a bubble pricked' 11 *Politics* 35

Oakes L. (1973) *Whitlam PM* Angus & Robertson, Sydney

— and Solomon D. (1973) *The Making of An Australian Prime Minister* Cheshire, Melbourne

— and Solomon D. (1974) *Grab for Power: Election '74* Cheshire, Melbourne

— (1976) *Crash Through or Crash: The unmaking of a Prime Minister* Drummond, Melbourne

O'Brien B. M. (1976) 'The Power of the House of Representatives over Supply' 3 *Monash Law Review* 8

O'Brien P. (1974) 'The Ermolenko Affair' 18 *Quadrant* 16 (No. 4)

— (1977) *The Saviours: An intellectual history of the left in Australia* Drummond, Melbourne

Odgers J. R. (1973) *Australian Senate Practice* (4th Ed.) AGPS, Canberra

Parker R. S. (1976) 'Political projections and partisan perspectives' 11 *Politics* 12

Penniman H. R. (ed.) (1977) *Australia At The Polls: The national election of 1975* American Enterprise Institute for Public Policy Research, Washington DC

Power F. R. (1975) *The Fight for "Life"* F. P. Power, Melbourne

Puplick C. J. (1974) 'The NSW Constitutional League and the "Double No" Campaign' 9 *Politics* 31

Rae P. (1976) 'Rejoice — extremes don't last' *Australian,* 6 May

Rawson D. W. (1966) *Labor In Vain?* Longmans, Melbourne

Reid A. (1976) *The Whitlam Venture* Hill of Content, Melbourne

Reynolds P. L. (1974) *The Democratic Labor Party* Jacaranda Press, Melbourne

Richardson J. (1976) 'The Legislative Power of the Senate in Respect of Money Bills' 50 *Australian Law Journal* 273

Rydon J. (1974) 'The Prices and Incomes Referendum 1973' 9 *Politics* 22

— (1976) 'Casual vacancies in the Australian Senate' 11 *Politics* 195

Sawer G. (1976) 'The Governor-General of the Commonwealth of Australia' 52 *Current Affairs Bulletin* (No. 10) 20

— (1976) 'The Whitlam Revolution in Australian Federalism' 10 *Melbourne University Law Review* 315

— (1977) *Federation Under Strain: Australia 1972-1975* Melbourne University Press, Melbourne

Sheehan N. (1971) *The Pentagon Papers as published by The New York Times* Bantam, New York

Smith R. F. (1977) 'Australian Cabinet Structure and Procedures: The Labor Government 1972-1975' 12 *Politics* 23 (No. 1)

— and Weller P. (1978) *Public Service Inquiries in Australia* University of Queensland Press, Brisbane

Solomon D. (1974) 'After the 1974 elections' 51 *Current Affairs Bulletin* 13 (No. 3)
— (1976) Elect the Governor-General! Nelson, Melbourne
— (1978) *Inside the Australian Parliament* George Allen & Unwin, Sydney
Staveley R. W. (1976) 'The Conventions of the Constitution: Kerr's folly' 11 *Politics* 16
Stretton H. (1976) *Capitalism, Socialism and the Environment* Cambridge University Press, Cambridge
Stretton, Hugh (1978) 'Capital Mistakes' in Bell, Colin and Encel, S. *Inside the Whale: Ten Personal Accounts of Social Research* Pergamon, Sydney
St. John E. (1973) 'Malcolm Fraser' 19 *Quadrant* 4 (No. 8)
— (1976) 'The dismissal of the Whitlam Government' 20 *Quadrant* 63 (No. 9)
Sugerman B. (ed.) (1963) *Alfred Conlon: A Memorial by Some of His Friends,* Benevolent Society of NSW
Troy P. N. (1978) *A fair price: The Land Commission Program 1972-1977* Hale & Iremonger, Sydney
Troy P. N. (ed.) (1978a) *Federal power in Australia's Cities* Hale & Iremonger, Sydney
Walker J. (1975) 'Labor in Government — The 1975 Federal Conference at Terrigal' 10 *Politics* 178
Weller P. and Cutt J. (1976) *Treasury Control in Australia* Novak, Sydney
Weller P. and Smith R. F. (1976) 'The bureaucracy: plus ca change . . .' 11 *Politics* 53
West F. (1976) 'Constitutional Crisis 1975 — An Historian's View' 48 *Australian Quarterly* 48 (No. 2)
Wheelwright E. L. (ed.) (1974) *Radical Political Economy: Collected Essays* ANZ, Sydney
Whitlam E. G. (1957) *The Constitution versus Labor:* Chifley Memorial Lecture Melbourne University ALP Club
— (1969) *An Urban Nation* Victorian Fabian Society
— and Grant B. (1972a) *Labor in Power — What is the Difference?* Victorian Fabian Society
— (1972b) Policy Speech: Opening of the 1972 election campaign, 13 November
— (1974) Policy Speech: Opening of the 1974 election campaign, 29 April
— (1975a) Chifley Memorial Lecture, University of Melbourne. 14 August
— (1975b) *The New Federalism: A Review of Labor's Programs and Policies* Address to Conference of the Centre for Research on Federal Financial Relations, Australian National University, 27 August
— (1975c) Curtin Memorial Lecture, Australian National University,

29 October
— (1975d) Policy Speech: Opening of the 1975 election campaign, 24 November
— (1979) *The Truth of the Matter* Penguin, Melbourne
Wilenski P. (1978) 'The Bureaucracy and Responsible Government' 3 *University of New South Wales Occasional Papers* 9
— (1978a) 'Labor and the Bureaucracy' in G. Duncan (Ed.) *Critical Essays in Australian Politics* Edward Arnold, Melbourne
Wilson H. (1976) *The Government of Britain* Weidenfeld and Nicholson and Michael Joseph, London
Woodhouse A. O. (1974) *Compensation and Rehabilitation in Australia: Report of the National Committee of Inquiry* (Vols. 1-3) AGPS, Canberra

Index